Then and Now
in the Gulf Islands

A Colourful History

Vicky Lindholm

Hidden Lighthouse Publishers

Publication

Hidden Lighthouse Publishers
A division of Diskover Office Software Ltd.
#55, 8193 West Coast Rd.
Sooke, BC V9Z 1H3
(250) 664-7366

© 2006-2009 Hidden Lighthouse Publishers

Extreme care has been taken to ensure that all information presented in this book is accurate and up-to-date, and neither the author nor the publisher can be held responsible for any errors.

Cover design, page design and composition by Vicky Lindholm
All photos, with the exception of those listed under Credits, by Ken and Vicky Lindholm

Front cover photo:
    Saturna Beach, Saturna Island

Back cover photo:
    Mouat's Store, Salt Spring Island

ISBN 978-0-9783367-6-9

Dedication

To Mr. Chevy Chase and the
people of Rosebud

Contents

Introduction 2
The Farms 3
The Roads 5
The Waterways 7
The Law 9
The Mail 10

Mayne Island 11
Miners Bay 12
Glenwood Farm 13
David Cove 14
First Nations Reserve 14
Miners Bay Wharf 15
Mayne Island Post Office 16
Bennett Bay 17
Mayne Island School 18
Village Bay Park 19
Active Pass Light Station 20
Marine Heritage Park 22
Miners Bay Community Park 23
Maude Bay 24
Piggott Bay 25
St. Mary Magdalene Church 25
Mayne Island Museum 27
Springwater Lodge 28
Mayne Island Agriculture Hall 29
Curlew Island 30
The Anchorage Heritage Home 30
Mayne Inn 31
Mayne Island Health Center 32
Miners Bay Trading Post 33
Active Pass Auto & Marine 34
Japanese Memorial Garden 34
Mayne Mast Restaurant & Pub 36
Horton Bay 37
Mayne Island Fire Department 37

Saturna Island 39
Saturna Beach 40
Saturna Beach 41
Brown Ridge 42
Breezy Bay B&B 43
East Point Regional Park 44
Narvaez Bay Park 45
Taylor Point 46
Saturna Island Post Office 47
Saturna General Store 48
St. Christopher's Church 49
Winter Cove Provincial Marine Park 50
Tumbo Island 51
Saturna Island Cemetery 52
Lyall Harbour 52
Saturna Island Community Hall 53
Thomson Community Park 54

Pender Islands 56
Hope Bay 57
Grimmer Bay 58
Hamilton Beach 60
Pender Islands Community Hall 61
North Pender Island Wharves 63
Pender Islands Post Office 64
Mount Menzies Park 66
Davidson Bay 67
Pender Islands School 67
United Community Church 69
Canned Cod Bay 69
Hyashi Cove 70
Pender Islands Museum 71
RCMP Boat 73
Oaks Bluff 73
Lilias Spalding Heritage Park 74
Hope Bay Stores 75
The Canal 77
Shingle Bay Park 78
Thieves Bay Park 79
Old Orchard Farm 79
Pender Islands Cemetery 81
Beaumont Provincial Marine Park 81
Cedar Creek 82
The General Store 82
Port Browning Marina Resort 84
St. Peter's Anglican Church 85
Bricky Bay 85
James Point 86
The Wool Shed 87
Church of the Good Shepherd 87
Pender Island Golf & Country Club 88
Poets Cove Resort 89
Arcadia By The Sea Lodge 90
Pender Islands Public Library 91
Pender Islands Fire and Rescue 92

Galiano Island 93
Sturdies Bay 94
Georgeson Bay 95
Galiano Island Post Office 96
Shaw's Landing 99
Murcheson Heritage Home 99
Whaler Bay 100
Mary Ann Point Light 101
Captain's Quarters Cottage 102
Home Hardware Store 103
St. Margaret of Scotland Church 104
Galiano Island Cemetery 105
Porlier Pass Light Station 105
Grand Central Emporium 106
Sturdies Bay Wharf 107
Spotlight Cove 108
Bellhouse Inn 108
Bluffs Park 110
North Galiano Community Hall 111

Contents

Morning Beach 112
Galiano Inn 113
Cain Peninsula 114
Galiano Community Hall 115
Retreat Cove 116
Spanish Hills 117
Montague Harbour 118
Galiano Island Fire Departments 119
Active Pass Caboose Cottage 120

Salt Spring Island   122
Ganges 123
Ganges Post Offices 124
Fernwood Point 126
Ganges Harbour 127
Vesuvius Beach 128
Mt. Maxwell Provincial Park 129
Salt Spring Elementary School 130
Fulford Harbour 131
Vesuvius Bay Wharf 133
Akerman Museum 134
Booth Canal 135
Seabright Beach 135
Ruckle Provincial Park 136
Heritage House Museum 137
Musgrave Point 138
Princess Margaret Park Reserve 139
Beddis Beach 139
St. Paul's Catholic Church 140
Dowry House Cottage 141
Beaver Point 142
St. Mary Lake 142
Russell Island Prov. Marine Park 143
Fulford Inn 143
Salt Spring Island Trading Company ... 145
Fulford Post Office 146
Old Farmhouse B&B 147
Salt Spring Cinema 148
Salt Spring Golf & Country Club 149
Hamilton Beach 149
Harbour House Hotel 150
Fulford Creek Guest House 151
Mahon Memorial Hall 151
Stitches Quilts & Yarns 152
Mouat's Mall 153
Embe Bakery 155
Salt Spring Centre of Yoga 156
Mouat Provincial Park 156
Booth Bay B&B 158
Stone Walrus Gallery 158
Lady Minto Hospital 158
Tree House Café North 159
Fulford Community Hall 159
Gulf Islands Secondary School 161
Hastings House Country Estate 161
Galleons Lap Photography 162
Salt Spring Island Fire Department 162
House Piccolo Restaurant 163

Long Harbour 163
Drummond Park 164
Mary Hawkins Memorial Library 164
Centennial Park 165
Harbour Building & Rotary Park 166

Preface

Bad Waters

Before the British arrived, First Nations people lived in the southern Gulf Islands. They were known as the *Coast Salish* and were members of the *Nanaimo, Chemainus, Cowichan, Saanich* and *Songhees* tribes.[1]

By the 1850's, the British had started negotiating with First Nations for the right to occupy their land. However, when some of the Indians in the Gulf Islands would migrate during the summer, the British would simply take their land.[2]

In 1863, a settler from Washington State decided to join a Mayne Islander in working his newly acquired land. On an Easter weekend, he set out to move his family to Mayne in two boats.[3]

When they encountered a storm, the settler and his daughter took shelter on Saturna Island. As they sat by their campfire, he was shot in the back. His daughter ran, but was caught and killed.[4]

Shortly thereafter, two other settlers were shot, on Pender Island. One of the settlers died of his wounds, but the other lived to describe his attackers as Indian.[5]

When the British learned of the attacks, they sailed a gunboat, called the HMG *Forward*, to Mayne Island. They took a half-breed Indian aboard to act as their interpreter. He guided them to where they could investigate the sites of the attacks.[6]

Their investigation prompted them to sail north of Salt Spring Island, to where a group of Indians lived on a neighboring island. There, they anchored their gunboat in the bay in front of the Indian village.[7]

Unknown to the British, Indian warriors were hiding on the bay when they arrived. When the British fired, the warriors returned their fire and a 16-year-old sailor was killed. He was the first and last British serviceman killed in action in British Columbia.[8]

After several hours, the British attack proved futile. Defeated, they pulled their boat out of the bay. It was the only strategic defeat ever imposed by a tribal group over the British Royal Navy.[9]

It is estimated that the Indians numbered just over 100 people, most of which were children. In spite of this, it took two more expeditions by the British, with three ships and 500 men, to overtake them.[10]

The Indian village was then burned and later confiscated. Seven natives were captured on Galiano Island. They were then tried and executed for the murders on Saturna and Pender Islands. The Indian war chief was never captured.[11]

Although it is not mentioned in most recorded histories, this battle was one of the largest military operations in the entire history of British Columbia.

By the late 1860's, the British had given up negotiating with the Indians. Instead, they implemented a system of creating Indian reserves within the boundaries of lands claimed by white settlers.[12]

A point on Saturna was named because of the killings that had occurred there. Now a part of the Gulf Islands National Park Reserve, it is called *Murder Point*.[13]

SOUTHERN GULF ISLANDS

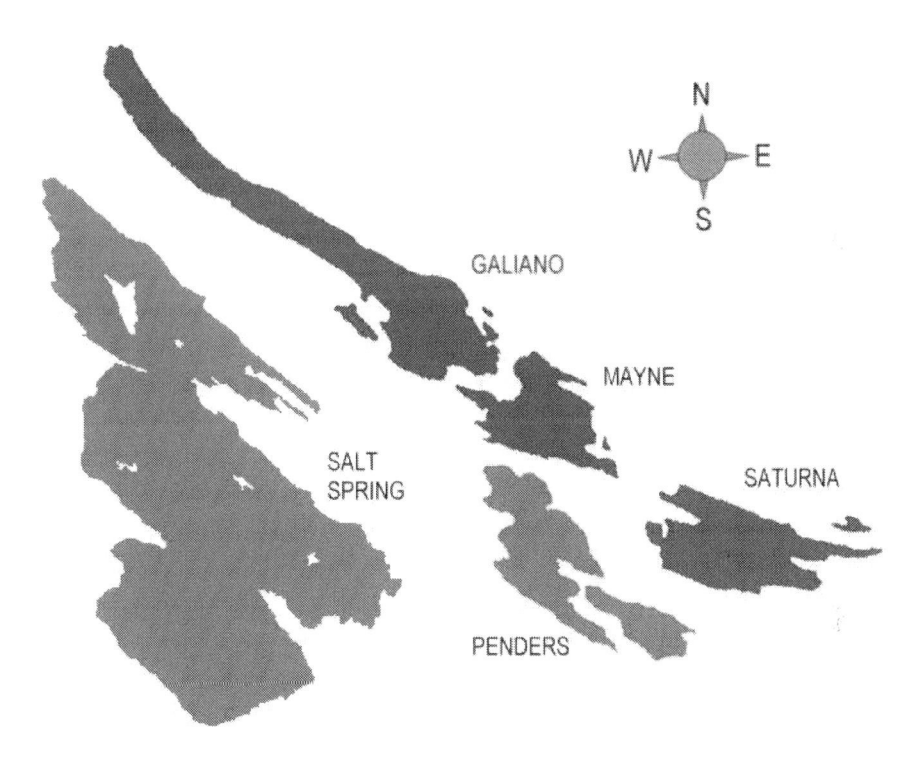

Introduction

Sunset in the Gulf Islands

Just sit right back and you'll hear a tale...

The southern Gulf Islands are centrally located between Vancouver Island and the mainland. They include *Salt Spring, Mayne, Pender, Galiano* and *Saturna*. Of these Islands, Mayne, Pender, Galiano and Saturna make up what is known as the outer Gulf Islands.

The Islands lie in the rain shadow of the Vancouver Island Mountains, which protects them from storms that blow in from the Pacific Ocean. Often referred to as the *Banana Belt of Canada*, they have Canada's only Mediterranean-type climate.

Although most of the Gulf Islands are uninhabited, the southern Gulf Islands have a combined population of over 14,000 permanent residents.

The rolling hills and roads on the Islands are reminiscent of an English *Illahee* (countryside). There are few streetlights, curbs or sidewalks, making them quite a quaint attraction.

The Islands enjoy an average of 2,000 hours of sunshine, annually. With the longest frost-free season in all of Canada, spring begins as early as February.

Because it rarely snows, a winter weekend can be quite cozy with some logs on a *paia* (fire). So much so that an early settler said this about them:

"We didn't notice until we left the Gulf Islands just how quiet it had been... But we loved it... When I think back on it, it was a really nice life."

Mrs. Peter Georgeson[14]

Introduction

The People

The southern Gulf Islands have not been in the mainstream of British Columbia's historical development. Generally, they were a place for people to pass through or to visit.[15]

After the first wave of settlement in the 1860's, an intriguing group of British immigrants began to call the Gulf Islands 'home'.[16]

British settlers at the turn of the century
Galiano Archives 2004017068

The majority of the Island settlers were British. When they emigrated, they brought their customs with them, carrying on their tennis, field hockey and cricket parties, and their formal dinners and dances.[17]

Many of these British settlers came from upper and middle classes and received incomes from England. Few other places in British Columbia could boast the nurses, nannies and governesses that were common in many of the families in the Gulf Islands.[18]

The Farms

The British settlers had to learn a lot about farming. The forest was thick with trees, right to the edge of the water.[19]

Salt Spring settlers falling a tree, 1930's
Salt Spring Archives 1994137078

The settlers had to learn how to use stumping powder to explode the stumps. Then, they would burn the larger ones.[20]

They also had to learn how to hitch a yoke of oxen and plough a field. It was backbreaking work.[21]

Fortunately, whenever a family was in dire need of getting a crop in or needed a new barn, the other Islanders would organize a *work-bee* (when neighbors work together) to help.[22]

Fruit farms were common sights in the Islands. However, around the turn of the century, the flavor of the fruit produced by

Introduction

growers in the interior of British Columbia proved superior, causing the Gulf Islands markets to die.[23]

Commercial dairy farming lasted longer, but there were problems transporting to the creamery on Salt Spring Island, which eventually caused its downfall.[24]

Farmers at a Galiano farm in the 1920's - Galiano Archives 2004026359

Because the rocky ridges on the Islands are not well suited to widespread farming, sheep farming proved to be the most suitable. The settlers received a good price for the wool and they could also sell their lambs.[25]

Much later, in the 1960's, many Islanders subdivided their large farms. This resulted in a 300 percent increase in the number of land owners than there were in the 1940's.[26]

Many new owners were mainland residents who had purchased lots for retirement, or as investment or vacation property.[27]

Today, some Islanders own cottages as their 'home away from home', living as *weekenders* (people who spend weekends in the Islands) on small lots during the summer.

Introduction

Many of the old homesteads have become parks for people to enjoy. An active Parks and Recreation Commission is working on an expanded trail system, enhancing the parks and developing several heritage sites.

The park trails range from short, lazy, seaside trails to forest hikes, so you might want to invest in a pair of *waffle stompers* (hiking shoes).

In the 1990's, a large amount of land was acquired by the Pacific Marine Heritage Legacy, a program to create an expanded and integrated network of coastal and marine protected areas on the West Coast. The land it acquired included areas on Mayne, Pender and Saturna Islands.[28]

Although First Nations can pursue traditional activities on these lands, including hunting and harvesting of plants and other materials, the lands are now protected as part of the Gulf Islands National Park Reserve.

The Islands do not have their own landfills, so private contractors must transport waste off Island. To ensure that nothing is left on the park trails, hikers take as much of their *iktas* (belongings) as possible off the Island.

The Roads

At the turn of the century, the Island roads were narrow dirt or gravel trails that were unsuitable for passing vehicles. So there were only a few horse-drawn buggies seen traveling the roads. When the early Gulf Islands settlers wanted to travel across land, they walked.[29]

Most of the settlers hauled materials and supplies by *stoneboat* (a heavy sled), which had runners made of driftwood planks set on their edges.[30]

It was the settlers who built the roads. The Road Act of 1862 forced them to spend six days each year working on the trails. In exchange, they were allowed to pay off their property taxes by improving the trails.

When there was a need for a road, the settlers decided on the route, and then staked it out. After they cleared the roadway, they brought in teams of horses or oxen, and with scrapers and stumping powder, they would grade it.[31]

5

Introduction

A road being made on Saturna Island in the early 1900's - BC Archives C-06972

Once a road was graded, the unwanted cedar tree trunks were split into fence rails, which the settlers used to make the 'snake' fences that can still be seen enclosing many of the old farmsteads today.[32]

There was very little asphalt on the roads before the late 1940's when most of the roads that exist today were built. A small highways crew, under the supervision of one settler who serviced multiple islands, kept the roads in good condition.[33]

Today, most of the Island roads are well maintained. Visitors often travel by bicycle or scooter, causing the roads to become congested with cyclists.

There are no shoulders on the roads and, although some appear to be there for casual country riding, many of them are major thoroughfares that are used by the Islanders to conduct their business.

Introduction

The Waterways

When the early settlers landed in the Gulf Islands, they encountered crystal clear waters. They soon learned that the easiest way to move people, supplies, livestock and lumber was across those waters.[34]

Initially, they traded with the Indians for their dugout canoes.[35] Later, they built their own rowboats. The sea was their highway.[36]

They had sloops and rowboats that were equipped with sails. However, winds were not always favorable or strong enough to allow significant progress against the tides.[37] So everyone used the *Armstrong Motor* (people power)[38] and learned how to take advantage of the currents.[39] Children learned how to *pull* (row) before they went to school.[40]

Unfortunately, passengers who wanted to leave the Islands had to row out to a steamer ship and climb up a ladder with the help of the ship's crew. When a settler had to ship cattle and other livestock across the water, they were dumped overboard to swim ashore.[41]

Although various ships traveled the Islands as early as the 1860's,[42] the building of the Salt Spring wharf in 1872[43] soon gave way to regular ferry service. The service was provided by a small steamship called the S.S. *Iroquois*.[44]

S.S. Iroquois in the Gulf Islands in 1907 – Salt Spring Archives 1994137285

In the year 1911, the *Iroquois* cast off from Vancouver Island. It was bound for Salt Spring with passengers and a large load of hay. Shortly thereafter, it was caught in a storm and capsized.[45]

Although Indians rescued many of the passengers into their canoes, a schoolteacher from Pender drowned in the accident, along with her two-year old son.[46]

In 1929, the Gulf Islands Ferry Company was formed. At that time, a ship, which was purchased from the Canadian Pacific Railway, was converted into a ferryboat, called the MV *Cy Peck*. It could carry 20 small cars.[47]

Introduction

In 1951, a Salt Spring Islander purchased the ferry company, and then drastically improved it.[48] The following year, the *Cy Peck* was carrying over 17,000 cars. At that time, it provided the only connection to Vancouver Island.[49]

A decade later, a ferry linking the mainland to Salt Spring was introduced, making the outer Gulf Islands more accessible. This caused their population to increase significantly over the next decade.[50]

When a second dock was added to the Mayne ferry terminal in 1982, vehicles could transfer from one ferry to another. This made it an important transfer hub for all the Island routes.[51]

Today, British Columbia Ferry Services operates scheduled ferry services to all the southern Gulf Islands, from the mainland and from Vancouver Island. At the time of this writing, it reported carrying 3.5 million passengers throughout the Islands each year.

Way back in the 18th century, the Spanish produced the first map to show the southern Gulf Islands. It depicted the area that was first charted by Spanish explorers.[52]

One hundred years later, in the mid-1800's, those waterways that had not already been named by the Spanish were then named by the English, after officers of the British Royal Navy or their vessels.[53]

Recently, over 400 modern-day Gulf Islanders celebrated the Spanish explorations of the 18th century by retracing the exact routes followed by the early explorers. They sailed in replicas of the original Spanish longboats.

Today, the waters surrounding the Islands are still crystal clear and the waterways are prime areas for sailing and kayaking. Late summer and fall is the best time to kayak because of morning and evening calms. Visitors can also travel by *stinkpot* (motorboat).

For people with car-top boats, there are various places to launch in the bays, including government docks and public wharves.

The many coves and inlets are ideal for boat moorage and the protected bays and shallow waters make it easy to find a cove to anchor in for the *poolakle* (night).

Introduction

The beaches in the Islands consist primarily of sedimentary rock. Most are public property up to where the driftwood ends.

The Law

Initially, law enforcement was the responsibility of the British Royal Navy. However, with the influx of gold miners in 1858, the Provincial Police Force was established to provide law and order to British Columbia.[54]

Later, in 1886, the first *gaol* (jail) to exist in the Islands was built on Salt Spring.[55] It was a small, square, white jailhouse that contained just two cells.[56] However, because Mayne is centrally located, a police constable was also appointed there, in 1893.

Provincial Police at Mayne Is. in the 1890's
BC Archives I-32839

The district patrolled by the Mayne Island police constable was named *Plumper Pass and the Islands*.[57] The constable assumed law enforcement duties for all the Islands, accomplishing his police work by boat.[58]

In 1905, police headquarters were moved to Salt Spring[59] and constables on Pender became responsible for law enforcement in the outer Gulf Islands.[60]

Much later, in the 1950's, the Provincial Police Force was merged into the Royal Canadian Mounted Police.[61] At that time, a small police detachment was set up on Salt Spring to handle law infractions in all the Islands.[62]

Today, there are over 6,000 *Queen's Cowboys* (RCMP) employed in British Columbia. However, the crime rate in the Islands is negligible and some people never lock their doors. As a result, only one Corporal, who is stationed at a two-person RCMP detachment on Pender, is in charge of the outer Gulf Islands. A separate detachment is located on Salt Spring.

Introduction

Wharf on Salt Spring Is., in the 1880's
Salt Spring Archives 50532

The Mail

Initially, postage was a tremendous expense. Settlers could purchase land in the Islands for just one dollar per acre. However, because the United States Postal System was responsible for the delivery of mail to and from British Columbia, postage on a letter to the U.S. cost 33 cents.[63]

Before wharves were built in the Islands, mail was carried by the fur-trading Hudson's Bay Company steamer ship, which sailed between the mainland and Vancouver Island. The settlers posted their mail by intercepting the ship and then handing their letters up to the crew.[64]

The first wharf in the southern Gulf Islands was built on Salt Spring, in 1872.[65] Two years later, postal service began from the Salt Spring Island Post Office.[66]

When a wharf was built on Mayne, it became the first of the outer Gulf Islands to offer postal service. Ships would first deliver the mail to Salt Spring, and then to Mayne. Postmen from Galiano, Pender and Saturna Islands would transport their mail, by boat, to and from Mayne.[67]

By the time the S.S. *Iroquois* was launched to carry the mail from Vancouver Island to the Gulf Islands,[68] each of the outer Gulf Islands had secured a post office from which they could receive and dispatch their own mail.[69]

The settlers would gather at the wharves to collect their mail on *boat days* (when the ships were scheduled to arrive) which became a social event.[70] The ships purser was the center of attraction. He handled the mail.[71]

Unfortunately, the handling of the mail was not without its problems. In the 1880's, the Postman from Pender submitted a petition to the postal authorities, claiming that the Postman from Mayne was opening letters and discussing their contents with the other settlers.[72]

Today, a private courier delivers the mail to each of the Islands by boat...

Mayne Island

Miners Bay Wharf

It was in the summer of 1862 that the notorious killer, Boone Helm, stopped an Englishman, named Tom Collinson, on a trail during the gold rush...

Helm aimed a shotgun at Tom's head, while his partner took Tom's six-shooter and his pack. Then, they chased him down the trail at gunpoint, claiming his cash for their own, but missing a large amount of gold dust in his shirt pocket.[1]

William Tompkins Collinson was born in the 1830's[2] and emigrated with his family from England to Canada.[3] In 1871, he moved to Mayne Island with his Indian wife,[4] where he earned the nickname 'Baron Munchausen of Mayne'.[5]

The story-telling Tom Collinson was an avid carpenter, having constructed several buildings on a bay on Mayne, including the first store.[6]

In the year 1880, Tom became **the Postman** for Mayne, operating the first post office from the home he had built there.[7] He was later made Justice of the Peace,[8] around the time this was said about him:

"Tall, lean Mr. Collinson was the postmaster, and held the record for having the largest feet, and being the island's champion liar - or shall we say, Romantic. No matter what the topic of conversation, he could lie... about his experiences and utterly impossible exploits... with a perfectly straight face, and then tell the same episode next time, with varying circumstances. It was a real gift!"

Winifred Grey[9]

Mayne Island

The Relaxed Island

Mayne is a relaxed island. At only 23 sq km, it is the smallest of the southern Gulf Islands. While idyllic meadows and wildflowers are its most distinguishing characteristics, the history behind the landmarks gives Mayne Island its unique charm.

Mayne has a population of about 900 permanent residents, a large percentage of which are over 55 years of age and retired. During the tourist season, the population swells to around 3,000.

Miners Bay

Before the 1850's, less than 500 settlers lived at the south end of Vancouver Island.[10] The only white people travelling between Vancouver Island and the mainland were employees of the Hudson's Bay Company who were trading furs with the Indians.

In 1858, when gold was discovered on the mainland, tens of thousands of *fifty-eighters* (miners living in the year 1858) came to British Columbia to seek their *tolla* (fortune) in the gold mines.[11]

Miners in Victoria in the mid-1800's
BC Archives A-04498

Many came from the United States, by way of a steamer ship that docked at Vancouver Island. Some gold miners continued the perilous journey to the mainland in a canoe or rowboat.

Since Mayne Island is located midway between the mainland and Vancouver Island, many of these miners began stopping overnight at the bay on its west side. The bay and its surrounding areas soon became known as *Miners Bay*.[12]

Over time, Mayne Island became one of the earliest summer resorts to ever exist on the West Coast of Canada. A surprising number of accommodations date back to the turn of the century when it developed into an important Pacific Northwest resort island.[13]

At that time, only approximately 100 residents lived on the Island. Nevertheless, they rapidly began to establish tourist facilities to capitalize on its growing popularity.[14]

Mayne Island

Miners Bay in the early 1900's, seen from the water, BC Archives A-09773

Today, Miners Bay is 'downtown' to Mayne Islanders - a seaside village where businesses and residents co-exist.

Miners Bay as it appears today

Glenwood Farm

In 1871, an Englishman, named Frederick Robson, set sail for the Gulf Islands and landed in a bay on the east side of Mayne.[15]

As he explored the area, he located a valley in which he started growing crops. He called his farm *Glenwood*. It was there that he built his first log home.[16]

Fred soon formed a partnership with Tom Collinson, the man who was destined to become **the Postman**. However, about two years later, the partnership was dissolved.[17]

Over time, Fred developed Glenwood Farm into a highly successful dairy farm.[18] Around the turn of the century, he started supplying cream to the creamery on Salt Spring Island.

Soon, the children attending the Island's school began picnicking at the farm, to celebrate the end of each school year. This became a tradition that continued for several years.[19]

During World War I, the farm was known for its herd of Record of Performance Jerseys, which won prizes at the provincial exhibitions for many years.[20] Fred paid his taxes each year by selling his fattest cow.[21]

Mayne Island

Today, Glenwood Farm is the oldest farm on Mayne and is one of the largest of the old homesteads in all the Gulf Islands.[22]

Although one of the first houses on the farm was destroyed by fire,[23] a descendant who lived in the third house to be built was still working it at the time of this writing.

Recently, a monument was erected to commemorate the farm and one of Fred's descendants.

David Cove

Soon after Fred Robson settled on the east side of Mayne, a schooner, called the *Zephyr*, set sail for San Francisco with a load of sandstone. During a *Squamish wind* (snowstorm), it struck Georgina Shoals on the north side of the Island. When it sank off a cove, it took the captain and one crewmember with it.[24]

The cove was originally named *Hidden Bay* but was later renamed *David Cove*, in honor of an early settler who once lived there.

The cove is a beautiful inlet with a rocky beach that provides for an abundance of clams, mussels, limpets, snails and crabs. It offers some safe boat anchorage.

Further out from David Cove is a favorite spot for scuba diving, where the wreck of the Zephyr exists.

The wreck is reported to be the oldest in the Gulf Islands and is protected under the Heritage Conservation Act of British Columbia. It was not discovered until the 1970's. A large block of sandstone that was recovered from the wreck a decade later[25] can be seen today at the Mayne Island Museum.

First Nations Reserve

In 1877, First Nations was allotted a 1.3 sq km reserve on a point, named Helen Point, which is located on the west side of Mayne.[26]

A decade earlier, in 1863, the area had made history when a half-breed Indian was brought aboard a British gunboat, to guide the Royal Navy to where they could investigate the sites of Indian attacks on Saturna and Pender Islands.[27]

Helen Point in the 1940's BC Archives I-20664

Mayne Island

One hundred years later, in the 1950's, the Saanich Tribe was divided into five bands. At that time, the *Tsartlip Band* was created.[28]

Helen Point as it appears today

The reserve on Helen Point is still owned by the Tsartlip Band today, but is occupied by members of the Cowichan Tribe. Helen Point contains the oldest, recorded, human settlement remains in the southern Gulf Islands.

Miners Bay Wharf

The first wharf to ever exist in the outer Gulf Islands was built in Miners Bay in 1878.[29] The wharf accommodated ships coming through the waterway that is officially called *Active Passage*, but was then known locally as *Plumper Pass*.[30]

In 1885, it was replaced with a larger wharf that was twice as wide and extended an additional 15 m into the Pass.[31] When the first steamer arrived at the new wharf, the settlers saluted it by firing their rifles.

Much later, in 1937, a bench was built at the foot of the wharf. For several decades, residents gathered to socialize around the bench on *boat days*.[32]

Miners Bay wharf in the 1930's, the post office shown in the background, BC Archives D-07435

Mayne Island

In 1952, the Miners Bay wharf was upgraded to accommodate a ship *Princess Elaine*.[33] Much later, in the 1990's, the wharf was destroyed by fire and a new wharf was built to replace it.[34] Today, it is used by sea planes and to transport schoolchildren to neighboring schools.

Miners Bay wharf as it appears today

Although the wharf is no longer a place for socializing, the bench still sits there. A little tree grows in the center.

Mayne Island Post Office

In 1879, a request for a post office on Mayne was approved by the Postmaster General. When a letter slot was cut into the side of the house belonging to Tom Collinson, postal service began from his home.[35] His 1879 tax records indicate that the total tax paid for the property on which the post office sat was 75 cents.[36]

In the 1890's, **the Postman** built a new home and store at the head of the new wharf, moving the post office to its second location.[37] At that time, the address of the post office was simply 'Plumper Pass'.[38] It was later renamed the *Mayne Island Post Office*.

The Mayne Island Post Office was the first to serve the outer Gulf Islands.[39] After steamer ships delivered the mail to neighboring Salt Spring Island, it would be delivered in a mailbag to Mayne. The mailbag would then be taken down to the boat on a wheelbarrow.[40]

The first building to serve as the post office was torn down in the 1970's.[41] The second building still sits in front of the wharf on the bay. It operates as the *Springwater Lodge*.

At the turn of the century, **the Postman** built a third building, on the north side of the wharf. Then he moved his store and the

Mayne Island

post office there.[42] He retained ownership of the building, but later sold his retail business to a farmer who operated it as *Deacon's Store*.[43]

Soon, his hands set to work on yet another building, for a retired Commander of the British Royal Navy. Located just up the street, the building was operated as the *Mayne Store*.[44]

The 3rd post office, 1920's
BC Archives B-03269

For decades, the post office operated from various stores at Miners Bay,[45] including Deacon's Store, the Mayne Store and what would eventually become the *Miners Bay Trading Post*.[46] Deacon's Store changed owners many times, becoming *Emery's Store*, *Bennett's Store* and others. Unfortunately, it was torn down in the 1960's.[47]

Site of the 3rd post office as it appears today

The Mayne Store became the telephone headquarters for the outer Gulf Islands in the 1940's. It now serves as a private residence on Georgina Point Road.

In 1974, the post office was moved to another building at Miners Bay.[48] Today, that building operates as a hair salon and the post office sits in a storefront. The post office celebrated its 125th Anniversary in 2005.

Bennett Bay

As the post office was being established at Miners Bay, a Scotsman, named Thomas Bennett, emigrated to Mayne with his family. With little or no farming experience, they began to develop a large successful farm on a bay on the east side of the Island.[49]

In the early 1890's, Thomas became the first proprietor of a grand hotel, where he lived with his family for a short time. By then, his wife had become well known as the midwife

Mayne Island

in the Gulf Islands and one of their own children was the first white man born on Mayne.[50]

Bennett Bay was named after this family. The beautiful bay provides for one of the finest sandy beaches in all the Gulf Islands.

If you launch a boat from the bay, you can sail through Georgeson Passage, toward Campbell Bay, or you can head toward Horton Bay. A cruise along the shoreline to Saturna Island is also quite intriguing. However, since it is exposed to winds, Bennett Bay offers only temporary boat anchorage.

Two smaller, rocky beaches on Bennett Bay exist south of the swimming beach. Both of these more secluded beaches are best visited at low tide, revealing the tidal pools. They are also good spots for scuba diving at a depth of up to 12 m.

Mayne Island School
In 1883, some property was donated in the center of Mayne Island for the site of a school. With **the Postman** also active in arranging for it, a schoolhouse was built. It measured just 40 sq m and contained only one classroom.[51]

When classes began, the enrollment numbered 20 children, which increased to 30 a year later.[52] The children who attended the school came not only from Mayne, but also from Galiano and Saturna Islands.[53]

In 1894, a second, larger school was built. Because there was no indoor plumbing, the daily drinking water was carried uphill from a well. To heat the schoolhouse, a student was paid to light the stove an hour before the morning classes.[54]

Second schoolhouse, 1890's, MIVF Archives

Unfortunately, when the Japanese-Canadians were taken from their homes at the start of World War II, 17 schoolchildren were evacuated from the Island. With only four children left in attendance at the school, it was closed for two years.[55]

In the year 1950, a third one-room school was built where the first schoolhouse stood. A decade later, the first schoolhouse was closed permanently and moved across the road.[56] It now functions as the social hall for the Mayne Island Volunteer Firefighters Association.

Ye Olde Schoolhouse as it appears today

Mayne Island

Since its construction, the new school has had many additions built all around it.[57] When the gymnasium was added in 1977, students collected items that represented current events, and then inserted them into a 'time capsule', which they buried beside the gymnasium door. Recently, a student from Galiano Island was chosen to open the capsule and reveal its contents.[58]

Today, the new *Mayne Island School* functions as an elementary and junior secondary school, serving the children of Mayne, Galiano and Saturna Islands. It accommodates about 65 full-time equivalent students, offering programs from kindergarten to grade 11.

Village Bay Park

Because the First Nations *rancherie* (village) existed on the southwest side of Mayne, the area eventually became known as *Village Bay*. All of the people who lived there were called *skeh-SUCK* (the Pass) people.[59]

As the Mayne Island School was being built in the center of the Island, a farmer, named John Deacon, purchased a large farm sitting in a valley on Village Bay. His family built a barn in the valley and a home at the edge of the farm overlooking the bay.[60]

A decade later, the family converted their home into a very popular resort they called *Kitty's Boarding House*.[61]

John's wife, Margaret, ran the resort. She did all the work in the boarding house herself. Sometimes, she would cater to 30 guests at a time.[62]

In 1892, they added a second wing to their boarding house. Unfortunately, a few years later, it was destroyed by fire.[63] Today, the barn is the only building that remains of their large farm and resort.

Barn at Village Bay in the 1950's, BC Arcihves NA-40412

Mayne Island

In the 1950's, an end-loading ferry terminal was built on the bay, where Kitty's Boarding House once stood.[64] For the most part, it replaced the wharf at Miners Bay.[65]

Village Bay ferry terminal, early 1960's
BC Ferries Archives

Today, British Columbia Ferry Services continues to use the land on Village Bay to operate scheduled ferry services from both the mainland and Vancouver Island.

Village Bay ferry terminal as it appears today

The pebbled beach on the bay sits in *Village Bay Park*. The park and beach can be accessed by car, from the end of Callaghan Crescent, or by way of two short, easy trails. However, the beach is closed to the harvesting of scallops, mussels, oysters and clams.

If you launch a boat from Village Bay, a cruise along the shoreline to Dinner Point is quite scenic. However, ferry traffic is heavy in the bay and because it is exposed to winds and ferry wash, the mooring facilities offer only temporary anchorage for small boaters.

Barn at Village Bay as it appears today

Active Pass Light Station

Way back in the 18th century, the British began surveying the West Coast. During one of their voyages, they landed on a point at the north entrance to the Pass.[66]

Mayne Island

One hundred years later, in 1881, **the Postman** discovered a British one-cent coin that had been lost on that point.[67] It was dated Seventeen Hundred and Eighty Four.[68]

Soon, construction of a lighthouse began on that same point.[69] It was called the *Plumper Pass Lighthouse*.[70] One of only two major lighthouses constructed before the turn of the century, it was the most important lighthouse on the entire coast.[71]

Active Pass Light Station in the late 1800's, Salt Spring Island Archives G39

The lighthouse was equipped with the first steam-powered foghorn ever used. The light was a coal-oil lamp with wicks and chimneys. It had a revolving, many-faceted magnifying glass, which was powered by a system of chains and weights and had to be wound up every few hours.[72]

In the 1940's, a new light station was built on the point.[73] At that time, one of the original buildings was moved to an organic farm where it is now being used as a house.

The new light station was named the *Active Pass Light Station*. Because the point, itself, had officially been named *Georgina Point*,[74] the lighthouse was renamed the *Georgina Point Lighthouse*.[75]

Active Pass Light Station as it appears today

In the 1980's, the Active Pass Light Station celebrated its centennial, a distinction held by only a few lighthouses on the entire West Coast.

Today, the grounds surrounding the light station are dancing with Arbutus trees,

Mayne Island

behind which is a Dahlia Garden. The grounds provide for breathtaking views of Active Pass and of Galiano Island. There are facilities for picnics if you want to stay awhile.

The tower was recently de-staffed and is now closed. However, the light station is still open to the public. In the year of this writing, it was acquired as part of the Gulf Islands National Park Reserve.

A short, easy trail through the park leads to a beach. At low tide, you can walk along the beach for *lele* (a long time) looking at the Sea Stars.

Georgeson Island

After originally settling on Galiano Island, a Scotsman, named Henry Georgeson, moved to Mayne in 1885. At that time, he became the first lighthouse keeper at the Active Pass Light Station.[76] Known locally as 'Scotty', he lived inside the lighthouse with his family.[77]

Each day, Scotty would light the oil lamp at sundown and blow it out at sunrise.[78] If the foghorn malfunctioned, he would ring the bell by hand whenever a steamer entered the Pass.[79]

One day, a family friend went around the corner of the lighthouse just as the ship *Princess Adelaide* crashed into the rocks on the beach in front of him. It had failed to sound its whistle in time.[80]

Scotty spent the first day towing passengers to shore in lifeboats. The ship, which had sustained only minor damage, remained on the beach for two more days before being pulled off by an American tugboat.[81]

When Scotty retired in 1921, he received the Imperial Long Service Medal for providing over 35 years of service to the lighthouse. He was succeeded by his son, George.[82]

Georgeson Island was named after this lighthouse keeper, whose name has become synonymous with the lighthouses in the southern Gulf Islands. For five decades, members of his family provided service to lighthouses on Mayne, Saturna and other Islands.[83]

The island is a beautiful ridge on the east side of Mayne. Its southern shore provides for great sandstone formations and you can often catch sight of a Bald Eagle flying across Georgeson Passage. However, it has been designated as a 'no access' area and there is virtually nowhere to land by boat.

Part of the Gulf Islands National Park Reserve, the island is highly valued as a Seal and Sea Lion haulout, as well as a nesting site for several species of birds.

The land that was acquired as part of the reserve also includes Bennett Bay and Campbell Point on Mayne Island. Today,

Mayne Island

Georgeson Island, Bennett Bay and Campbell Point are protected together as part of the park.

Campbell Point is accessible by way of an easy trail that loops around the point. Originally named *Paddon Point*, it is highly regarded for its Arbutus trees and is the place to see some of the most incredible examples anywhere on the West Coast.

At the end of Campbell Point, there is a view of Mount Baker, a 3,300 m strato-volcano located in Washington State. It is also a place to see Garry Oak or watch the Sea Lions while you picnic in the park.

Today, there are still ancient fruit trees growing along the trail that leads to the pebbled beach on *Miners Bay*. The beach sits in front of **the Postman's** very first home.

If you walk beneath the wharf in Miners Bay, you can watch the water as it trickles down the rocks. Although it has limited space and strong tides, you can find docking facilities at the wharf, from which you can walk into the village.

The short trail to the beach passes *Miners Bay Community Park*. It provides for great berry picking.

Miners Bay Community Park

By 1890, **the Postman** had become a member of the Islands Agricultural and Fruit Growers Association.[84] Reportedly, plum, pear and apple orchards could be seen on many of the farms, particularly a variety of apples called *King*.

Mayne Island

In the summer, the bandstand in the park provides a place for musicians to entertain visitors who come to attend events, such as the *Al'elen Music Festival*. There are also facilities for picnics if you want to stay awhile.

Maude Bay

In 1893, a magnificent hotel, called the *Point Comfort*, was built on a bay at the north end of Mayne.[85] Although the surrounding community was officially named *Lighthouse Point*, it soon became known locally as *Point Comfort*.

Thomas Bennett was the first proprietor of the hotel. However, one summer, in the year 1900, a water shortage forced him to sell to Eustace Maude, the retired Commander who was operating the Mayne Store at Miners Bay.[86]

Mrs. Maude would walk from the hotel to the church in the early morning hours, where she would play the organ in complete darkness.[87]

Because she did not approve of the hotel's bar, Commander Maude abandoned it and operated the hotel without it. Unfortunately, the hotel proved to be a financial failure. So, after operating it for just three summers, they made it their home.[88]

Initially, their home was a very attractive place to visit. The couple loved to host parties there. They would hold tennis parties on the lawn and dances in the ballroom. Mrs. Maude would wear beautiful dresses.[89]

Unfortunately, the couple did not maintain the building and, by the 1920's, it had become run down. So they decided to sell it. Subsequent owners renamed it the *Cherry Tree Inn*.[90]

The magnificent Point Comfort Hotel in the early 1900's BC Archives E-07867

At that time, Commander Maude, who had once served on Queen Victoria's own personal yacht,[91] attempted to sail his sailboat, the *Half Moon*, from Mayne to England, alone. He was 77 years of age.[92]

Mayne Island

After the Commander had spent almost 100 days at sea and had traveled over 6,000 km, he was caught in a storm off the coast of California. The storm caused the boom to strike him on the head and left him unconscious.[93]

A freighter soon spotted him but he refused their assistance. Despite having been blinded by the sun, he navigated his boat to Cape Flattery where he was rescued by his son. He returned to his home on Mayne only to succeed in his journey the following year.[94]

Maude Bay was named after this family who was the first British middle-class family to settle on Mayne. The bay is also known as *Cherry Tree Bay*.

Piggott Bay

Around the time the Point Comfort hotel was being built, a settler, named Sweany Colston, moved from the Pender Islands to Mayne.[95]

Whenever he wanted to visit his brother, Robert, Sweany would walk to a bay, and then light a fire or blow a horn made out of bull kelp to get his brother's attention.[96]

Robert would then row over to Mayne from North Pender and pick him up at what was then called *Brigg's Landing*.[97]

Other people from the Pender Islands also used the bay as a transfer point when traveling to Mayne, especially when picking up their mail. They would walk to the bay and row across the Channel.

Located on the south side of Mayne, *Piggott Bay* provides for views of Saturna Island. The sandy beach is lined with large pieces of driftwood and clams are plentiful. Because of its warm waters, the bay is a great place for a swim. However, it is exposed to the winds and offers only temporary boat anchorage.

St. Mary Magdalene Church

In 1893, **the Postman** offered to donate some land for the site of a church, but his offer was not acted upon. Instead, a famous explorer from Saturna Island provided the land.[98]

While the church was being constructed, a house that had recently been built on the land was used for services.[99]

The building of *St. Mary Magdalene Anglican Church* was completed on Mayne in 1898. It was the first church to serve the outer Gulf Islands.[100]

A few years later, a 180 kg piece of sandstone was discovered on the shore of Saturna. Because a natural basin had been carved into it by the tides, Canon Paddon, the Vicar, transported it by rowboat so it could be used as the baptismal vessel.[101]

Mayne Island

St. Mary Magdalene Anglican Church in the 1890's, BC Archives G-01421

Shortly after the turn of the century, a fire broke out on the church grounds and the house was destroyed. It had been serving as a residence for Canon Paddon. Fortunately, the church was saved by its parishioners.[102]

A decade later, the church accommodated an adjoining cemetery.[103] A Cowichan Indian, who lived in a home owned by **the Postman**, held the position as the grave digger.

In 1932, the Royal Canadian Legion constructed a *lych* gate in memory of the men who died in World War I.[104] It provided for a traditional, English, church yard entrance where wonderful examples of Arbutus trees grew.

Much later, in the 1990's, another fire ravaged through the forest behind the church. Reportedly, it loosened large boulders and sent them down into the church grounds where they now form part of a Centennial Memorial Garden.

St. Mary Magdalene Anglican Church as it appears today

Today, the church, which overlooks Miners Bay, is still very much the way it was at the

Mayne Island

turn of the century. The words, 'God and Ocean', can be read, in Japanese, on the steeple cross. They identify the church and its location in relation to the waters below.

Early in July, the church holds a long-lived annual fair called the *Country Fair,*. It is its only fundraising event.

Mayne Island Museum

In 1896, the famous explorer from Saturna Island donated some land near the wharf so a jail house could be built there. It was called the *Plumper Pass Lockup*.[105]

The jail measured just 32 sq m and contained a magistrate's courtroom and two holding cells. The reinforced doors of the cells in the jail were locked with iron crossbars.[106]

The jail was the police headquarters for all the southern Gulf Islands.[107] A constable, named Arthur Drummond, was the first to permanently police the Gulf Islands. He took residence in the building.[108]

The first prisoner to be held in one of the cells was arrested for larceny on Galiano Island. While **the Postman** was Justice of the Peace,[109] he presided over such cases when they were presented in the courtroom.

When police headquarters were moved to Salt Spring in 1905,[110] ownership of the building that operated as the Plumper Pass Lockup transferred to a physician.[111]

Mayne Island Museum in the 1950's, BC Archives B-07532

Mayne Island

Much later, in 1971, the jail was restored by the Mayne Island Agricultural Society, who converted it into the *Mayne Island Museum*.[112] Today, the museum is home to a variety of artifacts and historical data.

Mayne Island Museum as it appears today

Springwater Lodge

Around the same time the Plumper Pass Lockup was being built, **the Postman** was turning the two-story house he had built by the wharf into a boarding house.[113]

The Postman ran the boarding house for about 15 years, in an effort to supplement his income.[114]

After the turn of the century, his daughter, Emma, took over its operation, renaming it the *Grandview Lodge*.[115] Soon, the lodge had a false front and a six-bedroom wing off the side.[116]

Guests of the lodge were served berry pies, fresh garden vegetables and baked bread. They slept under hand-embroidered bed linens and quilts made of sheep's wool.[117]

The Springwater Lodge in Miners Bay in the early 1920's, BC Archives B-03269

By the 1930's, the lodge had developed such a good reputation that Emma was able to add indoor plumbing, electric lights and a walk-in refrigerator, in spite of the economic depression of that decade. She charged $14 for a single room, meals included.[118]

Mayne Island

The Springwater Lodge, 1930's
BC Archives D-07435

The Springwater Lodge as it appears today

In 1960, new owners changed the name to the *Springwater Lodge*.[119] Reportedly, a '67 Volkswagen van was impounded on Mayne after it crashed into the lodge. The owner who pressed charges was irate and unclothed.

Today, the Springwater Lodge is reputed to be the oldest, continuously operating hotel in all of British Columbia. Parts of **the Postman's** home still remain.

The lodge operates as a hotel during the summer months. It also provides for a year-round dining room and a seasonal seaside patio.

Mayne Island Agriculture Hall

By the turn of the century, Mayne had become the social center of the Gulf Islands. Even residents of Salt Spring would spend their weekends on Mayne.[120]

At that time, a community hall was built at Miners Bay. Because the Maple Leaf Club was formed to care for it, it was originally called the *Maple Leaf Hall*.[121] Later, it was renamed the *Mayne Island Agriculture Hall*.[122]

In 1925, an eccentric English woman, named Lady Constance Fawkes, started the *Mayne Island Fall Fair* at the Agriculture Hall and its fair grounds.[123] The fair grew and expanded until World War II, at which time it became dormant for seven years.[124]

Today, the agriculture hall is known locally as the *Ag Hall*. The hall and its fair grounds

Mayne Island

are the site of the famous *Mayne Island Farmer's Market*. They also host the annual Mayne Island Fall Fair.

The fair provides for a colorful parade and there is judging in a variety of categories, from produce and baking, to photography and crafts. It is the oldest fall fair in the outer Gulf Islands.

Curlew Island

In 1910, two brothers, named Ossian and Gottfried Bjornsfelt, emigrated from Norway to Canada.[125]

Ossian purchased a small island on the southeast side of Mayne. There, he raised goats and grew grapes.[126] He would often play his accordion at dances at the Agriculture Hall.

After he was badly wounded in World War I, Ossian returned to the little island and lived there until his death in 1931.[127]

At that time, his older brother, Gottfried, built a cottage on the east side of the island. He and his family used it as a summer residence. After his death in 1938, his family continued to vacation there into the '60's.[128]

Curlew Island contains less than .3 sq km of land. It is not serviced, except for a group of bighorn mountain sheep. The island is infested with domesticated peacocks that are living in the wild. If you listen carefully, you can often hear them squeal.

The Anchorage Heritage Home

Around the time that Ossian Bjornsfelt was settling on Curlew Island, an Englishman, named Richard Hall, purchased some land on Commander Maude's old property.[129] There, he established Mayne's first hothouse industry and pioneered the use of double-trussed greenhouses.[130]

In his greenhouse operation, he grew some of the first hothouse tomatoes in the province. However, in spite of the fact that he employed Chinese workers for 20 years, he never learned one word of the Chinese language.[131]

In the early 1920's, he built a larger operation, at Miners Bay. He called it *Mayne Island Nurseries* and specialized in flowers and tomatoes. His greenhouse was the largest in all of British Columbia.[132]

Eventually, Richard's hothouse industry became so large that his weekly shipments

Mayne Island

would often delay the steamer ships at the wharf for hours. As a result, he became well known on the West Coast as 'The Tomato King'.[133]

Unfortunately, Richard suffered in the stock market crash of 1929 and, subsequently, he retired in the 30's.[134]

Greenhouses near Miners Bay in the 1940's, BC Archives D-07434

When the Japanese took over his tomato industry, Richard began catering to guests from his home overlooking Miners Bay. He called his guesthouse *The Anchorage*.[135]

In the year 1950, The Anchorage ceased to operate as a guesthouse[136] but the hill on which it stands was named after this settler. It is called *Hall Hill*.

Today, Hall Hill is all that remains of Mayne Island Nurseries. A descendant of the settler still resides in the home.

Mayne Inn

In the year 1911, a French company began construction of a brick plant on Bennett Bay. The plant included a large wharf that extended into the bay and a boarding house accommodated the workers.[137]

At the onset of World War I, the plant was closed, without ever becoming operational. The Tudor-style boarding house remained empty until 1942, when it was converted into a hotel called the *Hollandia Hotel*. In the 1950's, the name was changed to the *Arbutus Lodge* and then to the *Mayne Inn* in the 60's.[138]

A decade later, the owners of the Inn attempted to build a large, commercial dock, adjacent to one of the best swimming beaches on Mayne.[139]

The project was estimated to cost as much as $60,000. However, before they received the necessary re-zoning, they started work

Mayne Island

on the dock. With half of the project completed, they were ordered to halt the work and begin its demolition.[140]

Today, the Mayne Inn is still operational. In the year prior to this writing, the new owners expanded the Inn by adding more guest suites called *Mayne Island Resort & Beach Homes*.

At the time of this writing, the historic Inn was also providing for a restaurant that emphasized locally grown and harvested Gulf Island products.

Mayne Island Health Center

Until the 1920's, pioneer women relied on the skills of Mrs. Robson and Mrs. Bennett who were midwives on the Island.[141]

In 1924, a retired Royal Canadian Northwest Mounted Police surgeon, named Dr. Christopher West, became one of the first resident doctors on Mayne.[142] He set up his practice in a building that extended out over Miners Bay.[143] His surgical tools sat on a little table, just inside the door.

A decade later, another doctor, named Dr. Thomas Roberts, set up his practice[144] in a small building that stands behind what is now the Springwater Lodge. It was simply called *Surgery*.[145]

In the 1930's, the Canadian Pacific Railway steamer would stop at Georgina Point to pick up seriously ill or injured patients, while on route from the mainland to Washington State.

Later, in 1965, a first aid station was built across from the school. At around the same time, an ambulance was purchased and a volunteer crew was appointed to operate it.[146]

A decade later, the *Mayne Island Health Center* was opened in the middle of the Island. An ambulance station was also established there.[147] Today, a resident physician and a visiting public health nurse provide health care to residents from the health center.

Mayne Island

The building where Dr. West had set up his practice is now a private residence on Georgina Point Road. It can be seen from the wharf.

Miners Bay Trading Post in the 1950's
Galiano Archives 2004026691

Miners Bay Trading Post

In 1926, a general store was built just east of the wharf at Miners Bay.[148] It changed owners several times until the year 1960, when it was run as a franchise called Bambrick Store Ltd. by a family on Galiano.[149] Reportedly, it was the only store on Mayne for a while.

Because there was no health centre on the Island at the time, three of its rooms were partitioned off to create a clinic for the doctors. This continued for many years.[150]

Soon, new owners changed the name of the store to *Hopkins Trading Post*. During much of the 1950's and 60's, the post office operated from this store. The name was then changed to the *Mayne Island Trading Post*, and then to the *Miners Bay Trading Post*.[151]

In the 1970's, an apartment that had been built above the Miners Bay Trading Post caught fire. The fire spread to the store beneath it and a new building was constructed to replace it.[152]

The Miners Bay Trading Post was the second business to be issued a liquor license in all of British Columbia.[153] At the time of this writing, it was operating as a grocery and liquor store.

Mayne Island

Active Pass Auto & Marine

Until the introduction of gasoline-powered vehicles, boat was the only means of transportation to and from Mayne.[154] However, in the 1920's, automobiles began to appear,[155] the first of which was a 1914 Model 'T' Ford.

In the 1940's, a roadside gas pump was set up at Miners Bay. The oil and gas drums were transported from the Miners Bay wharf by hand. In 1967, a pump was installed with a pipeline that led to modern storage tanks. A few years later, a building was constructed to enclose an automobile repair service.[156]

Today, you can gas up your vehicle at the *Active Pass Auto and Marine* station, from what is still a single gas pump. The station also offers 24 hour towing and a two-bay garage. At the time of this writing, you could also obtain fishing licenses, tackle and bait there.

Japanese Memorial Garden

The first Japanese to come to Canada were known as *Issei*. They settled on Vancouver Island where they encountered racism from the anti-Asian population of British Columbia, as well as from the government.[157]

The government denied the Japanese-Canadians the right to work in a profession. So when they came to Mayne in the 1890's, the first Japanese worked as laborers, cutting wood and making charcoal for the Fraser River canneries.[158]

Fishermen in the 1880's, believed to be the first Japanese in Victoria - BC Archives B-08405

Around the turn of the century, Japanese-Canadian fishermen began settling on the southeast side of Mayne, at St. John Point and at what is now Horton Bay.[159]

Within their own community they knew Mayne Island as *Gon Island*, which they named after one of the first Japanese settlers.[160] Fortunately, they were well received by the Europeans who had already settled on Mayne.[161]

The fishermen soon began concentrating on raising chickens. Their families produced market eggs from about 50,000 hens.[162]

Unfortunately, in the 1930's, freight increases made poultry farming unprofitable. So many Japanese families began to cultivate hothouse tomatoes and other vegetables, forming a successful marketing

Mayne Island

cooperative called *Active Pass Growers Association*.[163]

The cooperative boasted almost 35,000 sq m of greenhouses, made from glass imported from Japan.[164]

Label used by the Active Pass Growers Association in the 1930's

By the 1940's, the Japanese-Canadian community comprised one-third of Mayne's population.[165]

Unfortunately, when the Japanese attacked Pearl Harbor during World War II, the Japanese-Canadians were taken from their homes on Mayne and were dispatched to the interior of British Columbia where internment camps had been set up in remote towns.[166]

Japanese-Canadian internment camp, south of Slocan City, in the 1940's, BC Archives I-60959

At the same time, the Canadian Navy impounded all Japanese-Canadian fishing boats that existed in British Columbian waters.[167]

Some of the European settlers tried to buy the property belonging to their Japanese friends, but that soon became a criminal offence.[168]

After World War II, the property was sold off by government agents acting on orders made under the provisions of the War Measures Act. Ironically, their property was often sold to war veterans.

Even after the war, the Japanese-Canadian families were prohibited from returning to the British Columbian coast. They were only allowed to return to Japan or to travel east of the Rocky Mountains.[169]

Many traveled to the neighboring province of Alberta, to work as laborers on sugar beet farms.[170]

Eventually, the right to vote was returned to the Japanese-Canadians, who had lost it before the turn of the century. However,

Mayne Island

very few of them ever returned to Mayne to receive that right.

The *Japanese Memorial Garden* is a heritage park that was built by Mayne Islanders, on what was once a Japanese-Canadian fruit farm. The development was undertaken to commemorate the Japanese-Canadians who originally settled and worked on Mayne.

In the garden, Katsura trees, Japanese cherries, flowering plums and rhododendrons surround a large pond. Recently, a small group of individuals who quietly tend to the garden received the Islands Trust Community Stewardship Award for donating their time.

The Japanese Garden is visited by tourists during the summer and is decorated with an impressive display of festive lights during the Christmas season.

Mayne Mast Restaurant & Pub

In the 1920's, a Japanese fisherman, named Kumazo Nagata, purchased a turn-of-the-century, Victorian style home at Miners Bay.[171] Later, his family purchased a small greenhouse from Richard Hall, which they dismantled and moved, piece by piece, to Miners Bay.[172]

After re-assembling the greenhouse alongside his home, Kumazo began to use it to grow hothouse tomatoes.[173] It was he who established the Active Pass Growers Association.[174]

In 1937, Kumazo enlarged his home, only to have his family evacuated from it at the start of World War II.[175]

Much later, in the 1970's, the home was converted into a restaurant called the *Five Roosters Restaurant*.[176] Today, the home operates as the *Mayne Mast Restaurant and Pub*.

Mayne Island

Horton Bay

When the first Japanese settled on *Horton Bay* around the turn of the century,[177] it was called *Kawashuri Bay*.[178] One of the first Japanese-Canadians to settle on the bay was a Japanese-Canadian named Ei Kadonaga.[179]

In the 1930's, when the Japanese-Canadian families on Mayne formed the growers association,[180] Ei and his family built a portable sawmill on the bay to provide the lumber for the crates used in the shipment of their products.[181]

At the start of World War II, the family was evacuated from their home. It was later acquired to serve returning veterans of that same war.[182]

Horton Bay is located on the southeast side of Mayne. It provides for breathtaking views of Curlew Island to the east. The Kadonaga home still sits in a tiny cove in the bay. The face of a dock the family had built up with rocks[183] can be seen at the end of the road in front of their old boathouse.

Because of the government wharf that is located at the end of Horton Bay Road, Horton Bay is a great location for boat launching. However, thoro are *skookumchuck* (strong currents) on the east side of Curlew.

Boats can also be launched in the bay from a pebbled beach that is accessible by way of Steward Road. The road leads to a small point, known locally as *Spud Point*.

Mayne Island Fire Department

Because fires had destroyed so many buildings on Mayne in the first half of the century, it was incorporated into a fire protection district in 1964.[184]

The Agriculture Hall served as the fire hall. Ironically, it was made out of wood and the only fire protection available was a forestry pump and several hundred feet of hose.[185]

Within two years, a tanker truck was purchased for one dollar. It was followed by the purchase of an 800-gallon truck.[186]

When the *Mayne Island Volunteer Fire Brigade* began to meet with the *high muckymuck* (fire chief) for fire drills, the brigade moved to a three bay hall [187] In the

Mayne Island

year 1970, a modern, fire pumper truck was purchased and an electronic fire alarm system was installed.[188]

Today, the *Mayne Island Fire Department* consists of in excess of 20 *smoke eaters* (fire fighters). By their own admission, they "willingly rush toward a burning building that everyone else is rushing away from".

Saturna Island

Lyall Harbour Wharf

It was in the spring of 1896 that an Englishman, named Harold Payne, headed for Telegraph Creek to start a trading post in the gold mining fields...

To transport their gear, Harold and two other settlers purchased 150 mules. On the way to the gold fields, they encountered people celebrating Victoria Day. Alarmed, the mules started a stampede that the crowds mistook as part of the celebrations.[1]

Harold Payne was born in 1871. In 1891, he immigrated to Canada. Two years later, he settled on Saturna Island.[2]

The adventurous Harold Payne was a skilled traveler. He had spent 15 years sailing around the world and had taken many trips to British Columbia and the Arctic. He had dreams of becoming an officer. Unfortunately, they were shattered when he was found to be colorblind.

In 1894, Harold became **the Postman** for Saturna Island, operating a store and post office from buildings he constructed on a bay.[3] Years later, his daughter had this to say about him:

"Of course, Dad would let us. He never told us not to do anything because it was dangerous... Dad used to clear land and put up fences, and go cruising when he felt like it. And in the early days, of course, they always used to go off on these great trips – big game hunting up north with pack horses and guides."

Dora Payne[4]

Saturna Island

The Rugged Island

Saturna is a rugged island. At 31 sq km, it is the second smallest of the southern Gulf Islands. While rocky, sloping terrain and quiet seaside drives are its most distinguishing characteristics, the lack of commercialism gives Saturna Island its unique charm.

Saturna has more parkland per size and population than any of the other Gulf Islands and five mountains that are taller than 300 m. Its tallest mountain is the second highest peak in the outer Gulf Islands.

Although it is not the smallest of the Gulf Islands, Saturna is the most remote and least inhabited. Because its terrain makes it more difficult to develop than the other Islands, it has a population of only about 350 permanent residents.

Unlike the other Islands, where families have a continuous history, all of the early settlers have come and gone from Saturna, leaving a relatively new population.

Most of the permanent residents live near *Lyall Harbour*, where the services and facilities are located. During the tourist season, the population doubles to around 600.

Saturna Beach

As settlers started to emigrate from England in the 1870's, residential development of Saturna began on the west side. One of the first land owners to build on the Island purchased property at the harbour.[5]

Other settlements developed in secluded areas that were cut off from the harbour by tall peaks and steep cliffs. Those families who settled there learned to become self-sufficient.[6]

At that time, two brothers, named William and Charles Trueworthy, immigrated to Canada, from England. In 1883, Charles purchased some land on a bay, beneath a mountain on the southwest side of Saturna. He became the first permanent white settler on the Island.[7]

On the beach surrounding the bay, Charles constructed a house out of rough lumber. Because he was afraid that Indians might attack his property, he built holes into his home, through which he could fire a gun, if necessary.[8]

Unfortunately, only one year later, Charles was forced to put his beachfront property up for sale, due to health reasons.[9]

Saturna Island

Saturna Beach

In 1884, an explorer from England, named Warburton Pike, went into partnership with another Englishman, named Charles Payne. The two men decided to purchase the waterfront property that was for sale on the bay.[10]

There, on the beach, Warburton developed a ranch. He built a well-furnished bungalow with a vaulted ceiling and filled it with trophies of the big game he had killed.[11]

Initially, Warburton would row to Mayne or Pender Island for supplies, returning by way of the beach. Subsequently, the beach became known as *Pike's Landing*.

In the 1890's, he extended a wharf from the beach into the bay.[12] The wharf accommodated ships coming through the waterway called *Plumper Sound*.

Saturna Beach wharf at the turn of the century BC Archives C-06964

Warburton frequently went on sailing trips on his sloop called the *Fleetwing*. He would leave no word of his location and sometimes disappeared for months at a time. Whenever he went sailing, he would clean his dirty clothes by fastening them to the end of a long rope and letting them trail in the water.[13]

Referred to as 'Crazy Pike',[14] he was well known for not owning any decent clothes.[15] Once, while on a trip, **the Postman** left his trunk in town to lighten his load. Warburton went into the trunk and borrowed a good suit. It was a strange sight to see him dressed up, with nowhere to go but into the wilderness. He wore the suit until it fell apart.[16]

Eventually, Warburton gained a worldwide reputation, as a result of having written two books about his adventures.[17] Unfortunately, during World War I, he ended his life with a penknife, in an English sanitarium.[18]

In the 1920's, the wharf on the beach was torn down. A decade later, a new wharf was built and Pike's Landing was renamed *Saturna Beach*.

Although Warburton's house on the beach burned down[19] in the 1930's, his land is still known as the *Old Ranch*[20] and his memory is preserved in *Mount Warburton Pike*, the second highest peak in the outer Gulf Islands.

Saturna Island

Saturna Beach is situated at the foot of the 497 m peak, which provides for stunning panoramic views of the southern Gulf Islands, as well as of the San Juan Islands in the U.S.

The wharf on Saturna Beach has been moved many times over the years.[21] Today, it can be seen extending into the bay from the same location as the original turn-of-the-century wharf.

Saturna Beach wharf as it appears today

Brown Ridge

Before the turn of the century, sheep thrived on the hills of Saturna, roaming wild through the bush.[22] In the 1880's, an Indian sheep farmer, named Billy Trueworthy, lived in a shack on Warburton Pike's ranch. A nephew of Charles Trueworthy, he made a living tending several hundred sheep.[23]

Billy would run effortlessly up and down a ridge that rose above his home on the beach. Because he could run tirelessly for hours, the other settlers always called on him to help whenever they had to gather their sheep off the mountain.[24]

Billy ran bent over, as though he was heading into battle with a spear in his hand. He could run as fast as the little dog that helped him.[25]

Sometimes, the other settlers had to round up their sheep for earmarking the lambs.[26] Everyone would yell at the top of their lungs, while the sheep ran ahead. Billy had a wild, fierce, Indian yell that he would use whenever the sheep ran in the wrong direction. Dogs would crouch on the ground whenever they heard it.[27]

Saturna Island

Today, the hills and ridges of Saturna provide for some of the best hiking destinations in the Gulf Islands. The ridge, known as *Brown Ridge*, runs east from the top of Mount Warburton Pike.

Initially called *Prairie Hill*, Brown Ridge is protected within the Gulf Islands National Park Reserve. It provides for one of the most incredible hikes in all the Gulf Islands, with phenomenal views of the Pender Islands and of Washington State.

The slopes of Brown Ridge are significant habitat for falcons, eagles and large feral goats. There are numerous goat trails on the ridge. The feral goats that inhabit the area are descendants of domestic goats that were kept by families around the turn of the century.[28]

Breezy Bay B&B

In 1886, Charles Payne traveled to England and returned to Saturna with his younger brother, Gerald.[29] The first night on the Island, Gerald slept rolled up in a coat, on a shelf in Warburton Pike's fruit shed.[30]

The Payne brothers came from a wealthy family and received small incomes from England.[31] So, in 1892, Gerald purchased his own property, on a point on the west side of Saturna.[32] At that time, the point was called *Old Point*. It was later renamed *Payne Point*.[33]

Gerald established a farm on the point, where he built a green and white frame house near a bay. Although he was still a bachelor at the time, his home was well kept, the bed was always made and a basin, water jug and towels were always set out.[34]

Breezy Bay B&B in 1898 BC Archives C-06980

Six years later, Gerald joined the gold rush, along with his brother, Harold.[35] When he returned to Saturna, Gerald married and settled in to family life, building a separate schoolhouse on his property for his children's education. In the evening, he would tell them stories at the dining room table.[36]

On either side of Payne Point, he built docks from which he put his boat in the water. He built a stone dock just north of the Saturna Beach wharf and a wooden dock in a cove on the opposite side of the point.[37]

Later, in 1935, the property was sold to a resident named James Money.[38] James owned a pet goat that was often seen running along the roof of the house.[39]

Much later, in the 1980's, new owners restored the old house and added a verandah. Today, they run the property as the *Breezy Bay Bed and Breakfast*. The B&B is situated on a working organic farm, called *Old Point Farm*.

Saturna Island

Breezy Bay B&B as it appears today

East Point Lighthouse

As Gerald Payne was making a home on Saturna Beach, a ship carrying a large supply of coal ran aground on *Boiling Reef* on the opposite side of Saturna. It was coming through the Pass.[40]

The wreckage remained on the rocks for a year and prompted the government to purchase land for a light station at the Pass. The property they purchased belonged to Warburton Pike, whose property holdings also included land on the east side of the Island.[41]

Two years later, the *East Point Light Station* was built on East Point. It helped to keep the white Empresses and other ships off the reef.[42]

The *East Point Lighthouse* had a circular staircase that led to a wonderful view.[43] The light flashed once every 30 seconds. It had six wicks and burned coal oil. It operated on a pendulum system that had to be wound up like a grandfather clock, in the morning and at night.[44]

One of the first keepers of the lighthouse was a Scotsman, named James Georgeson. He was a brother of the lighthouse keeper on Mayne Island.[45]

In the year 1909, James' oldest son, Peter, took over the operation of the light station. He had been the first white child ever to be born on Saturna.[46]

Over time, Peter became an expert builder of flat-bottomed skiffs, which he sold to the other residents. They would use the skiffs to get to and from their boats. He used only an axe to work with the wood. Some of the skiffs could carry as many as six people.[47]

Peter produced a total of 80 boats, while he lived at the light station.[48] One of the boats, called *Irene*, was used for over 60 years.[49]

In 1939, his younger brother, Harry, took over the lighthouse. As a result, the lighthouse was in the Georgeson name for over 50 years.[50]

In the year of this writing, the lighthouse was acquired as part of the Gulf Islands National Park Reserve. Although it was recently de-staffed, the grounds, which are locally referred to as *Lighthouse Park*, are open to the public year-round. The existing lighthouse was built in the 1940's.[51]

Saturna Island

East Point provides for spectacular views of Mount Baker in Washington State. Seals and Killer Whales are frequently spotted in the waters off the point.

The beach on the point is called *Shell Beach*. It provides for a stunning shoreline that is dotted with interesting boulders and intricate sandstone formations. Along the rocks on the beach are tidal pools, which are home to an abundance of Sea Stars.

Narvaez Bay Park

In 1891, a settler, named Andrew Robertson, purchased some land on a bay on the east side of Saturna. Having lived several years in the West Indies, he wore a hard black cummerbund on his head.[52]

Andrew's cummerbund was made of tattered pieces of cloth that included an old school tie, a remnant of silk and some frayed rope. He would often conceal a knife or a gun inside it.[53]

Andrew lived on his land only part of the time. The rest of the time, he lived on his leaky boat named *Edith*.[54]

The top of the boat's cabin was covered with tin and, when it rained, the noise from inside was deafening. Whenever he chopped wood inside the cabin, his axe would hit the canopy, causing the sound to echo around the bay.[55]

Andrew was very fond of children. However, he liked to pick them up by the collar or belt, and then dunk them into the bay. Sometimes, he would leave them underwater too long.[56]

Originally called *Deep Bay*,[57] Narvaez Bay is located on the east side of Saturna. Two smaller bays, called *Little Bay* and *Echo Bay*, sit on either side. The bays provide for great swimming.

Saturna Island

Almost half of Saturna is parkland that is protected within the Gulf Islands National Park Reserve. *Narvaez Bay* is the largest acquisition in the Gulf Islands to date.

Narvaez Bay Park is one of the most diverse ecosystems on the entire west coast and is a recent addition to the Gulf Islands National Park Reserve. There are facilities for picnics if you want to stay awhile.

Taylor Point

In 1892, an Englishman, named George Taylor, emigrated to Saturna. He settled on *Potato Bay*, on the secluded southeast side of the Island.[58] Isolated by steep cliffs, he and his family was forced to become self-sufficient.

There was a small stone quarry on the property that had been started by Warburton Pike. George used sandstone from the quarry to build a two-storey home for his family.[59]

George was an inventor. He had a machine shop in which he built his own stationary threshing machine and hay baler. He could also turn four-cylinder engines into two-cylinder engines.[60] His wife, who looked like a tall Scottish gypsy, baked wonderful cakes.[61]

At the turn of the century, the Cedar shake roof of the family's stone house caught fire and the house was destroyed. Nevertheless, George continued to live in the bunkhouse, while his wife lived in a houseboat.[62]

Saturna Island

Taylor Point was named after this family. The remains of their stone house and sandstone quarry can still be seen there today.

The old growth forest of Douglas-Fir, Arbutus and Garry Oak on Taylor Point runs along one of the longest, continuous stretches of protected shoreline in the southern Gulf Islands.

Saturna Island Post Office

In 1893, Harold Payne settled on Warburton Pike's property. There, he began operating a post office from a little building on Saturna Beach. Initially, he would sail his small sailboat to Mayne Island to collect the mail.[63]

The Postman arriving at Saturna Beach in the 1890's - BC Archives C-07060

When the wharf was built at Saturna Beach, a steamer ship started delivering the mail to the wharf. It soon became the custom for **the Postman** to turn the mailbags upside down on the wharf and let the people scramble for their letters.[64]

Postal delivery was the center of Island social life for many years. The settlers would organize games of grass hockey, football or cricket while they waited for the mail. **The Postman** usually provided tea.[65]

Three years later, **the Postman** transferred the postal service to Arthur Drummond, the police constable from Mayne Island. He lived on Saturna occasionally.[66]

Soon, the mail was being hand-delivered to the settlers' homes by way of a police boat, called the *Constable*.[67] Those settlers who chose to wait for their mail at the post office would often be served bread and jam, and baked apples.[68]

In the 1930's, the post office was moved to a store at the harbour. Everyone would gather at the community hall to wait for the mail on boat days.[69] Two bachelors, who lived between two mountains, would leave a wheelbarrow near the harbour, which they would use to transport their mail.[70]

In the 1950's, the store was removed from the harbour. Subsequently, the post office was moved into a building up the road.[71]

Saturna Island

Meanwhile, **the Postman's** little building on Saturna Beach was being used for storage. Unfortunately, it was recently demolished.[72]

Today, the building up the road from the harbour functions as an Internet café and the post office operates from a newer store.

Saturna General Store

At the same time that **the Postman** built a little post office building on Saturna Beach, he also built himself a magnificent white house. From his house, he ran the first store ever to exist on Saturna.[73] It was called the *Saturna Island Store*.[74]

When the police constable took over **the Postman's** postal service, he also took over his store. The constable would deliver orders in his boat.[75]

A few years later, **the Postman's** brother-in-law, Major Bradley-Dyne, acquired the land on Saturna Beach, along with the store.[76] Later, the store became the home of George Taylor's son who was the caretaker for a resort. Unfortunately, the building burned down in the 1940's.[77]

Saturna Island Store, early 1900's - BC Archives C-070007

In the 1950's, James Money built another store, in the center of the Island. Called the *Saturna General Store*, it had apartments on the upper floor. A decade later, the store changed hands and the owners lived in an apartment at the back of the building.[78]

Today, the Saturna General Store functions as a grocery store, liquor store and post office. At the time of this writing, the new owners also operated an organic bakery that supplied baked goods to the store.

Saturna Island

St. Christopher's Church

In 1896, **the Postma**n brought his twin brother, Hubert, to Saturna. A few years later, Hubert, who was a Parson, purchased some land on the northwest side of the Island.[79]

On the property sat a Japanese boathouse that Hubert converted into a small church. Major Bradley-Dyne helped him build it. Then, the Major carved a large wooden cross and nailed it to the front gable.[80]

The church was named St. Christopher's Anglican Church. It seated just 20 people and was used for Sunday services.[81]

At that time, there were no roads into the area, so congregations came by boat.[82] The people would attend the church in black lace-up boots and little starched hats and white dresses.[83]

Hubert carried on his ministry with the help of an awkward motorboat called Gazelle.[84] It caused him a lot of grief.[85]

Because the church was never consecrated, it became a private residence when Hubert left the Island. Unfortunately, the resident wrapped a television antenna around the adorable rear gable of the church and strung a clothesline from one of its windows.[86]

By 1960, a Bishop from Pender Island was ministering to the residents of Saturna and Sunday services were being held in the community hall.[87]

Over time, a Saturna resident proceeded to build a replacement for the rundown old church. Some of the timber for the new church building came from the Point Comfort hotel on Mayne Island.[88]

The new St. Christopher's Church was designed as an upside-down boat. Beams were soaked with hot water so they could be curved to form arches. Then, every day, a clamp was twisted so that the top of the beams were gradually pulled to a precise curve. One by one, the arches were then raised and held upright with supports to form the shell of the building.[89]

On one side of the new church a wooden cross was set in a glass wall. On the other side a glass window was set in a wooden wall. A block of granite was donated as a corner stone and a small portable harmonium was donated to supply the church music.[90]

When the new church was complete, steel workers cast a bell in the tower.

Saturna Island

Unfortunately, a visitor pulled the rope and the bell fell and cracked.[91]

St. Christopher's Church in 1965
Jim & Lorraine Campbell

The new church was dedicated in the early 1960's. Later, in the year 1990, a couple donated some books and opened the *Eddie Reid Memorial Library* in the basement of the church.[92]

Eventually, the old St. Christopher's Church was restored. Today, it serves as a private chapel.

Winter Cove Provincial Marine Park

Like his older brothers, **the Postman** received a small income from England. In 1897, he purchased some land on a cove on the northwest side of Saturna. There, he built another home and started a family.[93]

The Postman's children were cut off from the other Islanders because there was no road into the cove. The only place they could walk was over a very rough trail to the lighthouse on East Point.[94]

The children learned to row in the cove by the time they were four years old. However, because the water was very cold, they did not learn to swim until much later.[95]

Once they learned how to swim, they would spend hours making rafts. Sometimes, they would trade apples from their orchard with the Indians, in exchange for old, leaky canoes. Then, they would patch them with tar and put sails on them.[96]

Saturna Island

The children earned extra money by salvaging logs. They would take a launch into the Strait, corral the logs, and then wrestle them down the beach. Then, they would pull the logs into the cove by hand, through a narrow passage.[97]

Much later, in 1979, a portion of the cove became *Winter Cove Provincial Marine Park*. Today, the park is a beautiful recreational area with a beachfront swimming area and a boat launch.

The park is also the site of the annual *Canada Day Lamb Barbeque*, one of the largest bashes in all the southern Gulf Islands. Each year, it draws hundreds of visitors from all over British Columbia.

Preparations for the barbeque begin long before people arrive. Lit in the early morning, an enormous bonfire is left to burn in a pit until a thick bed of smoldering coals remains. Metal crosses are then staked around the bonfire and whole lambs, which have been split down the middle, are skewered to the crosses to roast.

Winter Cove is a nature-lover's paradise, where Seals, Sea Lions and myriad birds can be seen. The beach consists of sandstone, shale and midden. There are areas for swimming and it is a good vantage point for spotting Whales during the summer.

A trail through the park leads to *Boat Passage*, which separates Winter Point on Saturna Island from Ralph Grey Point on Samuel Island. Once called *Canoe Passage*,[98] the passage provides whitewater excitement for experienced kayakers.

Tumbo Island

At the turn of the century, a German recluse, named Barnard Wensel, was living on a little island in the Georgia Strait.[99] During an evening storm in 1905, a visitor sought shelter on the island. Barnard, who was known locally as 'Jack The Ripper', warned the visitor to keep away.[100]

Saturna Island

When the visitor began to argue, Barnard retrieved a gun from his cabin and fired it at him. In self-defense, the visitor fired back through the darkness, and then fled.[101]

Worried that he had wounded or killed Barnard, the visitor reported the incident to Tom Collinson, the Justice of the Peace on Mayne Island. When a constable rowed to investigate the scene of the crime, he found Jack The Ripper dead on his doorstep.[102]

Tumbo Island is located off the northeast side of Saturna. Part of the Gulf Islands National Park Reserve, it is a day-use area that can be visited by small boat.

A short trail system through old growth Douglas-Fir and Garry Oak meadows provides for exploration of the island. However, the dock on the island is privately owned and the house is often inhabited.

Saturna Island Cemetery

In 1919, two people starting walking from either end of Saturna Island. Where they met became the site of its first school.[103] Unfortunately, during the depression of the 1930's, the population declined and the school was closed.[104]

After World War II, the school re-opened in a chicken house on the waterfront at the harbour. The children would make a habit out of intentionally dropping their pencils through the cracks in the old hen house as an excuse to go outside.[105]

A year later, Jim Money purchased some property for the building of a proper school nearby.[106] The builder donated a very nice book cabinet to the school. Unfortunately, the only reference books owned by the school was a set of The Book of Knowledge that had three volumes missing.[107]

When the new school was built the first school was torn down and the land became home to the *Saturna Island Cemetery*.[108]

Lyall Harbour

In the 1920's, the road to the harbour was just a narrow, single-lane track.[109] At that time, a wharf was built on Saturna Point. It extended into the harbour. For the most part, it replaced the wharf at Saturna Beach.

One day, an old man, who was living in a little shack at the harbour, took out an advertisement for a wife. When an interested lady responded to his ad, he sent her a photograph of himself.[110]

Eventually, the lady agreed to move to Saturna to be the man's bride. However, as her ship arrived in the harbour, she saw the old man and realized that the picture he had

Saturna Island

sent her was 40 years old. As a result, she refused to get off the ship.[111]

Lyall Harbour fits snuggly between Saturna Point and Winter Point. It provides for a boat launch at one end and a government wharf at the other. There is a sandy swimming beach at the head of the harbour.

Saturna Island Community Hall

In the 1930's, a community hall was built near the ferry terminal. It was called the Saturna Island Community Hall. For a while, church services were held there. Because there was no electricity, Coleman lamps were hung from a metal rod for light.[112]

The plans for the hall did not include a stage. So it was just large enough to serve as an indoor badminton court. The players had to avoid hitting the badminton birdie into the rod that held the lamps. Over time, a stage was built into the hall.[113]

During the 1950's, whenever there was a dance at the hall, James Money would pick up some of the other residents in his tractor-trailer and take them to the dance. Local accordion players provided the dance music and large Cedar trays were used to pass coffee around.[114]

Today, the community hall serves as the main venue for indoor events. It is also host to the annual *Saturna Island Farmer's Market*. The rod that once held the Coleman lamps now holds the lights for the stage.[115]

Thomson Community Park

In 1932, a resident of Vancouver, named Mr. Thomson, acquired the land on Saturna Beach from Major Bradley-Dyne. There, Mr.

Saturna Island

Thomson invested into the development of a resort. The resort was called the *Saturna Beach Resort*.[116]

Initially, three beachfront cottages were built at the resort, all of which had windows that opened like the windows on a tugboat. Within a couple of years, three more cottages were added, as well as a cookhouse that was set above ground on Cedar posts.[117]

In the 1940's, Mr. Thomson's daughter, Lorraine, inherited the property, along with her younger brother.[118]

A few years later, Lorraine and her brother divided the property between them and her brother claimed the portion that included Saturna Beach. As a result, Lorraine and her husband, Jim, moved onto a farm further inland.[119]

The Campbell Farm in 1956
Jim & Lorraine Campbell

Separated from their neighbors by a mountain, Jim and Lorraine became independent farmers on their portion of the property.[120]

They ploughed up an old pasture and established a potato farm, using a potato planter. Unfortunately, the pasture was infested with wireworm, which destroyed their first crop. Over time, the couple ceased growing potatoes and started raising sheep and cattle.[121]

In 1949, Lorraine's brother leased his beachfront property to an Argentinean sheep farmer. However, the Argentinean's luck soon turned bad and he decided to sell his flock and move off the Island. He sold all of his sheep, except for two lambs.[122]

The Argentinean had learned how to cook meat in Patagonia. So he offered to slaughter his two remaining lambs and hold an Argentine-style barbeque on Saturna Beach for the annual school picnic. At the picnic, he splayed the lambs out on the iron and roasted them over a fire.[123]

Canada Day Lamb BBQ in 1951
Jim & Lorraine Campbell

The lamb barbeque was so successful that, the following year, it was held on Canada Day and became the *Canada Day Lamb Barbeque*. Each year, the Argentinean would set up the lambs on the irons and oversee the barbeque.[124]

Saturna Island

Thomson Park in 1951 – Jim & Lorraine Campbell

Ironically, in 1964, the Argentinean died while preparing the spots for the irons at the next day's annual barbeque. Fortunately, the barbeque endured and, for 30 years, people traveled to the event by boat.[125] In the 1990's, Lorraine's brother sold Saturna Beach and the lamb barbeque was moved to Winter Cove Park.

Soon, plans were made to convert the family's Saturna Beach Resort into a park. Although the cottages were moved off the beach, the old cookhouse was left behind. Unfortunately, when the park was developed, the cookhouse was demolished.

Thomson Community Park is named after this family, who still use one of the resort cottages as their office.[126]

Thomson Park provides for a beachfront swimming area and there are facilities for picnics if you want to stay awhile.

A strenuous 4 km trail follows the shoreline, eastward, from the park. The trail passes *Murder Point*, which made history in 1863 when Indians killed a settler and his daughter there.[127]

Thomson Park as it appears today

Pender Islands

Port Washington Wharf

It was in the mid-1880's when an Englishman, named Washington Grimmer, purchased a herd of cattle from one of the southern Gulf Islands...

In a one-day cattle drive, Washington single-handedly drove his herd of cattle across the Island and hauled them onto the deck of a schooner by their horns. When the schooner reached the bay near his home, he lowered the cattle into the water and towed each one of them ashore in the darkness.[1]

Washington Grimmer was born in 1851 and immigrated to Canada with his family. In 1882, he crawled out of the window of a ship with his gun and dog, and set out for the Pender Islands.[2]

The ambitious Washington Grimmer was an ardent builder, having constructed several homes on North Pender.[3] With the help of his brother-in-law, he built the road that connects the two wharves.[4]

In 1891, Washington became **the Postman** for the Pender Islands, operating the post office from a home he had built there.[5] He was eventually made Justice of the Peace.[6]

Years later, his eldest son had this to say about him:

"...being of the restless type, he always found lots to do – a quick, wiry little man with a quick temper which, like a storm in a teapot, was over in minutes."

Neptune Grimmer[7]

Pender Islands

The Pristine Island

Pender is a pristine island. At 34 sq km, it is one of the largest of the southern Gulf Islands. While numerous beaches and dark forests are its most distinguishing characteristics, the spectacular festivals and events put on by the residents give Pender Island its unique charm.

North and South Pender in 1946
Pender Islands Museum

Pender Island is separated by a canal into two small islands known as *North Ponder* and *South Pender*. North Pender provides most of the services and facilities. South Pender is much more *illahee* (rural).

The two islands are, together, locally referred to as *the Penders* and a friendly rivalry has always existed between them. Because of the nationalities of the people who originally settled there, some of the settlers in the late 1800's referred to North and South Pender as *Little Scotland* and *Little England*.[8]

Pender is the second most populous of the southern Gulf Islands. Its population consists mainly of young *tillikums* (families), retirees and business professionals. Most of the 2,200 permanent residents live on North Pender. During the tourist season, the population doubles to around 4,000.

Hope Bay

In 1878, two settlers, named Noah Buckley and David Hope, purchased the entire northern half of North Pender, and then built a cattle fence that spanned the width of the island.[9]

On his portion of the land, David built one of the first homes on the Penders. Unfortunately, a wounded buck killed him, while he was on a hunting trip. Subsequently, his brother, Rutherford, inherited the home.[10]

The home was a little log cabin with a window on each side. The walls were built out of round Fir logs and the roof was made

Pender Islands

of split Cedar shakes.[11] The ceiling was so low that visitors had to lower their heads to move around.[12]

There was a stone fireplace at one end of the cabin. Behind it, was a chimney that was built out of square coal-oil cans. Above it, stretched a steel rod from which a kettle could be hung.[13] Across the end of the cabin was a lean-to shed, which was built out of poles and split Cedar.[14]

Hope Bay in 1946 - Pender Islands Museum

Hope Bay was named after this brother, who was famous for his home-baked bread.[15] He lived in the home until 1895.[16]

The bay is located on the northeast side of North Pender. If you launch a boat from the government wharf, you can travel north to Bricky Bay. However, tides there run up to 3 knots. Alternatively, you can travel across Navy Channel to Mayne Island and then on to Saturna Island, through a fascinating maze of islands and waterways.

Hope Bay as it appears today

Grimmer Bay

In 1882, Washington Grimmer went into partnership with his brother who had just bought out Noah Buckley. Two years later, Washington bought out his brother[17] and settled in what is now called the *Grimmer Valley*.[18]

In the valley, Washington built a four-room farmhouse.[19] Initially, as **the Postman**, he would row to Mayne Island to collect the mail.[20]

Because he found entering the bay near his home dangerous, he sometimes left his rowboat on a nearby island and swam to shore, instead.[21]

Walking up from the beach was also difficult. By the time he found the trail that led to his home, he had often used up a box of matches to light his way. Nevertheless, he soon brought his young bride to live in his home.[22]

The Postman's oldest child was the first white child born on the Penders. When his wife, Elizabeth, went into labor with their second child, he launched a boat to see a midwife on Mayne Island. However, before they reached their destination, she delivered their baby in the boat.[23]

In 1891, **the Postman** built a small cabin above the wharf,[24] only to sell it a few years

Pender Islands

later. At that time, he moved deeper into the valley where he developed a dairy farm.[25]

When his sons started entering his Jersey cows in all the major fairs in the province, his cattle became famous all over British Columbia.[26]

Shortly before the outbreak of World War I, he enlarged his home and turned it into a guesthouse.[27]

Grimmer Bay, early 1900's – Pender Islands Museum

Grimmer Bay was named after this Englishman, whose 1920's retirement home still stands overlooking the bay.

Grimmer Bay is located on the northwest side of North Pender. If you launch a boat from the wharf that extends into the bay, you can travel south to Mouat Point. The shoreline between Mouat Point and Stanley Point is quite captivating.

From there, you can continue all the way to Wallace Point. However, Swanson Channel can be dangerous and there are only a few places to pull out around Oaks Bluff.

Grimmer Bay as it appears today

Pender Islands

Hamilton Beach

At around the same time that **the Postman** was settling in his valley, a Scottish stonecutter, named Alexander Hamilton, was carving gravestones on Vancouver Island for the Mortimer Monumental Works Company.[28]

The company was also quarrying at the harbour on North Pender. Because they liked his work, they sent Alexander to the harbour to help with the quarrying.[29]

Soon, Alex purchased some land at the head of the harbour. There, he built a cabin where he and his family vacationed.[30]

Three years later, his younger brother, Hugh, emigrated from Scotland and moved into the cabin.[31] At the turn of the century, when Alex brought his family to live in the house full-time, Hugh built another home nearby.[32]

Whenever there was mail to be picked up at the South Pender Post Office, one of the Hamilton brothers would raise a flag on his property. Some of the other settlers would walk a long way just to see if the flag had been raised. If it had, they would then walk the rest of the way through the bush to pick up their mail.[33]

Hamilton Beach in the 1920's - Pender Islands Museum

Pender Islands

Hamilton Beach is located at the head of Browning Harbour. It was named after these two brothers who, in the year 1890, also brought the first horse to the Penders.[34]

The beach provides for a wharf and is a good place for a *soak* (swim). The Port Browning Marina at the harbour offers temporary boat anchorage and there are facilities for picnics if you and your boat want to stay awhile.

Mortimer Spit was named after the company who owned the quarry. Located on the most westerly tip of South Pender, the spit provides for one of the best swimming and clam digging beaches on the Penders.

If you launch a boat from Hamilton Beach, you can travel south to Mortimer Spit. At certain times, you can pass through the canal and on to Peter Cove. However, because the canal is only 12 m wide and tides run up to 4 knots, it should only be navigated at slack water.

Alternatively, you can travel south to Razor Point, and then head north to Bricky Bay. However, tides there run up to 3 knots.

Pender Islands Community Hall

The first community hall to be built on North Pender was constructed in the 1880's, on **the Postman's** land.[35]

In the year 1910, a second community hall was built,[36] beside a store at Hope Bay. It was called the *Hope Bay Community Hall*. Unfortunately, the hall was built on uneven ground, which caused its post foundation to become unstable.[37]

Two years later, a settler leased some of his land for a third community hall called the *Port Washington Community Hall*. It replaced the first hall in that community,[38] which had been disposed of at the turn of the century.[39]

By 1912, there were two halls in operation on North Pender; the Port Washington Community Hall and the Hope Bay Community Hall.[40]

Pender Islands

The Port Washington hall was initially a square box. It had a flat roof that was later replaced with a peaked roof. Because it had no electricity or indoor plumbing, water had to be brought in to the hall and gas lanterns were hung from the ceiling for light.[41]

For a while, the Port Washington hall was used as a school and for holding church services. A year after it was built, roller-skating was introduced to it and, soon, the floor became so uneven that dancing proved impossible and a new floor had to be laid.[42]

In 1932, some residents stayed up until midnight planning the Islands' first *Pender Islands Fall Fair* . It was hosted at the Hope Bay Community Hall and its fair grounds.[43]

In an effort to encourage them to plant vegetables to enter in the fair, the Farmers' Institute gave seeds to all the children living on the Island. Then, they came to the children's homes to inspect their gardens.[44]

Initially, the sponsoring community groups had to borrow folding tables for the fair and haul them across the Island for each and every event, including the evening dance, which was a highlight.[45]

In the first year of the fair, a settler's son won first prize for his entry. He took a vacation with his winnings.[46]

Another year, a woman decided to enter a cake decorated like the Union Jack, which was the national flag at the time. When she discovered that she had run out of blue food coloring, she used ink, instead. The cake won first prize.[47]

The fall fair was terminated at the onset of World War II and was not re-introduced until 1962.[48]

By then, the post foundation supporting the Hope Bay hall had deteriorated, causing it to be razed by fire.[49] Subsequently, it was torn down and the Port Washington hall became the social center for the Penders.[50]

Unfortunately, a decade later, the Port Washington hall was also razed by fire.[51] When its remains were torn down, its assets were transferred to a new school that had just been built.[52]

Port Washington Community Hall in 1963 - Pender Islands Museum

Pender Islands

The plans for the new school had included a community hall. It was the fourth hall to be built on the Penders.[53]

Recently, a fifth community hall was built. Under the guidance of a *Tsimshian* carver, a project was undertaken by about 60 women to carve three poles that now stand at the entrance to the new hall. The Women's Unity Welcome Poles display the figures of mother bears and a bear cub.

In addition to the *Pender Islands Fall Fair*, the *Pender Islands Community Hall* and its fair grounds are host to the *Pender Islands Farmer's Market*.

Visitors to the Island can bring their *tillicum* (friends) to the hall and enjoy a variety of other civic functions, from musical concerts to performing arts presentations.

The Pender Islands Fall Fair takes place in August. There are 1,000 exhibits entered each year, in a variety of categories. Judging takes place in numerous events and the fair is still followed by a dance.

North Pender Island Wharves

In the year 1891, the first wharf was built, on the northwest side of North Pender. It accommodated ships coming through the waterway called *Swanson Channel*.[54] The port was named *Port Washington*, in honor of **the Postman**.[55]

At the turn of the century, another wharf was built, in Hope Bay.[56] Because it was situated opposite Port Washington, a rivalry began between the largely English community of Port Washington and the Scottish community of Hope Bay.[57]

Pender Islands

In 1951, a ship, named *Princess Elaine*, was introduced to the waters surrounding the Islands. The Port Washington wharf was the only wharf in the outer Gulf Islands that could accommodate it.[58]

Port Washington Wharf in 1925 – Pender Islands Museum

Today, the Port Washington wharf is used to transport schoolchildren to neighboring schools, and by sea planes traveling between Pender and *Big Smoke* (Vancouver).

Occasionally, freighters can be seen at the Hope Bay wharf, waiting their turn to proceed to larger ports of call.

Pender Islands Post Office

When the Port Washington wharf was built in 1891, a steamer ship began delivering the mail directly to the wharf.[59] At that time, **the Postman** converted part of the porch in his cabin into a mailroom, from which he provided postal service.[60] The cabin was

Pender Islands

enlarged at the turn of the century.[61] Today, it is a private residence on an old orchard.

A year or so after **the Postman** accepted his postal duties, the post office was moved to a small building at the head of the Hope Bay wharf.[62]

The mail came in by way of an overland trail and the settlers would stand and wait at a little counter for their envelopes and parcels to be dispatched.[63]

A few years later, the first store ever built on the Penders was constructed near the Hope Bay wharf, by a settler named Mr. Corbett. He called the store *Corbett's*[64] and his small frame building soon became the home of the *Pender Island Post Office*. The address was simply 'Pender Island'.[65]

Pender Island Post Office in 1933
Hope Bay Rising Holdings Ltd.

In 1910, an Englishman, named Spencer Percival, built another store, at the head of the first wharf. The store was called the *General Store* and the *Port Washington Post Office* was established there.[66] Its address was 'Port Washington'.[67]

Port Washington Post Office, early 1900's
BC Archives D-08531

Soon, Corbett's store at Hope Bay was moved into a new building that had been constructed nearby. The Pender Island Post Office was then relocated to a large area at the back of the new store.[68]

Each time the store changed hands the new owners continued to use **the Postman's** original post office box in the post office.[69]

Much later, in the 1970's, the two post offices were consolidated as the *Pender Islands Post Office* and were moved into a mall in the center of North Pender. Unfortunately, within a decade, both stores had closed.[70]

A few years prior to this writing, the store at Hope Bay was restored.[71] The buildings are now being operated as offices, a gift store and a café.

Pender Islands

Ye Olde Pender Island Post Office as it appears today

Although the General Store at Port Washington changed owners several times, it was home to the Port Washington Post Office for over 70 years.[72] At the time of this writing, it was also being restored.

Ye Olde Port Washington Post Office as it appears today

Today, the Pender Islands Post Office sits behind the mall to which it had been moved in the 1970's. It serves both North and South Pender.

Mount Menzies Park

After **the Postman** converted his porch into a mailroom, he ran an ad for a farm hand to help him farm his land.[73] The settler who filled the position was named Mr. Menzies. He worked on the farm for three years.[74] Later, he purchased his own farm, in a valley.[75]

Mr. Menzies bred award-winning poultry on his farm, which he initially called the *Nob Hill Poultry Farm*, but later renamed the *Valley Home Farm*.[76] When he won second prize for his Ayrshire bull at the Victoria Fair, the showing of cattle from around the Penders began.[77]

Mr. Menzies entered animals at all the major fairs in the provinces. All of his cattle were on the Record of Performance Test. The first few cows of that breed ever to pass the test in Canada were from his herd.[78]

Soon, he purchased two Jersey cows and a bull, and established a fine Jersey herd that also won numerous prizes. One year, he won first prize for the most milk and butterfat produced by a single cow in two days.[79]

Mount Menzies was named after this settler, who lived on his farm for over 70 years.[80] Originally named *Bald Cone*, it is a 120 m peak on the east side of North Pender that provides for great views of Mayne and Saturna Islands.[81]

Pender Islands

Mount Menzies stands in *Mount Menzies Park*, which is part of the Gulf Islands National Park Reserve. The park provides for 2 km of moderately difficult trails through beautiful, dense Western Red Cedar and Douglas-Fir.

Davidson Bay

In 1892, **the Postman** sold some of his land on the bay to a Scottish settler named Andrew Davidson.[82]

Andrew was known for his rowing ability.[83] When he needed lumber to build his home, he rowed to Vancouver Island with his sons. Then, they walked the 30 km to Victoria to purchase it and towed it back to their property on a homemade raft.[84]

Davidson Bay was named after this settler,[85] but is now known locally as *Clam Bay*. The pebbled beach at the bay is accessible by way of a stunning 1.5 km trail of moderate difficulty.

The trail to the beach is called the *Found Road Trail*. It leads through lush forest of dense Douglas-Fir and Western Red Cedar, and passes through five ecological zones.

Pender Islands School

In 1893, **the Postman** and two other settlers chose a teacher for the children of North Pender. Classes were held on his property, in the Port Washington Community Hall.[86]

The hall was equipped with a painted blackboard, tables and benches. Students carried a lard pail lunch and their own textbooks to class, and completed their assignments on slates.[87]

The following year, a small outbuilding was built beside the hall. When it was equipped with desks, classes were then moved there from the hall. Water was carried to the building from a spring and a student was paid to stoke a fire for heat.[88]

At the turn of the century, the settlers decided that a new school was needed. Reportedly, they drew a circle around a map of North Pender and marked the building site in the centre, at Hope Bay.[89]

Upon completion of the school at Hope Bay, a couple made a home out of the old buildings at Port Washington.[90]

At the end of the first school year, 23 students wrote the high school entrance examinations. Of the four students who passed the exams, two attended the school at Hope Bay.[91] As a result, its teacher

Pender Islands

became well known in educational circles around British Columbia.[92]

At that time, the school consisted of only one room on a single level. Eventually, the front entrance was moved to the side of the building and a second level was added.[93]

Hope Bay School in 1946 - Pender Islands Museum

In the 1970's, a third school was built on North Pender. It was named the *Pender Islands Elementary Secondary School*.[94]

Ye Olde Hope Bay School as it appears today

When construction of the new school was complete, the old schoolhouse at Hope Bay was sold to the Recreation and Agriculture Hall Association for one dollar.[95] It is now home to a thrift store.

Today, the Pender Islands Elementary Secondary School serves the communities of both North and South Pender. The school

Pender Islands

accommodates over 100 full-time equivalent students.

United Community Church

The work of the Presbyterian Church began on North Pender in 1894. Services were held in the community hall, and a set of used Sankey hymnbooks and an organ were donated.[96]

Mr. Menzies' younger brother, George, accepted the task of pioneering the work. He made the first set of slatted benches and built a rowboat to provide transportation to and from the services.[97]

At the turn of the century, the first ordained minister was appointed and a gas-powered boat was built for his use.[98]

United Community Church in 1940
Pender Islands Museum

In 1905, some land was donated for the building of a church and the *Pender Island Presbyterian Church* was built on a hill overlooking Hope Bay. In 1921, a Manse was built below the church, for use as the Reverend's residence.[99]

Four years later, the Presbyterian Church merged into the United Church of Canada and the church building became known as the *United Community Church*.[100]

Much later, in the 1980's, when the Roman Catholics had no venue in which to hold church services on the Penders, the United Community Church building was used as a location for Catholic services.[101]

United Community Church as it appears today

Today, the United Community Church operates as a non-denominational church. As the oldest church on the Penders, it has changed very little since it was constructed at the turn of the century.

Canned Cod Bay

At around the same time that the Presbyterian Church was formed, two settlers, named Arthur Stanford and Elisha Pollard, settled on South Pender.[102]

Arthur purchased a farm on the waterfront. He called it *Southlands*.[103] Elisha helped him run it.[104]

Arthur made periodic trips to the U.S. to smuggle back cases of canned goods. The police had been suspicious of the smuggler for a while, but could not catch him.[105]

Pender Islands

One day, he arrived home with a load of cans. He carried them from his boat and hid them in some thick Alder trees. Then, he began falling the trees over the cans to hide them.[106]

Meanwhile, the police arrived to search his property for cans. As they searched, he continued falling trees. They searched everywhere, except under the falling trees. As a result, he was never caught.[107]

Canned Cod Bay is located on the southern tip of South Pender. It provides for great views of the San Juan Islands, the Strait of Juan de Fuca and Mount Baker, in Washington State. It is also a great place to spot whales.

The beautiful pebbled beach on the bay is lined with driftwood. At low tide, you can explore shallow caverns that have been carved out by the tides.

Hyashi Cove

In 1895, **the Postman** sold some waterfront property on a bay to a Japanese-Canadian sea Captain, named Mr. Hyashi.[108]

In a cove in the bay, Captain Hyashi started a herring saltery and fish processing plant. He then brought other Japanese families to the cove and became the boss of a Japanese camp that was established there.[109]

The saltery operated a fleet of seiners that fished in the Channel. At night, the fishing fleet displayed a spectacle of lights, while it traveled through the water.[110]

The saltery employed a large number of men, of various nationalities, who had a reputation for singing while they worked. As they sang, they packed the fish in cases, salting the fish heavily to escape paying a salt tax. Then, they sold them to countries in the Orient.[111]

Otter Bay in 1946 – Pender Islands Museum

Pender Islands

At the onset of World War II, when the Japanese-Canadian residents were taken from their homes on the Penders, the saltery was taken over. Unfortunately, the plant burned down in 1956.[112]

Hyashi Cove was named after the sea Captain who established the saltery.[113] Some remains of its concrete foundation can still be seen there.

The cove sits within a larger body of water, called *Otter Bay*, which is located on the northwest side of North Pender. It provides for the finest sandy beach on the Penders,.

The *Otter Bay Marina* at the cove provides for temporary boat anchorage. If you launch a boat from the marina, you can travel south along a fascinating shoreline to Mouat Point. From there, you can continue all the way to Wallace Point. However, there are few places to pull out around Oaks Bluff.

Pender Islands Museum

In 1896, a Scotsman, named Robert Roe, immigrated to North Pender with his family.[114] At the turn of the century, he purchased some land on a bay, where he and his wife established a farm.[115]

Soon, Robert built a cabin for their friends to vacation in. Their friends enjoyed it so much that the family decided to develop the property into a resort. They called it *Roesland Resort*.[116]

Each winter, the family added more cabins to the resort. Because the cabins only included the basic of necessities, their guests brought their own bedding and dishes, and carried their own water.[117]

By the mid-1920's, one of Robert's sons had taken over the resort. Robert Jr. built a general store on the property, for the use of his guests. He also maintained a gas station on nearby *Roe Islet* [118]

Pender Islands

By the 1950's, there were 17 cabins at Roesland Resort, each with its own bed, kitchen and outhouse. For those who could secure a reservation, it was one of the most popular vacation destinations in the southern Gulf Islands.[119]

In the 1970's, the property was sold to new owners who continued to run it as a resort. They built their own home on the property.[120]

In the 1990's, the resort was closed, after operating for over 70 years. Many of the regulars had been third and fourth generation guests.[121] When the land was purchased for use as a park, the Roe family was granted a life-long tenancy on the property.[122]

Recently, the Pender Islands Museum Society restored the family's house, and then converted it into an historical museum.[123] In the year prior to this writing, the *Pender Islands Museum* opened.

Roesland Park is located on the west side of North Pender. It is dense with Western Red Cedar and Douglas-Fir, and contains a highly sensitive ecosystem. Established in the 1990's, the park is now protected as part of the Gulf Islands National Park Reserve.

The easy, 600 m trail through the park leads to a footbridge that extends to Roe Islet. The islet is a good place to see Arbutus trees.

Roe Lake is located in Roesland Park. As one of the only natural, freshwater lakes in the Gulf Islands, it provides for good swimming.

Pender Islands

The easy 2 km trail to Roe Lake wanders through second-growth forest. Walking south along the trail will lead to the trail junction. At the junction, the trail to the left encircles the lake in a clockwise direction.

RCMP Boat

Before the turn of the century, rum running, hi-jacking, sheep stealing and wool smuggling were common occurrences on the Penders. At that time, the sheep farmers were all too familiar with a mysterious little smuggler from the U.S. who wore a very, very tall hat.[124]

Known locally as 'Old Burke', the smuggler would pay the farmers for their wool fleeces,[125] which they would store for him in their barns. Then, once a year, at dusk, the little smuggler would sail his big black boat into the harbours,[126] while he watched for Arthur Drummond's police boat on the beach.[127]

In the morning, the sheep fleeces, which had been carefully rolled up by the farmers, would be gone.[128]

Years later, when statistics showed that a tiny island had become the largest wool distributor in Washington State, the authorities became suspicious. So, to set a trap for the smuggler, they marked some fleeces that were stored in a shed at the harbour.[129]

Eventually, the marked fleeces were found in the possession of Old Burke, who was promptly arrested.[130] One of the farmers went to court to defend him and, subsequently, he was acquitted.[131] Nevertheless, wool smuggling ceased with the arrest of the smuggler in the tall, tall hat.[132]

Today, there is one Corporal stationed at the two-person RCMP detachment on North Pender. He is in charge of law enforcement for all the outer Gulf Islands. The RCMP boat can often be seen docked at one of the government wharves.

Oaks Bluff

With the help of his neighbor, Alexander Hamilton built a large fence on North Pender around the turn of the century. The fence enclosed a bluff that was used for raising sheep.[133]

Several times a year, the local men would hold a sheep run, herding the sheep from the bluff to the end of the point. The women and children would row to the end of the point to prepare a picnic lunch for when the men arrived.[134]

Oaks Bluff overlooks Swanson Channel at the south end of North Pender. Known locally as *The Oaks*, it is accessible by way of a steep trail, which provides for spectacular panoramic views of Bedwell Harbour and Swanson Channel.

Pender Islands

Lilias Spalding Heritage Park
At the turn of the century, a wharf was built in Bedwell Harbour. When the S.S. *Iroquois* began sailing through the Gulf Islands, the delivery of mail to South Pender began once a week via the new wharf.[135]

An Englishman, named Arthur Spalding, was the very first permanent settler on South Pender. In 1889, he married Lillias MacKay.[136]

Lillie was a good shot and would shoot at the deer if they ate the crops.[137] When the grapes were ripe, she made wine. She also baked bread, and made butter, cottage cheese and preserves. Whenever a pig was slaughtered, she rendered the lard, and cured hams and bacon.[138]

Arthur owned a library of 2,000 books. While he read, wrote poetry and sketched,[139] Lillie spun wool, which she then dyed[140] by hand.

Home of the South Pender Postmistress in 1908 – David Spalding

When the wharf was built in the harbour, Lillie became the Postmistress for South Pender, sorting the mail at the end of the wharf.[141]

Shortly thereafter, the crew of the HMS *Egeria* landed on the bay to study the tides. To carry out their duties, they built a small hut at the head of the wharf. When the crew departed three years later, Arthur and Lillie fell heir to the little building and converted it into the *South Pender Post Office*.[142]

The delivery of mail to the post office developed into a weekly social event. As the Postmistress, Lillie would drive her horse

Pender Islands

and buggy from the farm to the post office, along a dangerous wagon road.[143]

If the mail was late, she would often wait until after midnight for it to arrive. When the residents of South Pender turned up to discuss current events, she would serve them tea and cake.[144]

In 1932, the little hut from which she performed her postal duties was removed from the wharf. Although her farm was sold a few years later, Lillie continued to hold the position of Postmistress for South Pender until her death in 1951.[145]

Lilias Spalding Heritage Park was named after this pioneer woman, whose weaving loom can still be seen today, at the Pender Islands Museum.

The Spalding farm is now known locally as 'The Ranch'. A short trail through Lilias Spalding Park leads to the remains of one of the buildings there. The ruts, which are reported to have been left in the field by the settler's wagon, can still be seen there.

There is a steeper trail to the park, which is accessible from up the road. It leads to *Spalding Hill*, which provides for great views and beautiful rock faces. It is one of the best places in the Gulf Islands to see Turkey Vultures and Bald Eagles.

Located on the northeast side of South Pender, *Little Bay* provides for views of Mount Warburton Pike. Arthur and Lillie Spalding landed there upon returning home from their wedding on Saturna.[146]

Hope Bay Stores

At the turn of the century, Mr. Corbett moved with his family to North Pender.[147] The following year, he purchased some land on the northeast side of the Island. There, he established a farm, on which he built a house.[148]

Initially, the people of North Pender ordered their provisions and other goods by mail order, which were brought by boat to one of the two wharves.[149]

When Corbett's store opened at Hope Bay at the turn of the century,[150] it served local residents, as well as settlers from neighboring Saturna and Mayne Islands. It also provided a second home for the post office.[151]

Mr. Corbett asked all the ladies on the Island to make up grocery lists indicating their favorite brands.[152] They ordered long, black-beaded hatpins for their wide-brimmed hats, high-button shoes, as well as wool cashmere and pure silk stockings. The men generally shopped for gunpowder and buckshot. The supplies were then brought in to the store by the S.S. *Iroquois*.[153]

Corbett's store became very successful, eventually expanding into hardware and farm supplies.[154] Before the onset of World War I, a new store with two small warehouses was built on the site. A few years later, the two

Pender Islands

warehouses were replaced with a two-storey structure.[155]

In the 1920's, the store was modernized with an electric plant, refrigerator and ice cream cabinet. It was then further enlarged at the back.[156]

When the store was sold in the 1950's, it held claim to being the oldest, established, Gulf Islands general store to have operated under the same management for at least four decades.[157] On the firm's monthly accounts were many names of customers who had frequented the store when it first opened.[158]

The new owners changed the name of the store to *Smith Brothers*.[159] Later, it was shortened to *Smith's* and was then changed to the *Hope Bay Store*.[160]

In the 1960's, the Hope Bay Store ceased to operate as a grocery store and became home to various arts and crafts stores. It closed its doors in the 1980's.[161]

Hope Bay Stores in the 1970's – Kelly Irving

A few years prior to this writing, the original buildings at the Hope Bay Store were razed in an early morning fire. The property was partially restored, and then purchased in a foreclosure sale by a cooperative of Islanders who completed the restoration.[162]

The new, two-storey complex houses a variety of businesses. The renovation project was recently nominated for a Commercial Building Award, which recognized it for its exceptional quality.

Pender Islands

The original owners of the store still conduct business near the new stores, as *R.S.W. Corbett and Son*. Their company is one of the oldest firms still doing business in the Gulf Islands.[163]

At the time of this writing, Mr. Corbett's home was operating as a bed and breakfast called the *Corbett House Bed and Breakfast*.

The Canal

Initially, a strip of land, called *Indian Portage*, joined North and South Pender Islands. At that time, the Portage was a meeting place for settlers living on Saturna and South Pender Islands.[164] The area made history when Indians shot two settlers there in 1863.[165]

Whenever settlers wanted to travel between Bedwell Harbour and Browning Harbour, they would carry their boats across the Portage, in order to avoid having to make the dangerous voyage around South Pender.[166]

At the turn of the century, a petition was circulated around the Pender Islands requesting that a canal be dredged to enable the S.S. *Iroquois* to make a speedier passage around the Islands.[167] In 1903, a self-scouring canal was dredged.

The canal separating North and South Pender Islands, early 1900's - BC Archives G-06190

Pender Islands

The midden and surrounding areas of Bedwell Harbour are a burial grounds for the *Tsawout* and *Tseycum* First Nations, who lived in the area seasonally.[168] Unfortunately, when the canal was dredged, several artifacts left by the Indians were unearthed.[169]

Much later, in 1950, residents requested that a bridge be built across the canal. However, reportedly, the Federal Government disclaimed any responsibility for the blasting that took place when the canal was dredged.[170]

Eventually, the government accepted responsibility for the work that was done[171] and a single-lane bridge was built five years later, reuniting North and South Pender.[172]

The bridge, which links the two Islands at the two harbours, made Vancouver Island more accessible. This caused traffic traveling between the Penders and Vancouver Island to double.[173]

Today, the canal, which is now twice its original width, can be crossed by way of the bridge that was built. A monument, which was erected in the 1970's, commemorates the events that had unfolded at the site over the previous one hundred years.

The canal as it appears today

Helisen Archeological Site is now one of the largest archeological excavations in all the Gulf Islands. Excavations of the site have resulted in the discovery of thousands of Indian artifacts, some of which are on display at the Pender Islands Public Library.

Shingle Bay Park

While the canal was being dredged, two brothers, named Howard and Stanley Harris, purchased a portable sawmill and began to cut boards and shingles[174] out of a fine stand of Western Red Cedar that grew behind a bay.[175] Then, they built a scow and established the first mill ever to exist on the Pender Islands.[176]

The Harris brothers used a steam launch, called *Pearl*, to transport the lumber from the bay. It was the first powerboat ever used on the Penders.[177]

Shingle Bay is located on the west side of North Pender. The bay sits in *Shingle Bay Park*, which provides for playgrounds and facilities for picnics.

Pender Islands

Thieves Bay Park

While the Harris brothers were establishing their sawmill, the provincial police learned that two sheep rustlers were killing and salting down sheep on a bay. So the provincial police rounded up a posse of settlers, gave them guns and ammunition, and swore them in as special constables.[178]

The posse, which included **the Postman**, Rutherford Hope, Hugh Hamilton and others, all rowed to the bay to arrest the sheep rustlers.[179]

When the posse arrived at the bay, they apprehended the two criminals and handcuffed them. After the settlers went home, the policeman removed the handcuffs from the prisoners and made them do the rowing to the *gaol* (jail) on Mayne Island.[180]

Unfortunately, when they arrived on Mayne, the policeman made the mistake of getting out of the boat first and his prisoners seized the opportunity to push the boat away from the shore. Then, they quickly paddled into the Pass and were never seen again.[181]

Thieves Bay Park is a recreational park located on the west side of North Pender. It provides for playgrounds and facilities for picnics if you want to stay awhile. *Thieves Bay* provides for a sandy beach and marina.

Old Orchard Farm

In 1902, Spencer Percival purchased the farm from which **the Postman** had provided postal service. He called the farm *Sunny Side Ranch*.[182]

Over the years, Spencer and his wife made many changes to the single-gable cabin on the old farm. They substantially enlarged it, and then added a veranda and bay windows to it.[183]

Although it had an abundance of exterior doors, they never removed them. As a result, it is difficult for guests to determine which door to enter through.[184]

In the hall and study, the couple created a floor-to-ceiling collage of calendars, greeting cards, magazine clippings and photographs.[185]

At one end of the living room, they used oil paints to paint a large landscape. At the opposite end of the room, they painted a floral scene beneath the chair rails.[186]

Eventually, the space that had been used as a mailroom by **the Postman** was converted into a dining room.[187]

Pender Islands

Old Orchard Farm in 1925 - BC Archives C-07017

Throughout the orchard, Spencer installed an elaborate irrigation system of water pipes.[188] Later, he opened a tennis court on the lawn and the first tennis club was formed there.[189] It served as the site of many inter-Island tennis matches during the 1920's.[190]

In the late 1930's, new owners covered all the walls with plywood, concealing the collages and paintings. Then, they added a second storey as an apartment, which they rented to numerous tenants through the years.[191]

Much later, in 1979, the property was sold again and renamed *Old Orchard Farm*. Recently, when the new owners began restoring the old home, they discovered the artwork that had been boarded up by the previous owners.[192]

Old Orchard Farm as it appears today

Today, the meticulously restored Old Orchard Farm is a private residence on Port Washington Road. The house, which is nearly five times the size of the original building, can be seen through one of the finest ancient orchards on the Penders. The orchard is still producing over 40 varieties of apples, pears and plums.[193]

Pender Islands

Pender Islands Cemetery

In 1903, Mr. Menzies donated some land for the development of an Island cemetery. Maintenance of the cemetery was a community responsibility.[194]

Because there was no church on the Island at the time, funeral services were always held at one of the settlers' homes. A horse-drawn wagon would then travel to the cemetery and friends would prepare the grave.[195]

The *Pender Islands Cemetery* sits in the center of North Pender. Recently, the Pender Islands' Museum Society donated a 100-year time capsule to the cemetery. It had been started at the turn of the century by Rutherford Hope.

Beaumont Provincial Marine Park

In 1905, a settler wanted to transport a log house from Saturna Island to South Pender. So he arranged with a seaman to dismantle it, transport it to South Pender, and then reassemble it there. The seaman completed the task in less than two days. Later, he purchased the property.[196]

Over time, the seaman sold the property to a Captain, named Mr. Beaumont, who donated a portion of the property for use as a marine park.[197]

Beaumont Provincial Marine Park was named after this Captain.[198] Established in the 1960's, it is one of the most popular marine parks in the outer Gulf Islands and is one of the best places to see Garry Oak trees. You can access the park by boat or by way of a steep trail.

Mount Norman Regional Park is connected to Beaumont Marine Park. Acquired in the

Pender Islands

1980's, it was the first regional park established in all the Gulf Islands.

The moderately difficult trails through Mount Norman Park provide for one of the most beautiful hikes in all the Gulf Islands and lead through second-growth forest to the top of *Mount Norman*.

At 260 m, Mount Norman is the highest peak on the Penders and provides for incredible views of Vancouver Island and the San Juan Islands.[199]

Cedar Creek

In 1908, two brothers, named Wilfred and Godfrey Walker, emigrated from England and became apprentice farmers in the Spalding Valley.[200] The following year, they purchased some property from Arthur Spalding. They called the property *Cedar Creek*.[201]

Soon, the Walker brothers constructed a cabin on their property.[202] It had a fireplace and chimney, which they built out of granite that had been hauled over from Saturna Island.[203]

When one of the brothers was killed in action in World War I, the property was passed to the surviving brother's son.[204]

Cedar Creek is located on the north side of South Pender. It provides for a sandy beach. The cabin, which can be seen from the road, is reported to be the oldest log cabin still in use on the Penders today.[205] A descendent still owns the property.

The General Store

When Spencer Percival opened the General Store at Port Washington in 1910, it became the social center for the community and also the home of the post office.[206]

Spencer was the store's first proprietor. Reportedly, he had no experience as a storekeeper, but because he was a generous man, the store thrived.[207]

Pender Islands

One day, an evaporated milk salesman offered Spencer a discount on case lots. Although he had little hope of selling them, he ordered 50 cases. For a while thereafter, every time an Indian would arrive at Port Washington from Galiano Island, he would leave with a can of milk.[208]

Over the years, the store changed owners several times. Between the 1940's and 60's, a very small library operated from the store.[209]

The General Store in 1947 - BC Archives I-20737

When the store changed hands in 1974, the new owners ran it primarily as a grocery store.[210]

A decade after the post office was relocated, the store closed, having been continuously operated as a grocery store for over 75 years.[211] It then operated for several more years as a retail outlet for local artists.[212]

In the year prior to this writing, the community put it in Trust, using the strongest legal protection that exists for a heritage building. Then, they began to restore it

The General Store in the 1970's
Pender Islands Museum

Pender Islands

The General Store as it appears today

Port Browning Marina Resort

In 1912, Elisha Pollard arranged for a home to be built near a harbour on North Pender.[213]

Over time, Elisha built three cabins on the land, and he and his wife converted the property into a resort. Because there were large Maple trees on the property, they called the resort *The Maples*.[214]

Mr and Mrs. Pollard served meals to all of their guests and, over time, the Maples became one of North Pender's most popular resorts.[215]

Browning Harbour in 1946 - Pender Island Museum

The resort operated for more than 40 years, before closing in the 1970's.[216] The home and one of the cabins can still be seen from Browning Harbour today.

The *Port Browning Marina* provides for temporary boat anchorage at the harbour. A year-round resort, called *Port Browning Marina Resort*, offers self-contained cabins, as well as camping for tents, trailers and campervans.

Pender Islands

St. Peter's Anglican Church

Before the first church was built on North Pender, **the Postman** would row to Mayne Island to attend church services. Sometimes, his own home was used as a place of worship. Later, the Port Washington Community Hall was used for holding church services.[217]

Just before the outbreak of World War I, Spencer Percival donated some land for a church.[218] In 1915, the 50-person church was built. It was called *St. Peter's Anglican Church* and **the Postman** was instrumental in the building of it.[219]

Several items were donated to the church, including an antique silver chalice, a patent from England and an Italian marble font.[220]

In 1924, a cottage was built behind the church so the visiting clergy had a place in which to live during their visits. It was later renovated to provide a vestry for a resident Vicar.[221]

St. Peter's Guild grew out of a Women's Auxiliary, which included many pioneer women from Port Washington.[222] In the early 1930's, they started hosting a fair to raise funds for the Columbia Coast Mission, the Salvation Army and other causes.[223]

Reportedly, the fair was always held at a private residence, in their garden. Thereafter, it became known as the *Garden Party*.

During the 1940's, a Reverend served both St. Peter's Church and a church on South Pender. When his successor drowned in a storm shortly after starting parish work, a carved Oak lectern and a prayer desk were placed in the church, as memorials to both Reverends.[224]

Originally, St. Peter's Anglican Church was located at Port Washington. However, a decade ago, it was moved to a more central location, where it now sits beside a hall[225] called *Parish Hall*.

The annual Garden Party provides for games and prizes, as well as a flea market. It is held each year in July, at the Parish Hall beside the church.

Bricky Bay

Around the time St. Peter's Church was built on North Pender, the Coast Shale Company purchased some land on a bay. There, they

Pender Islands

constructed a brick factory with grinders, mixers and ovens. Then, they laid narrow track rails that led through a tunnel to a shale pit.[226]

Before it shut down and was demolished in the 1920's, the plant, which employed about 75 men, was producing up to 300,000 bricks every day. The bricks were then shipped from a wharf in the bay.[227]

Originally named *Colston Cove*,[228] Bricky Bay is located on the northeast side of North Pender. The sandy beach at the bay is strewn with bricks that are the remains of the brickworks.

James Point

During World War I, a sea Captain purchased some property that sat on a point. He then gave it to his daughter. It was called *Waterlea*.[229]

Vicki's husband was the first real estate agent to reside on the Penders. He would provide free room and board in their home, to prospective clients who came to the Island to view properties.[230]

Vicki soon became accustomed to providing for her husband's clients. So she converted their home into a resort, taking in guests in the summer.[231]

The resort had several rowboats, a tennis court and a pavilion that extended out over the water. Whenever the couple's children wanted to prevent the guests from using these facilities, they would wait until low tide, and then suggest to the guests that they have a picnic on nearby Betty Island. As a result, the guests would become stranded when the tide came back in.[232]

During the 1930's, the Canadian Pacific Railway steamers would pass by the resort. Sometimes, one of them would stop so guests could disembark. The guests would crowd onto one side of the ship, a rope ladder would be thrown over[233] and they would climb down.

James Point is located on the west side of North Pender. It has an ecologically

Pender Islands

sensitive sandy beach. The family lived on the point until 1945.[234] Their home can still be seen sitting on the point today.

The Wool Shed

In the 1920's, a settler, named Fred Smith, bought a small house on a bay. To supplement his income, he and his wife built three cottages on the property and opened their house to guests.[235]

Fred and his wife called their resort the *Welcome Bay Inn*. They supplied their guests with home-cooked meals, which they served in their dining room.[236]

The resort closed at the onset of World War II,[237] after which the Royal Canadian Legion used one of the guest cottages as their meeting place for a while.[238]

Today, the property is called *Welcome Bay Farm* and a descendant of the settler still resides there.

The owners of the farm raise goats and sheep on the property. At the time of this writing, they also ran a studio called *The Wool Shed*, in which they sheared, spun and hand-dyed wool.[239]

Church of the Good Shepherd

In 1937, an English woman donated land for the building of a church nearby.[240] She also donated a substantial amount of money to its construction.[241]

Hubert Payne, the Parson from Saturna, gave the fittings from a log chapel for use in the church and Fred Smith supervised its construction.[242]

The following year, the *Church of The Good Shepherd* was opened. Several items were donated to the church, including the altar and altar cloth, some furniture, the tower bell, the baptismal font and a stained glass window.[243]

At the front of the grounds was erected a *lych* gate, in memory of an early settler and his wife. To commemorate the coronation of King George VI, an Oak tree was planted on the church grounds.[244]

Pender Islands

Church of the Good Shepherd, early 1900's - Pender Islands Museum

Today, the charming Church of the Good Shepherd is very much the way it was when it was first constructed. The lych gate provides for a traditional English entrance.

Church of the Good Shepherd as it appears today

Pender Island Golf & Country Club

After **the Postman** divided his farm among his children,[245] his son, George, inherited his sheep pasture in the Grimmer Valley. One day, in the 1930's, George and his siblings decided to develop it into a golf course.[246]

A decade later, six people purchased the land so they could improve the course. They formed a golf club and worked hard at the tees. They set up the holes, cutting the greens with a push-type lawnmower.[247]

Initially, the golfers climbed down a ladder at the sixth hole. The club members later built steps there.[248]

On the pasture was a small two-room cabin, which the club members converted into a clubhouse. Much later, in 1981, a new clubhouse was built.[249]

Today, the *Pender Island Golf and Country Club* has over 350 members. The challenging, 9-hole RCGA and CLGA rated course has several different tee areas and plays as an 18-hole par 68 for men and par 69 for women. The *New Year's Golf Tournament* is an event held at the golf and country club each year.

Pender Islands

Open year-round, the course provides for a well-equipped golf shop where power carts, pull carts and golf clubs are available for rent. Volunteers recently contributed over 6,000 hours constructing a network of golf cart paths out of driftwood.[250]

Poets Cove Resort

Initially, settlers living on South Pender would row to Saturna Island for supplies.[251] In the 1930's, the first store to be constructed on South Pender was built at a harbour.[252]

Bedwell Harbour Marina, early 1900's – Pender Islands Museum

A few years later, a couple built a marina at the harbour. At the time, they were living in a building that was once a community hall. They had moved it to the harbour, and then expanded it to accommodate a cafe.[253]

In 1960, a hotel, called the *Bedwell Harbour Hotel*, was built at the harbour.[254] The hotel was later converted into a resort called the *Bedwell Harbour Resort*.[255]

Pender Islands

A few years prior to this writing, new owners expanded and renamed the resort *Poet's Cove Resort and Spa*.

Bedwell Harbour Marina as it appears today

Today, Poet's Cove Resort is the only center on South Pender. Located on Bedwell Harbour, it offers 46 rooms, villas and cottages, and provides for an activity centre, tennis courts and a swimming pool. At the time of this writing, a spa, called the *Susurrus Spa*, offered six treatment rooms.

The *Bedwell Harbour Marina* at the harbour is a full-service, deep-moorage marina and boat rental. A Canada Customs point of entry is located at the marina. It processes more than 9,000 vessels each year.

Because it attracts boaters from both sides of the border, Bedwell Harbour is the busiest port on the Penders.

Arcadia By The Sea Lodge

In 1941, a lawyer, named Wallace Lynd, purchased a 10-room, two-storey home on North Pender. The home was named *Mille Fleurs*.[256]

Soon, the lawyer's wife, Nefia, decided to remodel the interior of the home and convert it into a guest cottage. Because a friend supplied the bedrooms with Beautyrest® mattresses, Nefia changed the name of the home to the *Beautyrest Lodge*.[257]

Two years later, she employed an agency to find guests for her lodge, and then opened it for business.[258]

Eventually, Nefia added six more cottages and hired an off-island crew to build a separate building with a dining room and lounge.[259] Subsequently, the lodge became one of the most popular resorts in all the Gulf Islands.[260]

After 27 successful years, Nefia retired and the lodge was sold. New owners changed the name to *Otter Bay Lodge*.[261]

Pender Islands

Arcadia By The Sea in 1955 - Pender Islands Museum

In the 1960's, the lodge was renamed *Pender Lodge*.[262] It boasted a licensed lounge and dining room, as well as sleeping and housekeeping cottages. There was also a swimming pool and tennis courts on the property.[263]

At the time of this writing, the lodge was called *Arcadia By The Sea*. It offered three fully-equipped cottages.

Arcadia By The Sea as it appears today

Pender Islands Public Library

In the 1940's, a very small library operated from within the General Store at Port Washington. The library functioned from inside the store for more than two decades.[264]

Later, in 1973, a woman who had a large book collection decided to share them. When she approached the United Community Church, they agreed to let her store her books in a small room at the back of the church building. A few months later, a library was opened there. It was called the *Pender Lender*.[265]

Initially, only a few book borrowers came into the library. However, when the staff purchased 13 new books to add to their collection of used books, more borrowers started to show interest. Eventually, the library began receiving books from The Canada Council.[266]

The church room had an unreliable oil furnace. Whenever it malfunctioned, the library staff had to wear their coats and gloves to keep warm.[267]

When the new school was built a few years later, the staff moved the library into a small building on the old school grounds at Hope Bay. When they put child-sized furniture in a

Pender Islands

corner, even children started visiting the library.[268]

Recently, an architect designed a new building next door, in which to house the library. The building was named the *Auchterlonie Center*, in honor of a family of early settlers. When the library moved into the new building, the little building on the old school grounds became home to a playschool.[269]

Today, the *Pender Islands Public Library*, which is still jokingly referred to as the Pender Lender, is the Penders' fourth library. It is home to 13,000 books and enjoys the highest percentage of per capita support for rural libraries in all of British Columbia.[270]

Pender Islands Fire and Rescue

Because fires had destroyed so many buildings on the Penders in the first half of the century, they were incorporated into a fire protection district in 1971.[271] At that time, the *Pender Islands Volunteer Fire Brigade* was formed.[272]

The fire brigade consisted of a *high muckymuck* (fire chief), two crew heads and 14 *smoke eaters* (fire fighters). Their equipment consisted of four shovels, and a four-wheel drive power wagon that had a small pump in the front and a 1,500 liter water tank in the back.[273]

Soon, a fire hall was built on North Pender, on land that had previously been used as a skeet shooting area by the Rod and Gun Club.[274]

At that time, the society purchased a new fire truck and a fire siren. They were followed by a tanker truck the next year. In 1988, the *South Pender Fire Hall* was opened on South Pender.[275]

A decade later, a second hall was built on North Pender.[276] Today, there are a total of three fire halls on North Pender.

In the year prior to this writing, the *Pender Islands Fire and Rescue* acquired a new fire truck. Specially designed to provide fire protection to Poet's Cove Resort, it services the fire hall on South Pender.

Galiano Island

Sturdies Bay Wharf

It was in 1901 that an Englishman, named Stanley Page, came to Galiano Island and was given a portion of his father's land...

Stanley Page was born in the 1880's and immigrated with his family to Canada. In the year 1901, they moved to Galiano Island.[1]

In 1910, Stanley's mother passed away, leaving him and his siblings to be raised by his father, alone.[2] Two years later, Stanley built a home on his portion of the property and brought his bride to live there with him.[3]

In the 1920's, Stanley Page became **the Postman** for Galiano. Using a horse and a boat, he moved a little building onto his ranch, from which he operated the post office.[4]

In the 1940's, Stanley became Galliano's only taxi driver. After 30 years of service, he retired at age 89, as the oldest taxi driver in all of Canada.[5] He and his wife had lived on the same property for 60 years.[6]

Later, when speaking about how his father had felt about delivering the mail during his youth, one of his sons had this to say about him:

Dad was much happier working his farm, or building local houses and bridges
                                    Kenneth Page[7]

Galiano Island

The Friendly Island

Galiano is a friendly island. At 57 sq km, it is the second largest of the southern Gulf Islands. While shell beaches and endless forest drives are its most distinguishing characteristics, the lively, spirited people give Galiano Island its unique charm.

Called *The Jewel of the Strait of Georgia*, Galiano holds claim to having one of the largest provincial parks in all the Gulf Islands. Almost 75 percent of Galiano falls within a tree farm license held by British Columbia's forestry giant.

Galiano has a population of just over 1000 permanent residents, a large percentage of which are over 55 years of age and retired. Many of the residents live at the south end, where most of the services and facilities are located. During the tourist season, the population swells to around 2,000.

Sturdies Bay

Residential development began on South Galiano in the 1860's, along Active Passage. The community that developed was named *Sturdies Bay*, in honor of a family who settled there.[8]

Early settlers on Galiano
Galiano Archives 2004026505

Over the next 60 years, while South Galiano was becoming established, the community at the north end of the Island was also beginning to develop.[9]

By the 1920's, North Galiano had become one of the most prosperous communities in all the Gulf Islands, growing to several thousand people during the fishing season.[10]

In 1949, South Galiano acquired its own power company. However, because of the tree farm that exists between the north and south ends of the Island, power was not extended to North Galiano until the 1960's.[11]

By then, the communities on South Galiano had become more populous than those on North Galiano.[12]

Galiano Island

Sturdies Bay in the 1940's – Galiano Archives 2004026512

In the 1970's, South Galiano experienced a population explosion. When the last cannery on North Galiano closed, only about a dozen families lived there.[13]

Today, Sturdies Bay, on South Galiano, is 'downtown' to the Island residents. It is a seaside village where the residents and businesses co-exist.

Sturdies Bay as it appears today

Georgeson Bay

In 1863, Henry Georgeson, the Scotsman who would later become the lighthouse keeper on Mayno Island, purchased some land surrounding a bay on South Galiano. There, he built a cabin on the banks of a creek.[14]

A decade later, 'Scotty' purchased the remainder of the land around the bay. At that time, he established a farm and built another home.[15]

Galiano Island

Meanwhile, a tinker who lived on Mayne Island was shot to death and his cabin was looted. When a reward was posted by the police[16] Scotty gave evidence against an Indian, called 'Indian Tom'. The Indian was later executed as a result of Scotty's testimony.[17]

On returning home one day, Scotty found his wife lying on the floor. Indians had forced poison down her throat. Thereafter, he and his wife were in constant danger from the Indians.[18]

Georgeson Bay at the turn of the century
Galiano Archives MOR42

In 1921, after providing service to the lighthouse on Mayne for over 35 years,[19] Scotty's family built him a large retirement home at the head of the bay on his Galiano property. Two years later, he retired and the whole family moved into the house. Soon, it became known as the *Big House*.[20]

Georgeson Bay was named after this Scotsman. Located on the southwest side of Galiano, it provides for a rocky beach that is a great place to see Sea Lions.

Georgeson Bay as it appears today

Galiano Island Post Office

Well before the turn of the century, steamer ships delivered the mail to Salt Spring Island, and then it was delivered to Mayne Island. Residents of South Galiano would row to Mayne to collect their mail.[21]

By the turn of the century, a steamer ship began to deliver mail once a week to the wharf. Soon, the *South Galiano Post Office* began to operate from various homes at the south end.[22]

At that time, there was only a cow trail running between the north and south ends of the Island. If a settler on South Galiano had a package to send to North Galiano, he would use an axe to pin instructions to a tree at the south end of the trail and the next settler on route to North Galiano would carry the instructions on foot or by horseback.[23]

Galiano Island

Pack horse at the turn of the century
Galiano Archives M005

By the early 1920's, mail had ceased to be delivered to North Galiano by steamer. It was simply transferred there once a week from South Galiano.[24]

Soon, postal service for South Galiano was transferred to Stanley Page. As **the Postman**, he performed his duties from a little, shingled, post office building on his ranch.[25] Unfortunately, the Royal Canadian Legion decided that a war veteran should fill the position. So Stanley lost the post shortly thereafter.[26]

Today, the little post office building that **the Postman** used still stands in a backyard on Georgeson Bay Road.

In 1928, the South Galiano Post Office was moved again, to a house that was located about 5 km from the wharf. It was the fifth building to which it had been moved.[27]

The house was owned by a resident who had very tough feet. He would deliver the mail barefooted, even in winter.[28]

South Galiano Post Office, in the 1930's
Galiano Archives 2004020037

The house had originally been a barn. Postal services were performed from a room on the right-hand side of the house that was entered by way of a little door.[29]

The house served as the post office for several years. It was eventually passed down to a descendant[30] and still stands on Georgeson Bay Road today.

Ye Olde South Galiano Post Office as it appears today

Galiano Island

Post office at the Sturdies Bay wharf in the 1930's - Galiano Archives M309

South Galiano Post Office in the 1940's
Donald New 2004020078

At that time, a small building was set up at the wharf, for use as a mail sorting office.[31]

The sorting office building was opened an hour before the mail was due to arrive and the settlers would stand and wait at a counter for their envelopes and parcels to be dispatched.[32]

One day, after 15 years of sitting at the wharf, the sorting office building vanished. It was eventually located on another road, where a road crew had moved it.[33] The following day, it was moved near the main road, where it remained for two years.[34]

Later, in 1961, the government built a little post office out of bricks at Sturdies Bay. It operated until the 1990's, when it was sold. The post office was then moved further north, to a market.[35]

Today, the little brick building operates as an antique and gift store,[36] and the *Galiano Island Post Office* sits in a storefront across the road.

Galiano Island

Shaw's Landing

In 1877, an Englishman, named John Shaw, emigrated to Galiano.[37] At that time, he became the first man to settle on North Galiano.[38]

Because there was no store in the community, John would row to Vancouver Island for supplies. When steamers began stopping in a little bay near his home, he would row out to them, and pick up mail and groceries from one of the crew.[39]

Soon, he became the first person to offer postal service to the other residents of North Galiano.[40] The first *North Galiano Post Office* was operated from his house.[41]

Once a month, an Indian, who called himself 'Captain Peatson', would row to Salt Spring in a canoe and pick up the mail addressed to 'North Galiano'.[42] Later, when steamers began to dock in the bay, John would retrieve the mail from the crew.[43]

When John died in 1890, one of his sons took over the postal service.[44] John Jr. tended to the family orchard, while he continued his father's postal duties. Over time, he became adept at building large model sailboats.[45]

In the year 1912, the Postmaster General approved a request for a post office on North Galiano. It was established at the little bay near John's home.[46]

Unfortunately, much later, in the 1960's, John's house was demolished. Inside, were some priceless letters.[47]

Shaw's Landing was named after this family, who provided postal service to North Galiano for several decades. The beach on the bay provides for a seasonal waterfall.

Murcheson Heritage Home

In 1882, a prominent Scottish settler, named Finlay Murcheson, came to South Galiano and purchased some land near Sturdies Bay. There, he established a farm on which he built a square-timbered home.[48]

Finlay's eldest son was the first white child to grow up on Galiano. Unfortunately, he drowned at the turn of the century and his younger brother, Finlay Jr., inherited the family farm.[49]

Finlay Jr. eventually married and became the father of seven children, which earned him the nickname 'Father Finlay'.[50]

A single storey kitchen addition was added to the farmhouse just before the outbreak of World War I. An outside chimney was constructed much later, in the 1950's.[51]

Galiano Island

Oldest house on Galiano, in the 1960's – Galiano Archives 2004026157

Today, the Galiano Island Golf Course sits on part of the family's old farm.[52] Their 125-year old home can still be seen from Sturdies Bay Road. It is the oldest house on Galiano and is still very much the way it was at the turn of the century.[53]

Whaler Bay

Around the same time that Father Finlay arrived on Galiano, an Irishman, named Robert Wright, moved to South Galiano, from where he had been living on North Galiano.[54]

There, on a bay, Robert built a log cabin and started a family.[55] However, a few years later, his wife passed away.[56]

When his sister emigrated from Ireland to help him raise his two baby sons, he decided to build a larger home.[57]

Robert's new home had three large rooms on the main floor and three bedrooms upstairs, all of which were plastered on the inside.[58]

At one end of a long verandah, there was a milk-cooling room. At the other end, was a summer kitchen with an adjacent wood shed.[59]

Upon completion of the house, Robert's sister married and moved off the Island, leaving him with a large home to maintain.[60]

Galiano Island

Desperate, he hired a housekeeper, who managed his home and family well. Over time, he made her his second wife. Ironically, she died in childbirth shortly after the turn of the century.[61]

Unfortunately, on a New Year's Day in 1914, the ill-fated Robert Wright drowned while crossing from Mayne Island to Pender Island in his boat.[62]

Whaler Bay is a lovely bay on the southeast side of Galiano. The coves around the shores of the bay provide for good anchorages. Once an anchorage for small whaling boats,[63] it is now used as a home for commercial fishing boats.

Mary Ann Point Light

Sometime in the late 1880's, an English seaman, named Alexander Scoones, purchased some property on South Galiano. The property sat on a point called Mary Anne Point. There, he began to build a waterfront home.[64]

At the turn of the century, Alec moved to England, and then returned after World War I with his fiancé. In the 1920's, he exchanged the property for property owned by his brother, Paul.[65] Thereafter, Paul owned the home on the point.[66]

The windows in Paul's home faced a light that sat on the point. It was called the *Mary Anne Point Light*. Fuelled by carbide, it guided the ships through the Pass.[67]

A seaside trail led over flat rock and grass, down to the waters in the Pass, and then through the woods and down the hill to the house and the light.[68]

A garden of wildflowers grew among the rocks, behind which visitors could see the ships sailing through the rough waters.[69]

Galiano Island

Mary Anne Point Light, mid 1900's
Galiano Archives M297

Mary Anne Point Light as it appears today

In the 1950's, the Mary Anne Point Light was dumped into the sea[70] and the property was sold to a descendant for one dollar.[71] Today, a new light stands on the point. It can be seen from the ferries, as they travel through the Pass.

The 120-year old home that once belonged to Paul still stands nearby. The house was first enlarged in the 1920's. Subsequent owners have made modifications to it.[72]

Captain's Quarters Cottage

In the year 1890, a sea Captain, named Edward McCoskrie, emigrated from England to Galiano. A few years later, he established a farm on a bay on North Galiano. Initially, a simple lean-to with an earth floor served as his family's home.[73]

The following year, Captain McCoskrie and his son, Bill, built a log home with dovetailed corners. Because he worked off-Island, he hired a live-in governess for his children. She educated them in a lean-to classroom that was attached to the back of the log house.[74]

Later, Bill inherited the property. He lived in the home for the rest of his life. Unfortunately, the building was then left in an abandoned state for several decades, during which time much of the interior rotted away.[75]

In the 1980's, another sea Captain purchased the property. One hundred years after the house was originally built, he began

Galiano Island

to restore it.[76] At the time of this writing, the log home was being operated as a cottage rental called the *Captain's Quarters*.

Home Hardware Store

Initially, the children of South Galiano attended a school near the Pass.[77] The children who lived near the harbour on the western shore had to row to a trailhead, and then walk to the school.[78] So, sometime in the 1890's, a second school was built, on the southwest side of the Island.[79]

In the year 1900, a third school opened, on a bay on the southeast side of the Island.[80] The students would bring cans of pork and beans to the school, which they warmed on a heater.[81] For a while, church services were also held there.[82]

Five years later, a fourth school was opened further north. Called the *Retreat Cove School*, the tiny school served a community called Retreat Cove.[83]

In the year 1920, Father Finlay donated some land for a fifth school, near another cove, on the southeast side of the Island.[84]

The fifth school was called the *Galiano School*.[85] It had one room, in the center of which stood an iron stove. At the top of the stairs sat a container of drinking water.[86]

The first school was in use until just after the turn of the century and the third school was eventually demolished.[87]

The fourth school closed in 1939. Although another school opened in the same community after World War II, it was closed three years later when the population of North Galiano began to decline.[88]

Home Hardware in the 1930's – Galiano Archives 2004026356

Galiano Island

By that time, all of the schoolchildren on South Galiano were attending the Galiano School. So a second room and set of stairs were soon added to it.[89]

In 1954, a sixth school opened on South Galiano. Upon its completion, the Galiano School was sold. It now operates as a Home Hardware® store.[90]

Home Hardware as it appears today

St. Margaret of Scotland Church

Before the turn of the century, Catholic church services were held in a little shed on a South Galiano bay, where a fisherman had previously mended and dried his fish nets.[91]

Later, services were held in the old schoolhouse that sat near that same bay. At that time, Galiano was part of the parish of the church on Mayne Island.[92]

During World War I, a woman donated some property on the bay and a Mission Room was opened there. The altar, organ, lectern, prayer desk and silver communion vessels were all donations.[93] At least once a baptism was performed in a basin from the kitchen sink in a nearby home.[94]

Shortly thereafter, monthly services on North Galiano began at the Retreat Cove and North Galiano schools.[95] Eventually, the Mission Room was purchased by a man, named Ralph Stevens, who was the Island's undertaker. He made it his home.[96]

Mission Room in the 1950's
Galiano Archives 2004026171

In the year 1950, a resident, named Fred Robson, donated some land up the hill for the building of a proper church. A number of projects were undertaken to raise money for the building of it, including the first *Galiano Art Show*.[97]

Upon its completion, the church was called the *Church of St. Margaret, Queen of Scotland*.[98] A larger-than-life painting of The Crucifixion was hung above the altar.[99]

A stained glass window was placed in the rear of the church, in memory of a Reverend who drowned shortly after his appointment to the Gulf Islands' Parish.[100]

For many years thereafter, a resident, named Eddie Bambrick, would stop at the church with his family on his way to the Saturday night dance. He would light the oil stove in the church so it would be warm for the morning service.[101]

Today, the little St. Margaret of Scotland Church is the only church on Galiano.

Galiano Island

Galiano Island Cemetery

At one time, Indians buried their dead high in the trees on South Galiano, on a point that is now called Collinson Point. Over time, the point became Henry Georgeson's private burial ground,[102] which he donated for use as the Island's cemetery in the 1920's.[103]

Scotty placed two conditions on his donation; that there be no charge for burial of a resident of Galiano and that plots would be reserved there for members of his own family.[104]

Ralph Stevens, the local undertaker, cleared most of the property, which is still surrounded by huge Arbutus and Douglas-Fir trees.[105] The *lych* gate and the fence along one side were both donations.[106]

Ironically, the beautiful cemetery is accessible from what was once called *Dead End Road*. It was later renamed *Cemetery Road*.[107]

Porlier Pass Light Station

Initially, the passage at the tip of North Galiano was called *Cowichan Gap*, but was known locally as *The Gap*.[108] It was later renamed *Porlier Pass*.

At that time, an Indian village that belonged to the *Penelakut* Band resided on a point in the Pass. The point was called Virago Point. The small *rancherie* (village) on the point was named *xínepsem* (caught by the neck). It consisted of a few permanent houses that were occupied mainly in the summer for gathering food.[109]

At the turn of the century, construction of a major light station began at the Pass. It was called the *Porlier Pass Light Station*.[110]

There were two beacons at the light station. They overlooked what is now known as *Lighthouse Bay*. One beacon sat on Race Point and the other sat on Virago Point. Ships navigated the waters by lining up both lights.[111]

The first light keeper was a sailor, named Frank Allison, who was known locally as 'Sticks'.[112] At dusk, he would light the lamps in each tower so they would burn through the night. In the morning, he would fill the brass coal oil lamps, trim the wicks and polish the chimneys.[113]

Galiano Island

Race Point Tower in the 1950's
Galiano Archives 2004026354

Whenever the weather was foggy, Sticks would beat an old tin can to indicate to the boats where the Pass was.[114]

Sticks served the light station for 40 years. The wicks were in operation in the beacon towers until he retired in 1941.[115]

The tower on Race Point was recently removed and replaced with an automated beacon. However, the tower on Virago Point is still standing on the First Nations reserve and can be seen from Dionisio Point Provincial Park.

The Penelakut First Nation accounts for about 13 percent of the entire *Hul'qumi'num* Indian population.[116] The land on Virago Point is still owned by the band and permission must be attained prior to hiking it.

Grand Central Emporium

In 1896, an Englishman, named Joseph Burrill, immigrated to Canada. Three years later, he came to Galiano and purchased some property on a bay near Active Pass. There, he established a farm. Later, his older brother, Fred, moved to the Island and helped him run his farm.[117]

Because settlers initially had to row to Mayne Island for supplies,[118] the Burrill brothers were forever lending merchandise to their neighbors. So, in 1903, Joe built a store near the water. He called it the *Burrill Bros. Store*.[119]

Three years later, Joe built a larger store on the same property and the first store was then used as a shed.[120] While he ran the farm, Fred tended to the store.[121]

The store became a gathering place for the Islanders and, for many years, it had the only telephone on the Island.[122] The Burrill brothers hung a Swiss cowbell over the door, which their customers rang for service.[123]

Initially, the brothers used a sled pulled by a team of oxen to deliver large orders around the valley. Later, they purchased an old rheumatic horse to serve that purpose, which they hoisted up with a block and tackle each morning.[124]

Eventually, they added a post office, library and gas pumps to the store. They also added an apartment above the building, which they rented out.[125]

In 1947, the brothers sold the store. Subsequent owners dragged it further north, and then added a false front to it.[126] Today,

Galiano Island

it is known locally as the *Old Burrill Store* and is the home of a gift shop called the *Grand Central Emporium*.

In the year prior to this writing, the owners of the gift shop converted the attached deck into a 50's-style diner. They called it the *Grand Central Grill Restaurant*.

Sturdies Bay Wharf

At the turn of the century, a wharf was built at Sturdies Bay. The wharf accommodated ships coming through Active Pass.

There was no railing along the sides of the wharf at that time. Unfortunately, one day, a team of horses that was pulling a wagonload of bricks bolted, and then fell overboard and drowned.[127]

Much later, in 1952, a new wharf was built, to accommodate the ship named *Princess Elaine*.[128] It was built beside the original wharf so the piles could be driven deeper into the ocean floor.[129]

A decade later, a ferry linking the mainland to neighboring Salt Spring Island was introduced, making Galiano more accessible to Vancouver Island and the mainland.[130]

Sturdies Bay wharf in the late 1950's - Galiano Archives 2004026519

Galiano Island

Today, British Columbia Ferry Services uses the land at Sturdies Bay to operate scheduled ferry services from both the mainland and Vancouver Island.

Sturdies Bay wharf as it appears today

Spotlight Cove

While the Sturdies Bay wharf was being built, a sea Captain came to live at the Shaw residence on North Galiano.[131] With the help of John Shaw Jr., who was a model sailboat builder, he transformed a 50-year old dugout canoe into a sailing vessel.[132] They worked in a small boatyard in a nearby cove.[133]

The Captain strengthened the hull of the canoe with an Oak frame and added a cabin, floorboards, decking, a 135 kg keel, three masts and two watertight bulkheads. He called it the *Tilikum*.[134]

The Tilikum at the turn of the century
Galiano Archives MOR69

Later, the Captain sailed around the world in his boat, becoming the first person ever to do so in a boat of that size. The voyage took him three years to complete.[135] The Tilikum can be seen today at the Maritime Museum of British Columbia.

Spotlight Cove, on the northwest side of Galiano, provides for a long beach that is accessible by way of Porlier Pass Road.

Bellhouse Inn

In 1907, a settler, named John Bellhouse,[136] came to town wearing a Stetson hat. There, he purchased a farm called *Active Pass Stock Ranch*. On the farm was a little log home that he enlarged to accommodate his big family.[137]

In the 1920's, his son, Leonard, took over the house and farm. With the help of his stepmother, Leonard converted it into a nine-bedroom lodge called the *Farmhouse Inn*.[138]

The lodge had a main dining room. To polish the dining room floor, it became the custom for one person to sit on a pair of old

Galiano Island

long johns, while the other family members spun them around.[139]

Guests of the lodge arrived by steamer and were brought from the wharf to the lodge in a converted fishing boat.[140] When there was no vacancy at the Inn, they stayed in tents that had wooden floors and walls.[141]

The guests were free to explore the farm and often helped with the haying. Leonard would use his steam launch to take them on errands to the wharf or to the other Islands.[142]

A few years after it opened, the lodge caught fire. Leonard ran through the building in search of people who might need rescuing. When he found no one inside, he seized a vase on his way out. It was the only item that was saved from the fire. Subsequently, the Inn was destroyed and a new one had to be built.[143]

The new lodge had more bedrooms, and a larger kitchen and dining room. It had its own power plant and was the first home on Galiano ever to receive electricity.[144]

The Bellhouse Inn in the 1950's - Galiano Archives 2004026107

For many decades, Leonard and his own family operated the Inn. Their boats, the *Betsy Prig* and the *Betsy*, took guests to and from the wharf.[145]

The property was sold in 1966. The new owners used the house as their private residence.[146] Later, it was used as a medical center.[147]

In the 1990's, a couple purchased the property and renovated it. Then, they reopened it as the *Bellhouse Inn*.[148]

Today, the Bellhouse Inn is operated as a bed and breakfast. The B&B is located on the southern shore of South Galiano.

Galiano Island

The Bellhouse Inn as it appears today

Bellhouse Provincial Park was named after the Bellhouse family, who bequeathed the property to the province in the 1960's.[149] The park sits on a rocky peninsula, on the south side of Galiano.

The park is one of the most scenic parks in the Gulf Islands. It slopes to the sea at the entrance to Active Pass.

The park provides for wonderful sandstone and limestone formations on the shoreline around the Pass. Whale sightings are frequent there, and Sea Lions and Harbour Seals are in abundance. There are facilities for picnics if you want to stay awhile.

Bluffs Park

In 1907, an Englishman, named Max Enke, emigrated to Galiano from England.[150] He brought 11 Belgian people with him.[151]

Soon, Max purchased some land on Galiano, which was occupied by high bluffs that overlooked the Pass. There, he established a farm called the *Valley Farm*.[152]

In the year 1910, his daughter became the first white child born on Galiano.[153] Later, when one of his Belgian helpers went into labor, he delivered her baby with the help of a first aid book that was written in Spanish.[154]

In 1928, Max returned to Europe to live. After World War II, he and his wife sold the bluffs to the Galiano Island Development Association. At that time, a park was opened there. It was called *Bluffs Park*.[155]

Galiano Island

Bluffs Park sits in a beautiful, dark, old-growth forest on the southwest side of Galiano. There are 4 km of easy trails that wander through the park. The trails lead to a ridge that provides for views across the Pass and down the Channel.

North Galiano Community Hall

In 1918, a log schoolhouse was built on North Galiano.[156] It was called the *North-End School*.[157]

In 1927, George Baines, the owner of a marine shop, built a frame building beside the log schoolhouse. It was called the *North Galiano School*. For the most part, it replaced the log schoolhouse,[158] maintaining an enrollment of about 24 students.[159]

When the Retreat Cove School closed in the late 1930's, the schoolchildren were transferred to the North Galiano School. Their parents rented a cabin for the students to live in while they attended school there.[160]

North Galiano Community Hall in the 1930's - Galiano Archives M204

A decade later, the North Galiano School had four additional windows added to provide more light. In order for them to fit, they had to be placed in a staggered formation between the existing windows,[161] which gave the building a unique characteristic.

The North Galiano School closed in 1953. At that time, the schoolchildren were transferred to the Galiano School on South Galiano.[162]

In the 1970's, the North Galiano School became the home of the *North Galiano Community Hall*.[163] Today, the hall is host to many events, including the annual *Canada Day Jamboree*.

Galiano Island

North Galiano Hall as it appears today

Morning Beach

After World War I, Paul Scoones purchased some property that included Lion Islet, off the southeast shore of Galiano. He called the property *Lyons*. There, he built a large home.[164]

When he exchanged his property with his brother, Alec, in the 1920's, Alec became the owner of Lyons.[165]

In the year 1930, Alec leased Lyons to a family who ran it as a resort. A few years later, he returned to the property and ran it as a resort for another year, himself.[166]

Lyons on Lion Islet - Galiano Archives 2004021091

During World War II, the property was leased to the YWCA as a summer camp. It then changed owners several times until 1950, when it was operated as a large chicken farm.[167]

A decade later, the house was torn down and a new house was built on the property.[168]

Galiano Island

Lion Islet can be seen from Salamanca Point, on the southeast side of Galiano. The pebbled beach on the point is called *Morning Beach*.

Galiano Inn

Sometime in the 1920's, an English family built a large Elizabethan-style house at Sturdies Bay. They called it *Dunromin*.[169]

A decade later, Alec Scoones purchased the home and ran it as a resort. He renamed it *Greenways*.[170]

The resort served as the location for many parties, prospering until the end of World War II when new owners subdivided and sold the property.[171] Soon, it became the property of Fred Robson, who renamed it the *Galiano Lodge*.[172]

Galiano Inn & Spa in the 1930's - Galiano Archives 2004021043

The main floor of the lodge consisted of a large living room. It led off a spacious entrance that had a wide Oak staircase. On the second floor were eight bedrooms and a large bathroom with an extra large bathtub.[173]

The grounds, which had extensive rockwork, had been designed to simulate an English courtyard. There was also a riding stable and a tennis court.[174]

Because the main attraction to the lodge was the fishing, the Robson's built a wharf and float in the bay. Then, they purchased four small boats with gear and rented them to guests by the hour.[175]

113

Galiano Island

In 1951, the Galiano Lodge was destroyed by fire, leaving only the brick steps and stone verandah standing. The Robson's built a single-storied house on the same site and continued to operate it as a resort into the 60's. Subsequent owners added more rooms to the building.[176]

Today, the Galiano Lodge operates as the *Galiano Inn*. In addition to guest rooms, the Mediterranean-style Inn also features the *Madrona Del Mar Spa and Wellness Retreat*.

Cain Peninsula

In 1921, an Irishman, named Mr. Denroche, emigrated from Ireland to Canada. When he had borrowed enough money to purchase Gossip Island, off the southeast side of Galiano, he moved his family there.[177]

Although they had no experience living in the bush, the family initially lived in a tent. There was no water on the Island so the man rowed to Galiano every day to fetch water from a spring. Later, **the Postman** helped him dig a well and build a log cabin on his property.[178]

Soon, Mr. Denroche decided to start a resort. So he built some self-contained cottages on the property, each with its own bay.[179]

In 1929, he started a hotel on what his family called *Hotel Point*. He called it the *Gossip Island Hotel*.[180] It had 13 bedrooms, a large dining room and a sitting room with a fireplace. It hosted many dances.[181]

Mr. Denroche pioneered the use of propane as fuel for the hotel and, until it became too expensive, the family used it to cook, heat water and run the lights. The toilets ran on saltwater from the ocean.[182]

In the 1930's, **the Postman** built the Denroche's a summer house on the point. He also built a turnstile at the entrance to the hotel.[183]

Unfortunately, at the beginning of World War II, the hotel was closed down and partially dismantled.[184]

Today, Gossip Island can be seen from the *Cain Peninsula*. The peninsula provides protection to an adjacent bay from the winds blowing in from the Georgia Strait.

The rocky beach on the peninsula is dotted with large pieces of driftwood and provides for interesting sandstone formations.

Galiano Island

However, the beach is closed to the harvesting of scallops, mussels, oysters and clams.[185]

If you launch a boat from the Cain Peninsula, you can travel around Gossip Island and the coves nearby.

Galiano Community Hall

In 1925, **the Postman** donated some land beside the Galiano School for the building of a community hall.[186] Upon completion, it was called the *Galiano Community Hall*.[187]

The hall had a closed porch with a gable. There was a lean-to kitchen with a wood stove at one end and two dressing rooms at the back.[188]

A big steel drum between the windows generated heat. Light was provided by old Coleman mantle lanterns that hung off the walls and from the ceiling.[189]

The official opening of the community hall was a celebration. Special guests received a royal welcome at the wharf as they arrived by boat.[190]

In the 1930's, the hall was enlarged so that, during the winter, it could accommodate badminton matches and other events. Later, in the 1960's, heaters were installed, followed by indoor plumbing.[191]

Galiano Community Hall in the 1970's – Galiano Archives M103

Galiano Island

Today, the little Galiano Community Hall, which stands in the center of South Galiano, serves as a venue for various events throughout the year.

Galiano Community Hall as it appears today

Retreat Cove

In 1928, a Greek, named Tony Bell, purchased some property on a cove, where he and his wife established a farm.[192] On their farm, the couple lived in a little house overlooking a Japanese-Canadian owned herring saltery, where Tony worked.[193]

In 1933, Tony built a log cabin for his growing family. Because he had many children, he was known locally as 'Papa'.[194]

Papa raised Black Quebec mink on the farm. So his family called the farm the *Seven Sister Fur Farm*. During World War II, the mink became hard to find and the family was forced to sell them at a loss. Eventually, their farm was also sold.[195]

At that time, the area surrounding the cove was a thriving community, with a school, fish saltery and grocery store.[196]

One day, a party was held for all the fishermen at the Japanese owned saltery. During the party, a fire started on the dock.[197]

The fire spread through the saltery and all the stores, offices and homes at the cove. Ironically, the next day, news came of the Japanese attack on Pearl Harbour.[198]

Retreat Cove wharf, early 1900's – Galiano Archives 2004026520

Galiano Island

Retreat Cove is a beautiful cove on the northwest side of Galiano. It provides for views of Salt Spring Island.

The beach on the cove provides for overhanging rocks and a cavern. A government wharf that extends into the cove serves as a water access point.

You can launch a boat from the cove and take a relaxing, quiet tour around a nearby island called *Retreat Island*. However, the cove is exposed to westerly winds and the waters behind the island are shallow.

Spanish Hills

At one time, North Galiano had a sawmill, six salmon and herring canneries, and a marine shop called *Baines Motor Boat Repair Shop*. It was owned by George Baines, the builder of the North Galiano School.[199]

In 1949, the post office at Shaw's Landing was moved up the Island, to a store that had been opened at the turn of the century.[200] At that time, Tony Bell delivered the mail to North Galiano.[201]

The post office operated from inside the store and there were living quarters in the back. The store's new owners, Mr. and Mrs. Clutterbuck, changed the name to *Clutterbuck's Store*.[202]

A decade later, the store was destroyed by fire and was rebuilt. At that time, it was named the *North Galiano Store*.[203]

Spanish Hills Store in the 1950's
Galiano Archives M207

The North Galiano Store changed owners many times. In the 1960's, it was renamed the *Spanish Hills Store*.[204]

Ye Olde Spanish Hills Store as it appears today

Galiano Island

Today, the community of *Spanish Hills* provides mainly for wonderful scenery and great sports fishing. The store is now a private residence on Porlier Pass Road.

The area is a great spot for scuba diving at a depth of up to 30 m. The waters further north provide for some spectacular underwater scenery. However, the *skookumchuck* (strong currents) there can run up to 7 knots.

Montague Harbour

Montague Harbour was once an ancient Coast Salish Indian village.[205] Originally named *Stockade Harbour*,[206] the waters made history in 1863, when the British captured Indians there because of attacks they had carried out on Pender and Saturna Islands.[207]

Shell Beach at the turn of the century - Galiano Archives 2004021028

One hundred years later, in the 1950's, an end-loading wharf was built at the harbour. For the most part, it replaced the wharf at Sturdies Bay.[208] Shortly thereafter, the *Montague Harbour Marina* opened there.

Today, Montague Harbour is one of the most popular anchorages in the Gulf Islands. Located on the southwest side of Galiano, the wharf is used by sea planes and to transport schoolchildren to neighboring schools.

Shell Beach as it appears today

Galiano Island

The Montague Harbour Marina offers a wide range of services for boaters. In addition to moorage, fuel and boat rentals, it carries groceries, and camping and fishing supplies. There is also a seasonal restaurant.

Montague Harbour Provincial Marine Park was the first marine park to be established in all of British Columbia. It provides for lovely forest trails. There are also facilities for picnics if you want to stay a while.

During the summer, British Columbia Parks runs an extensive schedule of free interpretive programs that are held in the park at The Meeting Place and at The Marine Park Nature House.

The Gray Peninsula, which is connected to the head of the harbour, provides for a popular, white shell, swimming beach called *Shell Beach*. Underwater excavations are regularly performed there by *Montague Mudsuckers* (archeologists).

The easy 3 km trail that follows the waters around the peninsula is a great place to find clams and to see Great Blue Herons, Kingfishers, Bald Eagles and other birds.

Galiano Island Fire Departments

In the 1950's, the Galiano Chamber of Commerce purchased a Wajax pump and trailer. Along with some other pumps, this equipment was all that existed for fire fighting equipment on Galiano.[209]

A decade later, a pumper truck was purchased from Vancouver Island and an old building, which was originally operated by a power company, was used as a fire hall.[210]

Galiano Island

In an effort to pay for the property and equipment, two women designed a large thermometer that displayed 20 equally spaced lines, each representing one hundred dollars. Then, they hung it at Sturdies Bay and asked Galiano land owners for donations.[211]

It is assumed that each time a donation was made, the ladies moved a marker up on the thermometer,[212] a method that is still used to motivate Island residents during fundraising events today.

Within a few weeks, donations to the fire fighter's fund had amounted to over $2,000, exceeding the top line on the thermometer.[213]

At that time, because fires had destroyed so many buildings on Galiano in the first half of the century, it was incorporated into a fire protection district and the *South Galiano Volunteer Fire Department* was born.[214]

Shortly thereafter, a resident offered to let the fire department practice using their equipment by burning down some old buildings on his property on a bay.

However, when everyone went for lunch, a tree caught fire and help had to be brought in from Mayne Island to fight it.[215]

When the water tank on the pumper truck ran dry and the tide ran out, the pump in the bay began pumping sand, instead of water. Fortunately, the fire was eventually extinguished.[216]

In the 1970's, the founder of the Corner Store donated some land for a new fire hall.[217]

Today, there are two volunteer fire departments serving North and South Galiano. In the year prior to this writing, the North Galiano Volunteer Fire Department acquired its first new fire engine.[218]

Active Pass Caboose Cottage
In the 1970's, a turn-of-the-century Canadian Pacific Railway caboose was barged to Galiano from the mainland. She was then restored and converted into a guest cottage, complete with a tiny train station.

Galiano Island

At the time of this writing, the caboose was operating as a cottage rental on South Galiano. It is called the *Active Pass Caboose*.

Salt Spring Island

Vesuvius Bay Wharf

It was in the spring of 1861 that a Scotsman, named Jonathan Begg, was awakened by a band of Haida Indians who were stealing from his store...

With Jonathan aboard, the British Royal Navy pursued the Indians in the gunboat named the H.M.G. *Forward*. When they found the Indians camped on Vancouver Island, they fired on their camp. In the exchange of gunfire, four Indians and one crewman were killed.[1]

Jonathan Begg was born in Scotland, in the early 1800's. In 1859, he arrived penniless, in what was at that time the Colony of Vancouver Island.[2]

Jonathan was among the first settlers to reform the land pre-emption system for the colony.[3] He then settled in that colony, on Salt Spring Island. There, he became **the Postman**, operating the Island's first store and post office.[4]

The politically minded Jonathan Begg was a reporter of the news, having been Salt Spring's correspondent for the *British Colonist* newspaper.[5] In response to his request for a post office, another newspaper said this about him:

From Mr. J. Begg, one of the first, and most respectable of the settlers on Salt Spring Island, we are rejoiced to hear a most satisfactory account of the prospects of their happy little community.
New Westminster Times[6]

Salt Spring Island

The Bustling Island

Salt Spring is a bustling island. At 180 sq km, it is the largest of the southern Gulf Islands. While diverse scenery is its most distinguishing characteristic, the fact that it offers something for everyone gives Salt Spring Island its unique charm.

Salt Spring is the fastest growing and most populous of the southern Gulf Islands. It has a population of approximately 10,000 permanent residents, of which most are young families, retirees and business professionals.

Known as *The Art Lover's Gallery*, Salt Spring is home to the greatest collection of artists in all of Canada. During the tourist season, the population swells to around 20,000 when visitors tour the Island in search of local art.

Ganges

Urbanization of Salt Spring Island began at its north end, when a group of settlers arrived during the gold rush in the late 1850's. Most of these immigrants were Black men, who were former slaves from the U.S. They were followed immediately by Australians and settlers of other descents.[7]

Soon, a community called *Central Settlement* developed in the interior. Of the 26 families that settled there, 17 were Black.[8]

Central Settlement in the 1890's
Salt Spring Archives 1994137031

The settlers found the winter of 1862 to be unusually severe, which resulted in a 30 percent decrease in the Island's population.[9] Then, after the Civil War, many of the Black residents returned to the U.S.[10] However, as more women and children arrived in the 1870's[11] communities began to develop in each of the corners of the Island.[12]

Some of the families who settled at the south end were *Kanakas* (people of Hawaiian descent).[13] By that time, the Island's population had tripled[14] and it held claim to being the first agricultural settlement in all of British Columbia.[15]

Over the next decade, British and Irish immigrants began to settle on Salt Spring Island[16] and, soon, another community began to develop, near a harbour. The community became known as *Ganges*.[17]

Salt Spring Island

Main street through Ganges in 1948 – Salt Spring Archives CKC998162076

Ganges main street as it appears today

Today, Ganges is 'downtown' to Salt Spring Islanders. As the commercial hub of Salt Spring, it is the largest community in all the Gulf Islands.

Ganges provides for grocery stores, restaurants, banks, art galleries, retail stores and other businesses, as well as a marina.

Ganges Post Offices

Upon landing on Salt Spring in 1859, a few of the first settlers drew straws for their choice of sections of land. As the second settler to choose, Jonathan Begg selected a parcel of land overlooking a little bay on the northeast side of the Island.[18]

Soon, Jonathan began offering a postal service from his home.[19] A schooner would pass by his property three times a week[20] and he would row out into the Channel to collect the mail from one of the crew.[21]

Although it soon became a gathering place for the families living in the area,[22] the post office closed when **the Postman** left the Island in 1863.[23]

124

Salt Spring Island

A decade later, the *Salt Spring Island Post Office* opened[24] in a little one-room shack in Central Settlement. An obstinate mule delivered the mail. Whenever it decided to run past a delivery point, its rider would drop a note apologizing for not delivering the mail that day.[25]

In 1874, a Portuguese storekeeper opened a second post office, from his store. His store operated from a community now known as *Vesuvius*. Unfortunately, the post office closed shortly after it opened.[26]

Post Office in Vesuvius in the 1950's
Salt Spring Archives 02186028

Much later, in 1975, the 100-year old building in Vesuvius was destroyed by fire.[27] Today, the *Vesuvius Inn Neighborhood Pub* sits on the site.

Site of the Vesuvius Post Office as it appears today

In 1892, a settler opened another store on the Island, from his home in Central. Then, he took over the Salt Spring Island Post Office and moved it into his store.[28]

Salt Spring Island Post Office, 1890's
Salt Spring Archives 2005009001

The settler called his store *Broadwell's Store*. It was the largest store on the Island.[29] In 1933, the Salt Spring Island Post Office closed.[30] Today, a fire hall sits on the site.

Site of the Salt Spring Island Post Office as it appears today

In the year 1900, another post office opened, near a wharf in Ganges.[31] It operated from a building that was attached to the back of a boarding house.[32]

The S.S. *Iroquois* would deliver the mail to the wharf, at which time the ship's purser would often open up the ship's bar to the settlers who were waiting for their mail.[33]

Salt Spring Island

Ganges Post Office in the 1930's
Salt Spring Archives 1994137010

Much later, in the 1950's, the boarding house in Ganges was demolished, along with the addition that had served as the post office.[34] Today, a toy store, called *West of the Moon*, sits on the site and two post offices in Ganges serve the north end.

Fernwood Point

A few months after Jonathan Begg chose his property on Salt Spring, he began to build a log cabin. As he was building his small cabin, he discovered one of 14 valuable salt springs that existed at the north end.[35]

Jonathan's cabin had a mud floor and was covered with shakes on poles. It was heated by a small fireplace.[36]

By 1860, he had converted his cabin into the Island's first store and post office. As **the Postman**, Jonathan learned to save postage on his letters by writing a message down the page, rotating the paper, and then writing a second message across the first.[37]

The Postman's store was initially named the *Salt Spring Island Store*, but was later renamed the *Balmoral Store*.[38]

In his store, he sold groceries, dry goods and hardware. He would trade with the other settlers for the goods in his store, but would not extend them credit.[39] He would also not allow spitting in his store, nor would he allow swearing if ladies were present. He used a broom to enforce his strict policies.[40]

Over time, the area in which **the Postman** had lived and conducted his business was named *Beggsville*, in his honor.[41]

Today, Beggsville is part of a community known as *Fernwood*. There is an area in Fernwood, called *Fernwood Point*, to which there are three beach accesses. The beaches provide for views of Galiano Island.

One access leads to a public dock that is surrounded by the only live Sand Dollar beds

126

Salt Spring Island

on the Island. Another leads to Hudson Point, where the McFadden Creek Heronry is located.

If you launch a boat from Hudson Point, you can sail along the shoreline or across to Wallace Island. There is a marine park there that is a great place to see Seals and Bald Eagles.

The protected anchorages in the coves on the west side of Wallace Island make it easy to anchor in for the *poolakle* (night). However, there are sudden winds in *Houstoun Passage*.

Ganges Harbour

In the year 1860, 14 Bella Bella Indians were carrying a load of furs in a canoe.[42] Accompanying them was a renegade white man named John McCawley.[43]

The Indians stopped in a harbour where about 50 Cowichan Indians were already camped. The two tribes were long-time rivals and, as a result, a battle ensued.[44]

During the battle, John made his way to the home of a settler who lived nearby to tell him about the battle. When the settler went to the harbour to investigate, he discovered that eight Bella Bella Indian men had been killed and the remainder taken prisoner. It was a massacre.[45]

Ganges Harbour in 1912, the post office in the background - Salt Spring Archives 1994137020

Salt Spring Island

Ganges Harbour is located on the northeast side of the Island. First named *Admiralty Bay*,[46] it was the site of what is now known as the 'Massacre of Admiralty Bay'.

Ganges Harbour as it appears today

Ganges Harbour provides for two marinas and two government docks. There is an active Salt Spring Sailing Club at the harbour, as well as an outpost station for the Royal Vancouver Yacht Club.

Sea Star Point provides for a lovely beach on the north side of the harbour, with wonderful views of Goat Island and the Chain Islands.

One beach is accessible from the end of Churchill Road and another is located further south. If you launch a boat from either beach, you can sail out to those littler islands.

Vesuvius Beach

Soon after the Massacre of Admiralty Bay, a Black settler, named Louis Stark, arrived on the Island with his family and several head of cattle.[47]

Upon landing on the beach, Louis immediately sent one of his helpers to the home of **the Postman**, to ask for assistance in transporting his family's belongings.[48]

Suddenly, the Indians landed on the beach in their canoes. They were accompanied by John McCawley - the renegade white man.[49]

When Louis pointed his gun at the Indians, they climbed into their canoes and proceeded to leave the beach. Just then, a swarm of canoes carrying Indians from another band appeared in the bay. This prompted an Indian battle at sea, which culminated in another massacre.[50]

Salt Spring Island

Vesuvius Bay is located in the community of Vesuvius. The beach is called *Vesuvius Beach*. It is the most popular bathing beach on the Island and is one of the best places to watch the sun set.

The wharf in Vesuvius Bay provides for a small ferry terminal that services ferries traveling to and from the east side of Vancouver Island. There is also a public dock in the bay.

The village of Vesuvius provides for a general store, a restaurant, a pub and some quaint shops and studios.

Mt. Maxwell Provincial Park

One of the first settlers on Salt Spring was an Irishman named John Maxwell. When he moved to Salt Spring, he purchased land in a valley at the south end called the Fulford-Burgoyne Valley. There, he built a cabin at the foot of a mountain. He was the Island's first legal land owner.[51]

John started farming with 100 head of imported Texas Longhorn cattle. Soon, he became the Island's largest exporter of food, shipping about 20 head of cattle to Vancouver Island each month. Unfortunately, Indian cattle rustlers continuously plagued him.[52]

Mt. Maxwell in the 1890's
Salt Spring Archives 1994137251

When the government failed to provide him protection from the Indians, John and some other settlers set up an ambush on the mountain range behind his home.[53]

When the Indians arrived in their canoes, John McCawley was accompanying them. Upon seeing the Indians, the settlers fired

Salt Spring Island

down from the mountain. This panicked the Indians and they fled. Later, they slit McCawley's throat, blaming him for the attack.[54]

Mount Maxwell was named after John Maxwell, the Irishman, whose house operated as one of the first post offices at the south end.[55] The 590 m mountain, which can be reached by car, is also known as *Baynes Peak*. The views seen from the mountaintop at sunset are spectacular.

The mountain sits in *Mount Maxwell Provincial Park*, which is located in a secluded area on the west side of the Island. Established in 1938, it is one of the Island's first provincial parks.[56]

The old-growth forest park contains the largest Garry Oak, Western Red Cedar, Arbutus, Western Hemlock and Douglas-Fir trees on the Island. It provides for off-road cycling and there are facilities for picnics if you want to stay a while.

Salt Spring Elementary School

In 1861, a log schoolhouse was built in Central. It was called the *Vesuvius School*. A few years later, it was destroyed and a similar log building was built on the same site to replace it.[57]

Vesuvius School in the 1860's
Salt Spring Archives 1994137167

The first teacher to teach at the school was a Black man named John Jones. Each week, he would teach three days at the schoolhouse, and then walk to the property of **the Postman** where he would teach three days in an abandoned log cabin. For several years, he received no payment for his instruction.[58]

By the 1880's, a frame building had been constructed near the log schoolhouse and the school was moved there. At that time, the log schoolhouse became a location for community meetings and church services.[59]

By the turn of the century, there were five public schools on Salt Spring;[60] three at the north end and two at the south end. Over the next two decades, two more public schools opened.[61]

Unfortunately, by the year 1940, the depression of the previous decade had forced the Island to amalgamate most of its schools into one building, in Ganges.

Salt Spring Island

Named the *Consolidated School*, it provided for grades 1-12.[62]

When the Consolidated School opened, only two other schools remained in operation. In 1951, those schools also closed.[63]

Salt Spring Elementary School in 1940 - Salt Spring Archives 0001

By the 1960's, the Consolidated School had been renamed the *Salt Spring Elementary School*.[64] Today, there are five elementary schools on the Island.

Salt Spring Elementary School as it appears today

Fulford Harbour

In 1863, the gunboat, HMG *Forward*, was lost in a storm among the Gulf Islands. As the ship was being tossed about, the crew suddenly sighted a beacon light. So they pulled into a harbour to ride out the storm.[65]

By the 1890's, a wharf had been built in the harbour.[66] It provided a way for a very comfortable passenger vessel, called the *Joan*, to take settlers to and from Vancouver Island.[67]

At that time, most of the area was owned by Hawaiian settlers.[68] However, by the 1920's, a white settlement began to develop around the harbour and a general store, church, community hall and Inn were built nearby. There was even an ice cream kiosk at the wharf.[69]

Around that time, a carpenter built a ferry in the harbour. It was called *Hepburn's Ferry* and was powered by a farm tractor. It could

Salt Spring Island

carry four cars to Vancouver Island in two hours.[70]

There were several pulleys on the ferry's drive shaft. So, if the ferry needed more power during the voyage, the owner would just attach a belt from the rear wheel of a car to the ferry's drive shaft, and then start the car.[71]

Fulford Harbour in the 1920's - Salt Spring Archives 0011179041

Fulford Harbour wharf in the 1930's
Salt Spring Archives 1994137295

Fulford Harbour as it appears today

Fulford Harbour is located on the southeast side of the Island. The beach at the head of the harbour was once known locally as *Jackson`s Beach*.[72]

Salt Spring Island

The wharf in the harbour services ferries traveling to and from Vancouver Island. There are also two public docks in the harbour and a marina that provides for all season overnight moorage.

Fulford Harbour wharf as it appears today

The community of Fulford is located near the head of the harbour. It is a busy seaside village where businesses and residents co-exist. In addition to the store, church, community hall and Inn, which are all still standing, it offers some delightful galleries, shops and cafes.

Vesuvius Bay Wharf

During the 1860's, ships traveling to Vancouver Island sailed past both the east and west sides of Salt Spring. Passengers were landed by boat, off Trincomali Channel on the northeast side of the Island, or in Vesuvius Bay on the northwest side of the Island.[73]

The first wharf ever built on the Island was constructed in Vesuvius Bay in 1872.[74] It accommodated ships coming through the waterway called *Stuart Channel*. By the 1890's, five wharves had been constructed on the Island.[75]

Vesuvius Bay wharf at the turn of the century – Salt Spring Archives 50532

Salt Spring Island

A wharf in **the Postman's** community of Fernwood serviced the northern tip of the Island.[76] Wharves in Vesuvius Bay and Ganges Harbour serviced the communities on the northwest and northeast sides, while wharves in Fulford Harbour and Burgoyne Bay serviced the southeast and southwest sides.[77]

Wharf in Ganges Harbour in 1907
Salt Spring Archives 1994137002

In 1914, a new 300 m wharf was constructed in Ganges Harbour to provide deepwater docking on any tide.[78] By the 1930's, it had replaced the wharf in Vesuvius Bay as the main port of call.[79]

S.S. *Princess Elaine* at Ganges wharf in 1928
Salt Spring Archives CKC998162123

Today, there are three main wharves on Salt Spring. The newest wharf is located at *Long Harbour*, north of Ganges Harbour. Acquired in 1963, it services large ferries traveling to and from the mainland.[80]

The wharf in Fulford Harbour provides for the most demanding ferry terminal on the Island, servicing ferries traveling to and from the tip of Vancouver Island.

The Vesuvius Bay wharf still serves as a port of call, but for smaller ferries traveling to and from the east side of Vancouver Island.

Akerman Museum

Around the time the HMG *Forward* was pulling into Fulford Harbour to take shelter from a storm, an English settler, named Joseph Akerman, purchased some land in the Fulford-Burgoyne Valley. There, he built a log home.[81]

Two year's later, Joe and his new wife built a larger two-storey house beside a creek on their property. It was made from hand-hewn squared timbers.[82]

The following year, the couple converted part of their new house into the Island's first Inn and pub. They also ran the first store ever to operate in Fulford.[83] Called the *Traveler's Rest*, the Inn operated until the year 1910. The property was sold a decade later.[84]

One hundred years after Joe had first acquired the property, his great grandson, Robert, purchased it.[85]

Throughout his life as road foreman, Robert had collected artifacts and craft pieces from Indian village life. So after he had been living on the property a while, he built a museum beside the old Inn, in which to house his artifacts. He was over 80 years old at the time.[86]

Although the 140-year old Inn was recently demolished, Robert's museum still operates on the property. It can be viewed by appointment.

Salt Spring Island

Booth Canal

In 1868, a Scotsman, named John Booth, became the first representative of Salt Spring in the Legislative Assembly in Victoria.[87]

During John's reign as the Island's main politician, letters patent were issued for the incorporation of the Township of Salt Spring Island.[88]

Several municipal bylaws passed during the first meeting, which started a battle over the incorporation. This divided the Islanders politically for more than a decade.[89]

In the 1880's, the people charged John with retaining his political position without election because no one else was nominated to oppose him.[90] Eventually, the incorporation was cancelled and he went on to lose two provincial elections.[91]

Fortunately, in the year 1890, John won again, in a new riding called 'The Islands'. He held the seat until he passed away.[92]

Booth Canal was named after this politician, whose name also commemorates the adjoining bay. When he died, his funeral was the most impressive ever held on Salt Spring.[93]

Booth Canal is located near the village of Vesuvius. It provides for a pebbled beach.

Seabright Beach

In the 1870's, First Nations was allotted a reserve near Fulford Harbour.[94] The Indians would set up elaborate camps on the reserve and live there throughout the summers, digging for clams along the shore of the harbour.[95]

The Indians would make holes in the beach, into which they would place kindling. Then, they would light the kindling and throw rocks into the holes.[96] The bonfires and torches they used would light up the shoreline like a city.[97]

When the rocks became hot, the freshly-dug clams were dumped into the holes and covered with mats and bags. When the shells opened, the Indians would scoop the partially cooked clams out of their shells and thread them onto long, slender sticks. Each stick was then bent to form a hoop and hung over the fire until the clams browned.[98]

The clamshells the Indians left behind on the beaches produced lime in the soil. Later, when the settlers put in crops of potatoes, the lime caused them to become scaly.[99]

Located near Fulford Harbour, *Seabright Beach* sits beside Salt Spring's only Indian Reserve. The beach provides for some of the loveliest shoreline on the Island.

Salt Spring Island

Ruckle Provincial Park

In 1872, an Irishman, named Henry Ruckle, purchased some land on a point at the south end. There he established a farm. Three years later, he married a woman who had a son from a previous marriage.[100]

At that time, Henry built a one and one-half storey frame house and the couple started a family of their own. As the family grew, a small addition was added to the house.[101]

In the 1880's, Henry built a wharf, from which he operated one of the first post offices to be established at the south end.[102]

On his farm, he planted an orchard of 600 trees, establishing a variety of pears, called Ruckle Bartlet.[103] Reportedly, it was the first fruit orchard in all of British Columbia.

Henry also raised dairy Jersey cattle and transported cream to the creamery in Ganges.[104] He grew seed potatoes that produced as much as 60,000 kg of potatoes each year.[105]

A decade later, two of his sons built homes on his property and brought their brides to live there.[106] At that time, the farm was the largest on the Island.[107]

Ruckle farmhouse in the 1890's Salt Spring Archives 992112004

The settler's adopted son, Alfred, became very adept at woodworking. His magnificent home was fashioned in the Queen Anne style, with handcrafted woodwork and a

136

Salt Spring Island

sharply curved staircase with a gleaming cherry banister.[108]

In 1938, the family built yet another home on the property. The house was built for the settler's grandson, William, who planned to live in it with his bride. Unfortunately, their wedding was cancelled and, thereafter, the house was used to store their potatoes.[109]

Ruckle Provincial Park was named after this family, whose farm is the oldest family farm in all of British Columbia today.[110] The family was granted a life-long tenancy on the property[111] and continues to work it.

Ruckle Farmhouse as it appears today

The historical park, which was purchased in the 1970's, is located near Fulford Harbour. As the largest park in all the Gulf Islands, it provides for some of the Islands' best hiking through some of the largest Douglas-Fir and Western Red Cedar trees.

Ruckle Provincial Campground is the largest provincial campground in all the Gulf Islands. The spectacular campground offers 70 walk-in waterfront sites. The campground also provides for off-road cycling and there are facilities for picnics if you want to stay awhile.

Heritage House Museum

In the 1870's, a Portuguese, named Estalon Bittancourt, constructed a grand home on Vesuvius Bay for his growing family. Soon, he converted his home into a hotel called

Salt Spring Island

the *Vesuvius Bay Hotel*. At one time, it was also the home of a store and post office.[112]

In 1886, Estalon built a little house to be used as overflow accommodations whenever there was no vacancy at his hotel.[113]

Unfortunately, one hundred years after it was constructed, the hotel was destroyed by fire.[114] Fortunately, the little house survived the fire.[115]

Soon, the house became threatened by the expansion of the Vesuvius ferry terminal. So, in the year 1980, the Farmers Institute moved it to their grounds in Ganges. At that time, a seniors group obtained a grant to convert it into a museum.[116]

Today, the four-room house is the home of the Island's first museum. Named the *Bittancourt Heritage House Museum*, it can be viewed by appointment.

Musgrave Point

In 1874, four brothers, named Pimbury, emigrated from England to Salt Spring where they established a large sheep farm in a very secluded area. A decade later, another settler, named Edward Musgrave, purchased their farm.[117]

Musgrave Point was named after this settler who also purchased the brothers' 350 sheep.[118] The point is located on the southwest side of the Island. Until 1926, it was accessible only by water.[119]

The pebbled beach on the point provides for a government wharf. The point is accessible from the end of a long and rocky road.

Princess Margaret Park Reserve

In 1875, an Hawaiian, named William Naukana, came to the Gulf Islands, bringing with him a few other Hawaiians. They

Salt Spring Island

settled on a small Island, which they registered in their names.[120]

William had a unique way of curing tobacco. He would cut a round off a log, bore a hole through the middle, and then fill it with crushed, cured tobacco leaves. Then, he would pour in molasses and rum. When the hole was tightly packed, the log-round would split, producing a long tobacco stick that was ready for smoking.[121]

William's family liked to hold luaus. The parties would begin in his house, and then everyone would travel from home to home. They would remain at each house until they had consumed all the food and drink. Sometimes, the parties would last for weeks.[122]

Around the turn of the century, the Island was sold. William had lived there for over 30 years. When he died two years later, his descendants carried on his unique method of curing tobacco.[123]

Princess Margaret Park is part of the Gulf Islands National Park Reserve. Located on Portland Island, off the southern shore of Salt Spring, it provides for camping. There are facilities for picnics if you want to stay a while.

On the network of trails through the park can still be seen the fruit trees, roses and other plants that were grown by the Hawaiians who originally settled there. Bald Eagles and Turkey Vultures are also frequently seen there.

Beddis Beach

In the 1880's, an Englishman, named Samuel Beddis, purchased a sailing sloop and loaded it with food, a tent and some household items. Then, he set sail up the West Coast with his family.[124]

Eventually, Samuel landed on a beach, where he and his family constructed a log home.[125] Later, when he contracted pneumonia and died, his sons took over his business.[126] At the turn of the century, they built a new, two-storey, frame house for their family to live in.[127]

Salt Spring Island

Beddis Beach was named after this family of builders,[128] whose home and orchard can still be seen standing nearby.

The stunning white-shell beach is located near Ganges Harbour. It is one of the most beautiful beaches on the Island and provides for views of Prevost Island and Pender Island.

A buoy on a rock off the beach commemorates the family who, for many years, left a light burning in the front window of their home to guide ships through the Pass.[129]

At the north end of the beach is a five-storey structure called Winsor Castle. It was built from thousands of kilograms of stone that were handpicked by an artist, from beaches all over the Gulf Islands.[130]

You can launch a boat from the beach and travel south along the shoreline to the Channel Islands. Alternatively, you can sail to Prevost Island.

St. Paul's Catholic Church

In the year 1880, the construction of a Catholic church began on Salt Spring.[131] Much of its construction was performed by Hawaiians, who were later buried in the adjoining cemetery.[132] Thereafter, the church was the center of Hawaiian life for many years.[133]

The windows, door and bell for the church came from an Indian reserve on Vancouver Island. The materials were transported by canoe to a bay on the southwest side of the Island, and then by stoneboat to Fulford.[134]

Eventually, the exterior siding and part of the interior were faced with imitation stone,[135] making it one of the most beautiful churches on Salt Spring.

St. Paul's Catholic Church and rectory at the turn of the century - Salt Spring Archives 083a

Salt Spring Island

St. Paul's Catholic Church as it appears today

Today, there are at least six historic churches that visitors to the Island can admire. *St. Paul's Catholic Church* is the oldest church on the Island.

Dowry House Cottage

In the 1880's, Estalon Bittancourt constructed three houses on Vesuvius Bay.[136] They were built as dowries for three of his six daughters. However, because the vacant homes were built to be lived in after his daughters were wed, they were often rented out.[137]

Eventually, Estalon's dowry houses were sold and remodeled. One of the homes was moved up a hill[138] where it overlooked the bay.

Dowry House Cottage on Vesuvius Beach in the 1890's - Salt Spring Archives 093a

At the time of this writing, the dowry house on the hill was one of three cottage rentals operated by *Salt Spring Cottages*. They call the cottage the *Dowry House*. It still looks out over the bay.

Dowry House Cottage as it appears today

Salt Spring Island

Beaver Point

In 1885, Samuel Beddis constructed a one-room schoolhouse on a point, with the help of his two sons. The school was named the *Beaver Point School* and his sons were the first of the initial 17 students enrolled.[139] Children from Hawaiian and Indian mixed families made up at least one-half of the enrollment at the school.[140]

Much later, in 1951, the school closed.[141] When it closed, it held claim to being the oldest continuously running school in all of British Columbia.[142]

Beaver Point is located near Fulford Harbour. There are numerous little coves and bays surrounding the point. A rocky beach is accessible by way of trails through Ruckle Provincial Park. The `Little Red Schoolhouse` now operates as a preschool.

St. Mary Lake

While Samuel Beddis was building the Little Red Schoolhouse on Beaver Point, a Scotsman, named Thomas Mouat, emigrated from Scotland with his wife, Jane. Soon, they purchased a farm that was sitting on a lake at the north end.[143]

The house that stood on the farm was not a desirable one. So, in the 1890's, Tom hired a man to build a new home on the property.[144]

St. Mary Lake at the turn of the century
Salt Spring Archives 50550

Unfortunately, six years later, Tom died, due to poor health, and Jane was left to raise 11 children on her lakeside farm, alone.[145] Her youngest child was an infant who passed away soon after her father.[146]

With the help of her remaining children, Jane continued to run her farm for a decade. After she moved into a boarding house in Ganges, she rented out the farm. At the end of World War I, it was sold.[147]

Salt Spring Island

St. Mary Lake is the largest freshwater lake in the southern Gulf Islands. Jane's home can still be seen standing on the southwest side of the lake today.

The lake is located near Fernwood. The sandy beach is accessible from the north end of the lake. It is a great place for a swim.

St. Mary'Lake as it appears today

Russell Island Prov. Marine Park

In 1886, an Hawaiian, named William Haumea, emigrated to a tiny island. There, he developed a farm, where he established an orchard and raised sheep and cattle.[148]

In 1902, William died, leaving his entire farm to a young Hawaiian woman named Maria Mahoi Fisher. She and her husband built a small frame house on the property and continued to raise sheep and care for the orchard.[149]

Russell Island Provincial Marine Park is located on *Russell Island*, which sits off the southeastern shore of Salt Spring.

The park is part of the Gulf Islands National Park Reserve and provides for a forest of Douglas-Fir, Arbutus and Garry Oak. There are stands of Shore Pine that grow around its perimeter.

The frame house that was owned by the Hawaiian immigrant still stands on the Island. The Island is protected by a resident caretaker.

Fulford Inn

By the 1890's, a settler, named Mr. Rogers, had opened a tavern, called *Roger's Saloon*, at the head of Fulford Harbour. Unfortunately, in 1901, it was destroyed by fire[150] and Mr. Rogers sold the property to another settler, named Mr. McFadgen.

Salt Spring Island

One day, Mr. McFadgen heard a rumor that the highways crew were planning to build a road over the bank across a nearby creek. That caused him concern because it could cut off the corner on which his property sat.[151]

Mr. McFadgen knew that a bylaw existed to prohibit the destruction of a fruit orchard during the construction of a highway. So he promptly planted fruit trees all over his newly acquired property. Subsequently, a bend in the road from Fulford to Ganges was created at the head of the harbour.[152]

A few years later, the property was sold again. The new owner, Arthur Eaton, was known locally as 'Pop'. He erected a store on the property, beside the bend in the road.[153] Soon, he converted his store into a hotel.[154]

Initially, the hotel was called the *White House Hotel*, but was later renamed the *White Lodge*.[155] During the 1920's, it also served as the home of the post office at Fulford Harbour.[156]

The Fulford Inn in 1920 - Salt Spring Archives 1994137041

The hotel was destroyed by fire in the mid-1930's. When it was rebuilt, it was renamed the *Fulford Inn*. In the 1950's, it was again destroyed by fire and rebuilt as a Tudor-style Inn.[157]

Today, the hotel is one of the oldest Inns in all the Gulf Islands. As a licensed pub and restaurant, the Inn has the largest organic wine selection under one roof in all of British Columbia.

Fulford Inn as it appears today

The pub also provides for live music from some of the best performers in Canada.

Salt Spring Island

Musicians and singers, such as Randy Bachman, Valdy and Harry Manx, have all performed there.

Salt Spring Island Trading Company

In 1892, a wealthy, but generous, Englishman, named Harry Bullock, immigrated to Salt Spring. He was always formally dressed, with a satin top hat and a long black frock. He liked to be called 'the Squire'.[158]

In 1911, Harry and some other settlers incorporated the *Salt Spring Island Trading Company*.[159] The following year, they built a general store in Ganges.[160]

The Trading Company soon became a direct competitor of a store run by Jane Mouat and her family. Nevertheless, the relationship between the store owners remained friendly.[161]

Salt Spring Island Trading Company in the 1930's - Salt Spring Archives 02186020

Salt Spring Island

The Trading Company operated until 1969, when it was bought out by the Mouat family.[162] At that time, it was renamed the *Gulf Islands Trading Co. Ltd.*[163]

Over time, additional businesses were established alongside the store. Today, the building complex is, once again, called the Salt Spring Island Trading Company.

At the time of this writing, the businesses included a long-lived shoe store, as well as a health food store, a fitness center, a bookstore and a café.

Salt Spring Island Trading Company as it appears today

Fulford Post Office

By 1893, three post offices had opened at the south end.[164] At the turn of the century, two of them were moved into the Fulford-Burgoyne Valley.[165]

When they were moved, they were consolidated as one post office called the *South Salt Spring Island Post Office*.[166] It served the two communities there.

The consolidated post office operated from a store called *R.P. Edwards' Store*. The storekeeper was known locally as 'Old Edwards'.

Old Edwards would wait until he heard the ship's whistle before loading the mail bags into his cart. The ship's Captain would then wait impatiently as he wheeled the cart down the long road to the Fulford Harbour wharf.[167]

During its final voyage of 1911, the S.S. *Iroquois* was delivering the mail to the post office. After the ship sank in a storm, a mailbag that was on board washed ashore. One of the letters it contained was addressed to Robert Akerman's father, George. It was from the government, appointing him Justice of the Peace.[168]

In 1918, the post office was moved into the White Lodge overlooking Fulford Harbour.[169]

**Fulford Post Office in 1920
Salt Spring Archives 1994137040**

In 1923, another post office opened, at Musgrave Landing.[170] Once again, there were three post offices serving the south end; one at Fulford Harbour, a second at Musgrave Landing and a third at Beaver Point.[171]

In the 1940's, the Fulford Harbour Post Office was moved into a store at the wharf. A decade later, the building was converted into a concession, called *Mary Lee's Snack Shop*. Four years later, new owners changed the name to *Nan's Coffee Bar*.[172]

Salt Spring Island

Fulford Post Office in the late 1950's
Salt Spring Archives 02186003

Around that time, the other post offices at the south end closed, leaving only the Fulford Harbour Post Office in operation.[173]

Today, the building that housed the post office is home to a café, called the *Tree House Café South*, and the post office operates from around the corner.

Old Farmhouse B&B

In 1895, a British dairyman, named John Collins, settled with his family on Salt Spring. At that time, he rented a cottage on Harry Bullock's estate.[174]

Two years later, Harry permitted John to convert his barn into a creamery called the *Salt Spring Island English Creamery Company*. The business operated near a pig farm. Unfortunately, it was not a success.[175]

In 1898, the Island founded a branch of the Farmer's Institute to educate farmers and improve agriculture. John was an active member and officer in the organization.[176]

Over time, he purchased some property at the north end, where he built a tall farmhouse for his family.[177] There, he established a farm. Over time, an Arbutus tree could be seen growing in front of the farmhouse.

Old Farmhouse B&B, early 1900's
Management of Old Farmhouse B&B

One hundred years later, new owners of the property converted the fine heritage building into a bed and breakfast.

At the time of this writing, it was operating as the *Old Farmhouse B&B*. The Arbutus in the yard is now the largest on the Island.

Salt Spring Island

Old Farmhouse B&B as it appears today

Salt Spring Cinema

In 1896, an agriculture hall was constructed beside the school in Central. It was named the *Central Community Hall*.[178]

That year, the hall hosted the Island's first agricultural fair.[179] However, when it became apparent that the building was more suited to hosting indoor events, the fair was moved[180] and the hall went on to serve as a community center.

During the 1950's, events organizers would set up wooden folding chairs in the hall for special events. Then, a projectionist would display slides on a screen, while the local piano teacher played background music for the audience.[181]

Salt Spring Cinema in the 1930's - Salt Spring Archives 02186024

In the 1970's, two wings, a stage and a porch were added to the hall.[182] Today, the hall serves as a movie theatre called *Salt Spring Cinema*.

Located in Central, the cinema seats 120 people and offers a full concession stand. A highlight of the cinema is the dynamic slide show that is shown before the feature film.

Salt Spring Island

Salt Spring Cinema as it appears today

Salt Spring Golf & Country Club

In the 1890's, a Reverend, named Edward Wilson, took over a run-down farm in Central. There, he lived in a log cabin on a dirt floor. Later, when his family arrived, a new home was built on the property.[183]

Eventually, Reverend Wilson turned the property into a successful farm called *Barnsbury Grange*.[184]

In the 1920's, the Reverend's son took over the property. He converted the farm into a golf course and the farmhouse into a clubhouse. Unfortunately, the clubhouse was destroyed by fire in the 1960's.[185]

Today, the farm is the home of the *Salt Spring Island Golf and Country Club*. The 9-hole course, which is open year-round, plays as a par 36. It features 10 tees and various teeing areas.

Hamilton Beach

In 1897, an Irishman, named William Hamilton, moved his large family to Salt Spring on a tugboat called the *Alert*.[186] The tugboat pulled into Fulford Harbour dragging two scows that were loaded with the family's household supplies, some lumber, a cat and a canary.[187]

After negotiating with the highways crew for a public road to be built to their property, William settled on the waterfront. Unfortunately, the only building standing on the property was a small, bug-infested, log cabin.[188]

The Hamilton family soon planted hundreds of fruit and nut trees on their property. Then, they began to build a large two-storey house on the beach. They called it *Dromore*.[189]

Unfortunately, the carpenter never fulfilled his obligation and, as a result, the house was never finished. Subsequently, the boys who slept upstairs would awaken on cold mornings to find icicles hanging above their heads.[190]

Hamilton Beach was named after this family, who discovered an Indian burial ground on the *Skull Islands* at the entrance to Fulford Harbour.[191]

The wide pebbled beach, which is dotted with driftwood, is located on the harbour. It is home to dozens of swans that feed at an estuary there.

If you launch a boat from the beach, you can sail around Isabella Point. You can continue around the south end and up to Musgrave Landing. Near Cape Keppel is a marine ecological reserve that is a good place to see wildlife.

Salt Spring Island

Harbour House Hotel

In 1898, an Irishman, named Alfred Crofton, emigrated from Ireland to Salt Spring. Initially, he worked on a farm overlooking Ganges Harbour. A decade later, he purchased the farm and renamed it *Harbour House*.[192]

While Alfred was serving in World War I, his wife, Nona, decided to convert the farmhouse into a guesthouse by adding some bedrooms and a dining room. She also set up some tents on the property.[193] They called the guesthouse the *Harbour House Hotel*.

The hotel became a popular destination and, soon, Alfred and Nona expanded it and added a tennis court.[194] In the 1920`s, they added two additional tennis courts, a beer parlor and a glassed-in dance pavilion called the 'Sun Room'. There was also a drawing room and a lounge, in which they kept roaring fires.[195]

The guests of the hotel participated in crab races on the billiard table, bridge, beachfront swimming and scavenger hunts. The hotel dances attracted as many as 100 people.[196]

At that time, they acquired a cook who did not like customers gathering in his kitchen. When too many people came in at one time, he would throw pepper on his stove. The burning pepper would cause the customers to leave.[197]

In the 1940`s, the tents on the grounds were replaced with cabins[198] and by the 60's, a swimming pool had replaced one of the three tennis courts.[199]

Unfortunately, a decade later, the hotel was destroyed by fire[200] and rebuilt. Today, it offers 35 rooms and facilities for special events.

At the time of this writing, the hotel featured a licensed pub and restaurant called *Porter`s Restaurant and Lounge*. Burning pepper is not on the menu.

Salt Spring Island

Fulford Creek Guest House

At the turn of the century, a settler established a farm for his family in the Fulford-Burgoyne Valley. Initially, a small cabin was their homestead.[201]

When the family outgrew the cabin in the 1920's, they built a four-bedroom farmhouse nearby. During the 1940's, the house was used as a boarding house for migrant farm workers. A decade later, it became a nursing home.[202]

At the time of this writing, the farmhouse was being operated as the *Fulford Creek Guest House*. The family's little cabin still sits on the property.

Mahon Memorial Hall

Because the new hall in Central was not suitable as an agriculture hall, the Islands' Agricultural and Fruit Growers' Association built a new hall on a Ganges farm in 1902. The land provided for adequate exhibition grounds to host the fall fair.[203]

The society borrowed some of the funds from a settler named Ross Mahon.[204] Unfortunately, the following year, Ross drowned while swimming in Long Harbour. At that time, his family forgave the debt and the hall was named the *Mahon Memorial Hall*, in his honor.[205]

Mahon Memorial Hall in the 1920's – Salt Spring Archives 1994137111

Salt Spring Island

The hall was host to dances, recitals, drama productions, school concerts and indoor recreation.[206] The fall fairs held at the hall were called the *Salt Spring Agricultural Exhibitions*. They were so spectacular that they rivaled the famous exhibitions in Vancouver.[207]

Unfortunately, the Salt Spring Exhibition was terminated during World War II. After the war, smaller fairs were held, but those soon ceased, as well.[208]

Much later, in 1980, the annual art show was moved to Mahon Hall. It featured arts and crafts produced by artists throughout the Gulf Islands.[209]

Today, the art show is called *ArtCraft*. The internationally renowned exhibition is the largest and longest-running art show in all the Gulf Islands. The show represents over 200 local artists and artisans.

ArtCraft is open in Mahon Memorial Hall each year, from May to September. Other, shorter ArtCraft exhibits are held in the hall, in the spring and during the Christmas season.

Mahon Memorial Hall as it appears today

Stitches Quilts & Yarns

In the year 1904, the building of the *Vesuvius Bay Methodist Church* began in Central. Jane Mouat had driven her horse and buggy across the Island to raise the necessary funds.[210]

In the 1920's, when several Protestant churches joined to form the United Church of Canada, the front portion of the church building was moved to Ganges and became the *Ganges United Church*.[211]

By the 1950's, the church had outgrown the structure. So they sold it to the Royal Canadian Legion,[212] who converted it into their hall.[213] The structure served as the centre of Legion and Auxiliary activities until the 1980's.[214]

Stitches Quilts & Yarns in the 1960's
Salt Spring Archives L1

At the time of this writing, the front of the Vesuvius Bay Methodist Church was operating as *Stitches Quilts & Yarns*. The store carries notions, fabric art supplies, embellishment kits, yarns and fabrics.

Salt Spring Island

Stitches Quilts & Yarns as it appears today

Mouat's Mall

In 1904, two settlers went into partnership and purchased Broadwell's Store in Central. Then, they constructed a large building at Ganges Harbour and moved the store there.[215]

Their new store included a blacksmith shop and some sheds that sat near the Ganges wharf. Using two boats, the partners operated a large export business from their store.[216]

When one of the partners died three years later, Jane Mouat and one of her sons purchased the business.[217]

Jane and her son sold everything from groceries and shoe polish, to tools and furniture.[218] They also operated the post office in Ganges.[219]

Because her son's name was Gilbert James, Jane named the store *G.J. Mouat and Company*.[220] When another son joined the business later, it was renamed *Mouat Brothers Company Ltd*.[221]

By then, the wharf had become known as *Mouat's Landing*. Customers would gather there to socialize on boat days and when they shopped at the store. They would leave their saddle ponies, ox teams, buggies and wagons all around the wharf.[222]

Mouat's Mall in the 1920's - Salt Spring Archives CKC998162061

Salt Spring Island

Just before the outbreak of World War I, a new building was constructed next door and the store was moved there.[223]

The new store had a wide staircase and a long counter that spanned the length of the store. The staircase led to a landing, and then split into two sets of stairs that continued up to the second floor.[224]

There was a large feed shed at Mouat's Landing, with a separate room for kerosene, naphtha gas and lubricating oil. The shed had an office inside, with a stand up desk on which sat a telephone that was connected to the store.[225]

In 1969, the company assets were purchased by a group of individuals that included Jane's grandsons. At that time, a new company was formed and the store was renamed *Mouat's Trading Company Ltd.*[226]

Over time, the feed shed was connected to the store to form a building complex. It was called *Mouat's Mall*.

Today, the store provides for hardware and housewares, and the mall is leased to businesses that are known collectively as *Seaside at Mouat's*. At the time of this writing, the businesses in Mouat's Mall included a salon, a bookstore, a gallery and a restaurant.

Mouat's Trading Company will celebrate its centennial in the year 2007. The busy mall is located in Ganges.

Mouat's Mall as it appears today

Embe Bakery

At the same time that Broadwell's Store was being bought out, Estalon Bittancourt's

Salt Spring Island

brother, Reid, constructed a stone building in Ganges for use as a creamery.[227] Named the *Salt Spring Island Creamery*, it was a cooperative of dairy farmers.[228]

Initially, only farmers in the Ganges community sent their cream there. However, over time, other farmers started supplying cream to the creamery. By 1928, the creamery was producing over 60,000 kg of butter.[229]

During that time, a truck driver would drive around the Island picking up the cans of cream from all the farms along the road.[230]

When the ships would dock at Mouat's Landing, the driver would leave the empty cream cans and wait for the full ones to be unloaded from the ship. Some of the cans came from neighboring Galiano, Mayne and Pender Islands.[231]

One year, the creamery's butter was entered in the Canadian National Exhibition where it was awarded the distinction of being the best in all of Canada.[232]

Embe Bakery in the 1950's - Salt Spring Archives 02186016

The Salt Spring Island Creamery closed in 1957. After several additions were attached to the front of the building,[233] it became home to the *Embe Bakery*. Today, the popular bakery is still in business and offers soups, subs, breads, pastries and cakes.

Embe Bakery as it appears today

Salt Spring Island

Salt Spring Centre of Yoga

In 1907, a Scottish settler, named Alan Blackburn, purchased an acreage on Salt Spring that he named *Ostaig*. Then, he hired Samuel Beddis to begin construction of a large two-storey house. The plans for the house included a turret, a tower and a chapel.[234]

Unfortunately, in 1913, Alan ran out of money and abandoned the unfinished house. In the 1920's, he passed away and his family moved off the Island. At that time, the house was rented out.[235]

Eventually, the government took over the property. They renovated it, and then used it to run rehabilitation programs until after World War II.[236]

Later, in the early 1980's, the Dharma Sara Satsang Society converted the home into an holistic center.

Today, the elegant house is known locally as the *Blackburn House*. At the time of this writing, it was operating as the *Salt Spring Centre of Yoga*.

The Salt Spring Centre of Yoga offers programs that concentrate on body and spiritual awareness, and self-help techniques, such as yoga and tai chi. It is famous for its Swedan massage.

Mouat Provincial Park

In 1912, after running Mouat's Store in Ganges for three years, Jane Mouat converted it into a boarding house. Then, she moved herself, her sons and her store employees into it. Her boarding house was called the *Ganges Inn*, but became known locally as *Granny's Boarding House*.[237]

By the onset of World War I, Jane's sons had become successful businessmen. As Mouat Brothers Company Ltd., they acquired the Island's Ford automobile dealership, installed a gas pump at the corner of the store and built a garage across from the

Salt Spring Island

boarding house. They also started a taxi service.[238]

Unfortunately, Gilbert Mouat soon contracted polio, which left him paralyzed. Neverthe-less, he continued to conduct business from his wheelchair.[239]

Mouat's property holdings in 1912 - Salt Spring Archives 1994137008

Mouat Provincial Park was named after this family of entrepreneurs, whose company also owns and operates *Mouat's Clothing Company* and *Old Salty Greetings, Gifts and Gourmet* at Mouat's Landing.

The park provides for beautiful Western Red Cedar trees. There are also facilities for picnics if you want to stay a while.

At one time, Mouat Park was the Island's only drive-in campground.[240] Today, it provides for a frisbee golf course called the *Hart Memorial Disc Golf Course*. The *Hart Memorial Disc Golf Tournament* takes place there each year.

Salt Spring Island

Booth Bay B&B

Around the same time that Jane Mouat opened her boarding house, a boat builder began construction of a large, waterfront, frame house on land he had acquired on Booth Bay.[241]

The following year, he sold his property to Alfred Crofton`s brother, Ernest. Ernest completed the house and added upswept ends that gave the building a unique characteristic.[242]

In 1948, the property was sold to a resident, named John Acland, who converted it into a resort called *Aclands*. John and his wife opened up some rooms in the house and served meals in their dining room.[243]

Several years later, the property was sold again. The new owners built some guest cottages on the property and changed the name of the resort to the *Booth Bay Resort*.[244]

In the 1970's, the property was sold yet again and a restaurant, called *The Bay Window*, was opened on the property.[245] The resort ceased to operate in the 1990`s.[246]

Today, the home is operated as the *Booth Bay Bed and Breakfast*. The beautiful building still retains much of the character that was instilled by its original owners.

Stone Walrus Gallery

At the onset of World War I, the first bank on Salt Spring moved into a new building in Ganges.[247] At that time, the building that had originally been its home became the private residence of the manager of the Salt Spring Island Trading Company.[248]

At the time of this writing, the building was operating as the *Stone Walrus Gallery*. The gallery offers a collection of world art that visitors can purchase for *tillicum* (a friend).

Lady Minto Hospital

While the first bank was moving into its new quarters, a retired British army doctor, named Lionel Beech, donated some land for a hospital near Ganges. The hospital was first named the *Gulf Islands Hospital*, but was later renamed the *Lady Minto Gulf Islands Hospital*.[249]

Initially, the hospital had two wards, each of which contained three beds. The year following its construction, a third ward was added.[250]

A small shed that was used as the Morgue stood behind the hospital. The medical staff would prepare the dead, put them on a stretcher and carry them down a dark path to the Morgue.[251]

In 1936, a nurse's residence opened and the facility grew to become an 18-bed hospital. A decade later, an x-ray machine and sterilizer were installed.[252] Unfortunately, the

Salt Spring Island

sterilizer was so old that every time they used it, the staff was afraid it would explode.[253]

Old Lady Minto Hospital in the 1930's
Salt Spring Archives 02186014

For 40 years, the Lady Minto Hospital was the only hospital in all the Gulf Islands. Then, in 1958, it was replaced with a larger building that was built nearby.[254]

For a while, the old hospital building served as a dormitory for schoolchildren from the other Gulf Islands who attended the secondary school in Ganges.[255]

In the 1970's, the building was taken over by the Salt Spring Island Community Society.[256] At the time of this writing, it was operating as a community center.

Ye Olde Lady Minto Hospital as it appears today

Tree House Café North

In the 1920's, a small building was built behind Mouat's Store. It housed an electric generator that powered the store. Later, it became a place where the butcher made sausage and prepared hams for smoking.[257]

At the time of this writing, the building was operating as an outdoor café called the *Tree House Café North*. The café provides for live entertainment and features over 50 entertainers during 123 consecutive nights of music. On Thursday nights there is an open mike under a plum tree.

Fulford Community Hall

While the Mouat brothers were installing their electric generator behind their store, the South Salt Spring Island Women's Institute was constructing a community hall in Fulford.[258]

Salt Spring Island

The *Fulford Community Hall* became a venue for several events at the south end, such as fairs, dances, card parties and movies.[259]

Four years after it was built, the furnace was overloaded with paper, causing the chimney to set the roof on fire. The fire destroyed the hall and the Women's Institute was forced to reconstruct it.[260]

In 1936, an arsonist burned the hall to the ground. However, fortunately for the Women's Institute, members of the community rebuilt it.[261]

In the 1940's, Robert Akerman purchased 100 pairs of second-hand roller skates for the hall. Soon, the neighborhood children were roller-skating there.[262]

Fulford Community Hall in the 1950's - Salt Spring Archives 02186006

Over the years, a lean-to entrance was added to the west end of the hall. It included a balcony where people could watch the roller hockey games.[263]

Today, the little Fulford Community Hall at the south end serves as a venue for various activities. It is also host to some of the events that take place during *Fulford Days*, a week-long festival that is held in August.

Fulford Hall as it appears today

Salt Spring Island

Gulf Islands Secondary School

Initially, Salt Spring students could only attain grade eight. In 1926, classes for grades 9 and 10 began in a former police building.[264]

A few years later, the Salt Spring Island Farmers Institute offered the school a more suitable building, which had been used to house poultry during the fall fair.[265]

The school was named the *Ganges High School*, but was jokingly referred to as the *Chicken House School*.[266]

The first year, 23 students in grades 9 and 10 attended the school. The students paid a monthly fee to attend and were responsible for their own books and transportation.[267]

The Chicken House School, early 1900's
Salt Spring Archives CKC998162047

In the 1960's, a new high school was built, on a hill beside the elementary school. It was called the *Gulf Islands Secondary School*.[268]

Recently, the high school was moved into a new building. The *Scholar Ship* (a water taxi that carries school children) transports children to the high school, from neighboring Islands.

Hastings House Country Estate

In the 1930's, a naval architect, named Warren Hastings, immigrated to Canada from England. Shortly thereafter, he purchased some waterfront property overlooking Ganges Harbour.

On the property stood a fortified trading post that had been established by the Hudson's Bay Company in the mid-1800's.[269] The trading post was the first structure ever built on Salt Spring.

When Warren began to establish a farm on the property, he moved the trading post inland[270] and built a Sussex-style Manor House on the site. In his home, he worked on secret designs for the British Royal Navy.[271]

Today, the property operates as a world-renowned luxury Inn called the *Hasting's House Country Estate Hotel*. The Inn, which has won numerous awards, offers 18 guest suites in seven restored buildings.

The Tudor-style home and farmhouse each provide for two suites. The original barn contains additional suites and a spa. The original Hudson's Bay trading post serves as a two-room cottage called 'The Post'.

Salt Spring Island

The *Hasting's House Restaurant* provides for a formal dining room and superb wine cellar. At the time of this writing, it offered a five-course dinner menu featuring West Coast cuisine.

The dining room is described as one of the top 10 in North American Inns. Those who wish to dress in more casual attire can dine in 'The Snug', which is adjacent to the wine cellar.

Galleons Lap Photography

In 1940, one of the Mouat brothers donated some land for the building of *St. George's Anglican Church*.[272]

Much later, in the 1990's, the church was moved across the street.[273] However, the church hall was not moved[274] and, at the time of this writing, it was the home of a gallery called *Galleons Lap Photography*.

The gallery promotes the work of both contemporary and historic photographic artists. It hosts shows in a broad spectrum of themes.

Salt Spring Island Fire Department

In the 1940's, a Salt Spring Islander, named Dick Toynbee, used a welding torch to add a tank and a pump to an old black Buick. The Buick was then painted bright red and it

Salt Spring Island

became Salt Spring's first fire truck. The fire chief used an old motor horn as a siren.[275]

At that time, the Salt Spring Island Trading Company looked out over the ocean.[276] In 1961, a landfill was created in front of it and a fire hall was built on the site.[277]

A few years later, the Island hired its first official *high muckymuck* (fire chief)[278] and a volunteer fire brigade was formed.

Today, the *Salt Spring Island Fire Department* provides for eight fire trucks, one emergency vehicle, four *smoke eaters* (fire fighters) and 31 volunteers.

House Piccolo Restaurant

Around the same time that Salt Spring was acquiring its first fire truck, the Dominion Government Telegraph and Telephone Company was constructing a building in Ganges to house a telephone exchange on the Island.[279]

When the telephone company changed its system to dial telephones in the 1960's, the building became the home of an ice cream and candy store. Since then, it has operated as various restaurants.[280]

At the time of this writing, the building was home to a restaurant called the *House Piccolo* restaurant. It features European and Scandinavian cuisine.

Long Harbour

In the 1940's, the Canadian Pacific Railway provided ferry service to and from the mainland. The ferry docked at Fulford Harbour four days a week. The trip took eight long hours.[281]

In 1964, another ferry terminal was built, in *Long Harbour*.[282] It acquired the sailings that were bound for the mainland.

Long Harbour sits snugly between Nose Point and Scott Point, just north of Ganges Harbour. There are two accesses to the beautiful beach.

If you launch a boat from the beach, you can travel to the tip of Nose Point. From there, you can continue to Prevost Island, which is part of the Gulf Islands National Park Reserve. It offers some of the most scenic shoreline in all the Gulf Islands. However, there are *skookumchuck* (strong currents) around Nose Point.

Salt Spring Island

Drummond Park

In the 1950's, a tall, barefooted, Black resident, named Jim Anderson, would go down to the beach every morning to see what the tide had brought in.[283]

Jim would use a broom to sweep the beach. Then, he would put bunches of wild poppies and ferns into soup tins that he would place in the hollows of old tree trunks.[284] He treated the beach as his own little 'park' and loved to invite people from the north end to attend weekend picnics there.[285]

Drummond Park is a recreational park on Fulford Harbour. Established in the early 1970's,[286] it offers playgrounds and a beachfront swimming area. There are also facilities for picnics if you want to stay a while.

Mary Hawkins Memorial Library

As Jim Anderson was sweeping his beach, 12 women established a library as a centennial project in a back room of Mouat's Store.[287] The library was named the *Centennial Library* and it opened with 1,300 donated books.[288]

Within a decade, the library had acquired more than 5,000 books. When it was decided that a larger building was required, a boat-building workshop was purchased and the library was moved there the following year.[289]

Several years later, the library, which had doubled in size, purchased a small house on an adjacent property. The staff enlarged the library by attaching it to the house. At that time, it was the only library in British Columbia that contained a bathtub.[290]

In 1974, the library was renamed the *Mary Hawkins Memorial Library*.[291] At last count, it maintained a collection of at least 43,000 books.

Salt Spring Island

Today, about 150 volunteers staff the library, making it the largest all-volunteer library in Canada. The bathtub has been removed.

Centennial Park

In 1964, when a boat basin and dock were created in Ganges, the dredging produced enough land for a waterfront park to be created. So the clamshells that were part of the fill were leveled and topsoil was brought in[292] in preparation for the park's development.

The park was named *Centennial Park*. After it was completed, a memorial cenotaph was relocated to the center of the park, from across the street.

In the 1970's, the infamous *Saturday Market* began in the park. At that time, vendors could sell virtually anything at the market.

Today, over 100 artisans of various types contribute to the Island's international reputation for fine, world-class artists and organic farmers. However, the vendors must now make, bake or grow their wares themselves.

The market, which takes place every Saturday, from April to October, frequently provides for live music, crafts, food and activities.

Centennial Park also provides for a marina, wharf and playgrounds. The wharf is secluded behind a secure breakwater and isolated from the floatplanes and powerboats that pass through the harbour.

The bandstand in the park provides for outdoor entertainment, while the boardwalk offers a wonderful view of Ganges Harbour.

Salt Spring Island

There are facilities for picnics if you want to stay a while.

Harbour Building & Rotary Park

Even after Centennial Park was developed, the area behind the fire hall was still a tidal inlet that contained log booms.[293]

**Site of the Harbour Building, 1960's
Salt Spring Archives CKC998162110**

In the year 1970, the site was filled in to provide more parking and retail space for Mouat's Store.[294] Today, a building, called the Harbour Building, sits on the site of the tidal inlet. It provides for retail outlets, restaurants and galleries.

Behind the Harbour Building is another park called *Rotary Marine Park*. Like Centennial Park, it also provides for a beautiful seaside boardwalk.

Recently, the Rotary Club of Salt Spring organized a fundraiser whereby visitors to the park could personalize commemorative paving stones that were then used to pave the entrance to the park.

Salt Spring Island

A

Admiralty Bay. *See* Ganges Harbour
Akerman Museum, 137
Arbutus tree, 131, 147

B

bakeries, 160
Barnsbury Grange. *See* Salt Spring Golf & Country Club
Baynes Peak. *See* Mt. Maxwell Provincial Park
Beaver Point, 145
bed and breakfasts, 151
Beddis Beach, 142
Bittancourt Heritage House Museum. *See* Heritage House Museum. *See* Heritage House Museum
Blackburn House. *See* Salt Spring Centre of Yoga
Booth Bay B&B, 162
Booth Canal, 137
Burgoyne Bay, 136

C

cafés, 160
camping, 140, 142
Centennial Library. *See* Mary Hawkins Memorial Library
Centennial Park, 170
Central Community Hall. *See* Salt Spring Cinema
Central Settlement, 125
Chain Islands, 129
Channel Islands, 143
Chicken House School. *See* Gulf Islands Secondary School
community halls, 152, 165
Consolidated School. *See* Salt Spring Elementary School
cottage rentals, 144

D

disc golf, 162
Douglas-Fir tree, 131, 140, 147
Dowry House Cottage Rental, 144
Drummond Park, 169

E

eagles, 127, 142
Embe Bakery, 159

F

fabrics stores, 157
fairs, 156
Fernwood, 126, 127, 136
Fernwood Point, 126
ferry service, 130, 133, 137, 140, 168
festivals, 165
fire department, 168
First Nations, 138
Fulford, 136
Fulford Community Hall, 164
Fulford Creek Guest House, 155
Fulford Harbour, 133, 136, 147
Fulford Harbour Ferry Terminal, 136
Fulford Inn, 147
Fulford Post Office, 150
Fulford-Burgoyne Valley, 130, 137, 150, 155

G

G.J. Mouat and Company. See Mouat's Trading Co.
Galiano Island, 127, 159
Galleons Lap Photography Gallery & Atelier, 167
Ganges, 123
Ganges Harbour, 127, 136, 154, 171
Ganges High School. See Gulf Islands Secondary School
Ganges Post Offices, 124
Ganges United Church. *See* Stitches Quilt Shop
Garry Oak tree, 131, 147
Goat Island, 129
golfing, 153
Gulf Islands National Park Reserve, 142, 147, 169
Gulf Islands Secondary School, 166
Gulf Islands Trading Co. Ltd.. See Salt Spring Island Trading Company

H

Hamilton Beach, 153
Harbour Building, 171
Harbour House. *See* Harbour House Hotel
Harbour House Hotel, 154
hardware stores, 159
Hastings House Country Estate Hotel, 166
Hawaiians, 133, 141, 143, 145, 146
health care, 163
Heritage House Museum, 140
historical parks, 138
hospitals, 163
House Piccolo Restaurant, 168
Houstoun Passage, 127
Hudson Point, 127

I

Indian Reserve. *See* First Nations
Inns, 147, 154, 166

Salt Spring Island

J

Jackson's Beach, 134

L

Lady Minto Gulf Islands Hospital, 163
Long Harbour, 136, 168
Long Harbour Ferry Terminal, 136

M

Mahon Memorial Hall, 155
markets, 170
Mary Hawkins Memorial Library, 169
Mary Lee's Snack Shop. *See* Fulford Post Office
Mayne Island, 159
McFadden Creek Heronry, 127
Mouat Brothers Company Ltd.. See Mouat's Trading Co.
Mouat Provincial Park, 161
Mouat's Landing, 157, 177
Mouat's Mall, 157
Mouat's Trading Co., 159. See
movie theatres, 152
Mt. Maxwell Provincial Park, 130
museums, 137, 141
Musgrave Landing, 150
Musgrave Point, 141

N

Nan's Coffee Bar. *See* Fulford Post Office
Nose Point, 168, 169

O

Old Farmhouse B&B, 151

P

Pender Island, 142, 159
photography, 167
picnic facilities, 131, 140, 142, 162, 169, 171
playgrounds, 169, 170
Portland Island. *See* Princess Margaret Marine Park
post offices, 124, 125, 126, 131, 138, 147, 150, 151, 157
Prevost Island, 142, 143, 169
Princess Margaret Park Reserve, 141
pubs, 137, 148, 154

R

recreational areas, 169, 170
restaurants, 148, 154, 163, 167, 168
Roger's Saloon. *See* Fulford Inn
Rotary Park, 171
Royal Canadian Legion, 157

Royal Vancouver Yacht Club, 129
Ruckle Provincial Park, 138
Russell Island Provincial Marine Park, 146

S

S.S. Iroquois, 126
Salt Spring Centre of Yoga, 160
Salt Spring Cinema, 152
Salt Spring Elementary School, 131
Salt Spring Golf and Country Club, 153
Salt Spring Island Creamery. *See* Embe Bakery
Salt Spring Island Farmers Institute, 140, 166
Salt Spring Island Fire Department, 168
Salt Spring Island Post Office. See post offices. See post offices. See post offices. See post offices
Salt Spring Island Trading Company, 149
Salt Spring Sailing Club, 129
Scholar Ship. *See* Gulf Islands Water Taxi
schools, 131, 166
Scott Point, 168
Sea Star Point, 129
Seabright Beach, 138
seals, 127
Seaside at Mouat's, 159
Skull Islands, 153
SS Iroquois, 150
St. Mary Lake, 145
St. Paul's Catholic Church, 143
Stitches Quilts & Yarns, 156
Stone Walrus Gallery, 163
Stuart Channel, 135
swimming, 146, 169

T

tai chi, 161
trails, 142, 145
Traveler's Rest, 137
Tree House Café North, 164
Trincomali Channel, 135
Tsawout Band. *See* First Nations
Turkey Vultures, 142

V

Vancouver, 136, 168
Vancouver Island, 130, 133, 134, 135, 137, 143
Vesuvius, 136
Vesuvius Bay, 135
Vesuvius Bay Ferry Terminal, 137
Vesuvius Bay Methodist Church. *See* Stitches Quilt Shop
Vesuvius Beach, 129
Vesuvius School, 131
viewpoints, 127, 129, 131, 171

Salt Spring Island

W

Western Hemlock tree, 131
Western Red Cedar tree, 131, 140, 162
wharves, 126, 130, 133, 134, 135, 136, 137, 138, 141, 150, 157, 170
White House Hotel. *See* Fulford Inn

White Lodge. See Fulford Inn. See Fulford Inn
World War I, 146, 154, 158, 161, 163
World War II, 156, 161

Y

yoga. *See* Salt Spring Centre of Yoga

Galiano Island

A

Active Pass, 94, 102, 107, 108, 112
Active Pass Caboose Cottage Rental, 124
Active Pass Stock Ranch. See Bellhouse Inn
Agriculture Hall. See Galiano Island Community Hall
Arbutus tree, 106

B

Bald Eagles, 123
bed and breakfasts, 111
Bellhouse Inn, 110
Bluffs Park, 112
boat rentals, 122
Burrill Bros. Store. See Grand Central Emporium

C

Cain Peninsula, 116
camping, 122
Captain's Quarters Cottage Rental, 103
clams, 123
Clutterbuck's Store. See Spanish Hills Store
Coast Salish Indians, 121
Collinson Point, 106
community halls, 113, 117
Corner Store, 123
cottage rentals, 103, 124
Cowichan Gap. See Porlier Pass

D

Dionisio Point Provincial Park, 107
Douglas-Fir tree, 106
Dunromin. See Galiano Lodge

F

Farmhouse Inn. See Bellhouse Inn
ferry service, 109
fire department, 123

G

Galiano Art Show, 105
Galiano Community Hall, 117
Galiano Inn, 115
Galiano Island business sections, 94
Galiano Island Cemetery, 106
Galiano Island Fire Departments, 123
Galiano Island Post Office, 96
Galiano Light and Power Company, 123
Galiano School. See Galiano Trading Company. See Galiano Trading Company
Georgeson Bay, 95
Georgia Strait, 117

gift shops, 108
Gossip Island, 116
Gossip Island Hotel, 117
Grand Central Emporium, 107
Gray Peninsula, 123
Greenways. See Galiano Lodge
grocery stores, 119, 122

H

halls, 113, 118, 123
hardware stores, 104
Home Hardware, 103
Hotel Point, 117

I

Indian Reserve. See First Nations
Inns, 110, 116

J

Japanese-Canadians, 119

L

Lion Islet, 114
Lyons. See Lion Islet

M

Madrona Del Mar Spa, 116
mainland, 109, 124
marinas, 121
Marine Park Nature House, 122
Mary Ann Point Light, 102
Mary Anne Point, 102
Mayne Island, 96, 105, 123
Meeting Place, the, 122
Montague Harbour, 121
Montague Harbour Marina, 121
Morning Beach, 114
Murcheson Heritage Home, 100

N

North Galiano Community Hall, 113
North Galiano School, 120. See North Galiano Community Hall
North Galiano Store. See Spanish Hills Store
North-End School. See North Galiano Community Hall

O

Old Burrill Store. See Grand Central Emporium

Galiano Island

P

Pender Island, 121
Penelakut Band. *See* First Nations
picnic facilities, 112, 122
Porlier Pass, 106
Porlier Pass Light Station, 106
post office. *See* North Galiano Post Office. *See* Galiano Island Post Office

R

Race Point, 106
restaurants, 108
Retreat Cove, 119
Retreat Cove School, 104, 113
Retreat Island, 120
Royal Canadian Legion, 97

S

Salamanca Point, 115
Salt Spring Island, 96, 108, 119
Saturna Island, 121
schools, 103
scuba diving, 120
sea lions, 96, 112
seals, 112
Shaw's Landing, 99
South Galiano School. *See* Galiano School & Activity Center
Spanish Hills, 120

spas, 116
Spotlight Cove, 109
St. Margaret of Scotland Anglican Church, 105
Stockade Harbour. *See* Montague Harbour
Sturdies Bay, 100, 115
Sturdies Bay Ferry Terminal, 109
Sturdies Bay Wharf, 108
swimming, 123

T

The Gap. *See* Porlier Pass
trails, 112, 122, 123

V

Vancouver, 108
Vancouver Island, 99, 108, 109, 123
viewpoints, 112, 119
Virago Point, 106

W

Whaler Bay, 101
whales, 112
wharves, 96, 99, 108, 118, 119, 121
World War I, 100, 102, 105, 114
World War II, 104, 112, 114, 115, 117, 119

Pender Islands

A

Arcadia By The Sea, 95
Arcadia By The Sea, 94
Auchterlonie Center, 96

B

Bald Cone. *See* Mount Menzies
Bear Mother Project, 63
Beaumont Provincial Marine Park, 84, 85
Beautyrest Lodge. *See* Arcadia By The Sea
bed and breakfasts, 79
Bedwell Harbour, 75, 79, 93, 94
Bedwell Harbour Marina, 94
Bedwell Harbour Resort. *See* Poet's Cove Resort and Spa
Betty Island, 90
Bricky Bay, 57, 61, 89
Browning Harbour, 61, 79

C

camping, 88
Canal, the, 79
Canned Cod Bay, 71
Cedar Creek, 85
Church of the Good Shepherd, 91
Clam Bay. *See* Davidson Bay
Colston Cove. *See* Bricky Bay
community halls, 61, 68, 70, 88, 97
Corbett's store. *See* Hope Bay Stores
Corbett's Store, 66. *See* Hope Bay Stores
cottage rentals, 88

D

dances, 62
Davidson Bay, 68

F

fairs, 62, 63
fire department, 96
Found Road Trail, 68

G

Galiano Island, 86
General Store, 66, 67, 86, 95
gift shops, 77
Grimmer Bay, 57
grocery stores, 78
Gulf Islands National Park Reserve, 68, 74

H

Hamilton Beach, 59

Hope Bay, 56, 64, 65, 66, 69, 70, 77, 96
Hope Bay Stores, 77, 78
Hope Bay Wharf, 64
Hyashi Cove, 71

I

Indian Portage. *See* Canal
Inns, 94

J

James Point, 89
Japanese-Canadians, 71, 72

L

libraries, 95
Lilias Spalding Heritage Park, 76

M

marinas, 61, 72, 82, 88, 94
markets, 63
Mayne Island, 57, 67, 77, 81, 88
midden, 80
Mille Fleurs. *See* Arcadia By The Sea
Mortimer Spit, 61
Mouat Point, 58, 72
Mount Baker, 71
Mount Menzies, 67, 68
Mount Menzies Park, 67
Mount Norman, 85
Mount Norman Regional Park, 85
Mount Warburton Pike, 77
museums, 73

N

Navy Channel, 57
North Pender Fire Hall. *See* Pender Islands Fire & Rescue

O

Oaks Bluff, 58, 75
Oaks, the. *See* Oaks Bluff
Old Orchard Farm, 82, 83
Otter Bay Lodge. *See* Arcadia By The Sea
Otter Bay Marina, 72

P

Parish Hall. *See* St. Peter's Anglican Church
Pender Island Golf and Country Club, 92
Pender Islands Cemetery, 84
Pender Islands Community Hall, 61

Pender Islands

Pender Islands Elementary Secondary School, 68
Pender Islands Fall Fair, 62
Pender Islands Farmer's Market, 63
Pender Islands Fire and Rescue, 96
Pender Islands Museum, 73
Pender Islands Post Office, 65
Pender Islands Public Library, 81, 95
Pender Lender. See Pender Islands Public Library
Peter Cove, 61
picnic facilities, 61, 81, 82
playgrounds, 81, 82
Poets Cove Resort, 92
police, 75
Port Browning Marina, 61, 88
Port Browning Marina Resort, 87
Port Washington Community Hall, 62

R

RCMP Boat, 74
recreational areas, 82
resorts, 88, 92, 94
Roe Islet, 73, 74
Roe Lake, 74
Roesland Resort. See Roesland Park
Royal Canadian Legion, 90

S

Saturna Island, 57, 68, 77, 79, 84, 85, 92
Shingle Bay Park, 81
Smith Brothers. See Hope Bay Stores
South Pender Fire Hall. See Pender Islands Fire & Rescue
South Pender Post Office, 59, 76
spas, 93
SS Iroquois, 76, 77, 79

St. Peter's Anglican Church, 88
Stanley Point, 58
Strait of Juan de Fuca, 71
studios, 91
Sunny Side Ranch. See Old Orchard Farm
Susurrus Spa, 93
Swanson Channel, 58, 64, 71, 75
swimming, 61, 74, 93

T

tennis, 89, 93
Thieves Bay Park, 81
trails, 68, 74, 75, 77, 85
Tsawout Band. See First Nations
Tseycum Band. See First Nations

U

United Community Church, 70

V

Vancouver, 65
Vancouver Island, 68, 80, 85
viewpoints, 67, 71, 75, 77, 85, 89

W

Wallace Point, 58, 72
Washington State, 71, 75
Waterlea, 89
Welcome Bay Farm. See The Wool Shed
Welcome Bay Inn. See The Wool Shed
wharves, 57, 58, 61, 64, 65, 66, 76
Wool Shed, The, 90
World War I, 58, 85, 88, 89
World War II, 62, 90

Saturna Island

A

Arbutus tree, 47

B

barbecues, 51, 54
bed and breakfasts, 43
Boat Passage, 51
Boiling Reef, 44
Boundary Pass, 44
Breezy Bay B&B, 43
Brown Ridge, 42, 43

C

Canada Day, 54
Canoe Passage. *See* Boat Passage
community halls, 53

D

Douglas-Fir tree, 47, 52

E

East Point, 44
East Point Regional Park, 44
Echo Bay, 45

G

Garry Oak tree, 47, 52
Georgia Strait, 51
grocery stores, 48
Gulf Islands National Park Reserve, 43, 46, 52

H

halls, 53

K

kayaking, 51

L

libraries, 50
Lighthouse Park. *See* East Point Regional Park
liquor stores, 48
Little Bay, 45
Lyall Harbour, 52

M

Mayne Island, 41, 44, 47
Mount Baker, 45
Mount Warburton Pike, 43

Murder Point, 55

N

Narvaez Bay, 46
Narvaez Bay Park, 45

O

Old Point. *See* Payne Point
Old Point Farm. *See* Breezy Bay Bed and Breakfast

P

Payne Point, 43
Pender Island, 41, 43
picnic facilities, 46, 55
Plumper Sound, 41
post office, 48. *See* Saturna Island Post Office
Prairie Hill. *See* Brown Ridge

R

recreational areas, 51

S

Samuel Island, 51
Saturna Beach, 40, 52
Saturna Beach Resort. *See* Thomson Community Park
Saturna Beach Wharf, 41
Saturna General Store, 48
Saturna Island Community Hall, 53
Saturna Island Farmer's Market, 53
Saturna Island Post Office, 47
Saturna Point, 52, 53
schools, 52
sea lions, 51
sea stars, 45
seals, 45, 51
St. Christopher's Anglican Church, 49
swimming, 45, 51, 53, 55

T

Taylor Point, 46
Thomson Community Park, 54
trails, 52, 55
Tumbo Island, 51

V

viewpoints, 42, 43, 45

Saturna Island

W

Washington State, 43, 45
whales, 45, 51

wharves, 41, 47, 52
Winter Cove Provincial Marine Park, 50, 51
Winter Point, 51, 53
World War I, 41

Mayne Island

A

Active Pass, 15, 20, 22, 24
Active Pass Auto & Marine, 37
Active Pass Growers Association, 38, 40
Active Pass Light Station, 22, 24
Anchorage Heritage Home, the, 33
Anchorage, the, 34
Arbutus Lodge. See Mayne Inn

B

Bambrick Store Ltd., 36
beaches, 41
Bennett Bay, 19, 25, 35
Brigg's Landing. See Piggott Bay
British, the, 22, 23

C

Campbell Bay, 19
Campbell Point, 25
Canadian Navy, 39
Centennial Memorial Garden, 29
Cherry Tree Bay. See Maude Bay
Christmas, 40
Church Fair, 29
community halls, 32
Cowichan Indian Tribe, 15
Curlew Island, 33, 41

D

David Cove, 14
Deacon's Store, 18
Dinner Point, 22

F

fairs, 29, 33
Fall Fair. See Mayne Island Fall Fair
Farmer's Market. See Mayne Island Farmer's Market
ferry service, 21, 22
fire department, 41
First Nations, 14, 20
fishing, 37
Five Roosters Restaurant. See Mayne Mast Restaurant
Fraser River, 12, 38

G

Galiano Island, 19, 20, 24, 30
gardens, 24, 29, 38
gas stations, 37
Georgeson Island, 24
Georgeson Passage, 19, 24

Georgina Point Lighthouse, 23
Glenwood Farm, 13, 14
Grandview Lodge. See Springwater Lodge
greenhouses, 34, 38, 40
grocery stores, 37

H

Hall Hill, 34
health care, 35, 36
Helen Point, 14, 15
Hidden Bay. See David Cove
Hollandia Hotel. See Mayne Inn
Hopkins Trading Post. See Miners Bay Trading Post
Horton Bay, 19, 38, 40, 41

I

Indian Reserve. See First Nations

J

Japanese Memorial Garden, 38
Japanese-Canadians, 20, 38, 39

K

Kawashuri Bay. See Horton Bay
King apples, 25
Kitty's Boarding House. See Village Bay

L

Lighthouse Point. See Georgina Point
liquor stores, 37

M

Maude Bay, 26, 27
Mayne Inn, 35
Mayne Island Agricultural Society, 30
Mayne Island Agriculture Hall, 32, 33, 41
Mayne Island Fall Fair Parade, 33
Mayne Island Fire Department, 41
Mayne Island Health Center, 35
Mayne Island Museum, 14, 29
Mayne Island Nurseries, 34, 35
Mayne Island Post Office, 17
Mayne Island School, 19
Mayne Island Trading Post. See Miners Bay Trading Post
Mayne Island Volunteer Firefighters Association, 20
Mayne Mast Restaurant & Pub, 40
Mayne Store, 18, 26
Miners Bay, 17

Mayne Island

Miners Bay Community Park, 25
Miners Bay Trading Post, 18, 36
Mount Baker, 25
museums, 30

P

Paddon Point. See Campbell Point
parades, 33
Pender Island, 28
picnic facilities, 24, 25, 26
Piggott Bay, 27
Plumper Pass. See Active Pass
Plumper Pass Lighthouse. See Georgina Point Lighthouse
Plumper Pass Lockup, 30
Point Comfort. See Georgina Point
post office. See Mayne Island Post Office
pubs, 40

R

recreational areas, 26
restaurants, 35, 40
Royal Canadian Legion, 29

S

Salt Spring Island, 13, 17, 32
Saturna Island, 19, 20, 28, 29
schools, 13, 19, 20, 36
scuba diving, 14, 19

Springwater Lodge, 17, 31
Spud Point, 41
St. John Point, 38
St. Mary Magdalene Anglican Church, 28
swimming, 28

T

trails, 22, 24, 25
Tsartlip Band. See First Nations

V

Vancouver, 22
Vancouver Island, 12, 22, 38
viewpoints, 25
Village Bay, 20, 22
Village Bay Ferry Terminal, 21
Village Bay Park, 20

W

Washington State, 25, 36
wharfs, 41
wharves, 15, 17, 21, 25, 26, 31, 34, 35, 36, 37
World War I, 13, 33, 35
World War II, 20, 33, 39, 40

Z

Zephyr, the, 14

Introduction

Notes

[1] **A Gulf Islands Patchwork**: Some Early Events on the Islands of Galiano, Mayne, Saturna, North and South Pender – British Columbia Historical Association, pp. 1

[2] **The Terror Of The Coast:** Land Alienation And Colonial War On Vancouver Island And The Gulf Islands – Chris Arnett, pp. 31 & 317

[3] **The Terror Of The Coast:** Land Alienation And Colonial War On Vancouver Island And The Gulf Islands – Chris Arnett, pp. 112

[4] **The Terror Of The Coast**: Land Alienation And Colonial War On Vancouver Island And The Gulf Islands – Chris Arnett, pp. 112

[5] **The Terror Of The Coast:** Land Alienation And Colonial War On Vancouver Island And The Gulf Islands – Chris Arnett, pp. 112

[6] **The Terror Of The Coast:** Land Alienation And Colonial War On Vancouver Island And The Gulf Islands – Chris Arnett, pp. 128

[7] **The Terror Of The Coast:** Land Alienation And Colonial War On Vancouver Island And The Gulf Islands – Chris Arnett, pp. 131 & 132

[8] **The Terror Of The Coast:** Land Alienation And Colonial War On Vancouver Island And The Gulf Islands – Chris Arnett, pp. 132 & 135

[9] **The Terror Of The Coast:** Land Alienation And Colonial War On Vancouver Island And The Gulf Islands – Chris Arnett, pp. 139

[10] **The Terror Of The Coast:** Land Alienation And Colonial War On Vancouver Island And The Gulf Islands – Chris Arnett, pp. 157, 202, 235, 247 & back cover

[11] **The Terror Of The Coast:** Land Alienation And Colonial War On Vancouver Island And The Gulf Islands – Chris Arnett, pp. 140, 184,254, 304 & 308

[12] **The Terror Of The Coast**: Land Alienation And Colonial War On Vancouver Island And The Gulf Islands – Chris Arnett, pp. 308

[13] **More Tales from the Outer Gulf Islands:** An Anthology of Memories and Anecdotes – British Columbia Historical Association, pp. 149

[14] **The Gulf Islanders:** Sound Heritage, Volume V, Number 4, pp. 76

[15] **The Gulf Islanders:** Sound Heritage, Volume V, Number 4, pp. 1 and **Homesteads and Snug Harbours:** The Gulf Islands – Peter Murray, pp. 9

[16] **The Gulf Islanders:** Sound Heritage, Volume V, Number 4, pp. 1 and **Homesteads and Snug Harbours:** The Gulf Islands – Peter Murray, pp. 9

[17] **The Gulf Islanders:** Sound Heritage, Volume V, Number 4, pp. 1

[18] **The Gulf Islanders:** Sound Heritage, Volume V, Number 4, pp. 1

[19] **The Gulf Islanders:** Sound Heritage, Volume V, Number 4, pp. 41 & 42

[20] **The Gulf Islanders:** Sound Heritage, Volume V, Number 4, pp. 41 & 42

[21] **The Gulf Islanders:** Sound Heritage, Volume V, Number 4, pp. 41 & 42

[22] **The Historical Pender Islands:** Limited Edition Calendar, 2006 – Pender Islands Museum Society

[23] **The Gulf Islanders:** Sound Heritage, Volume V, Number 4, pp. 1, 5 & 43

[24] **The Gulf Islanders:** Sound Heritage, Volume V, Number 4, pp. 1, 5 & 43

[25] **The Gulf Islanders:** Sound Heritage, Volume V, Number 4, pp. 5 & 38

[26] **Mayne Island & The Outer Gulf Islands:** A History – Marie Elliott, pp. 91

[27] **Mayne Island & The Outer Gulf Islands:** A History – Marie Elliott, pp. 91

[28] **Gulf Islands National Park Reserve of Canada website**: Visitor Information, Parks Canada

Introduction

[29] **More Tales from the Outer Gulf Islands:** An Anthology of Memories and Anecdotes – British Columbia Historical Association, pp. 53 & 155 and **A Gulf Islands Patchwork:** Some Early Events on the Islands of Galiano, Mayne, Saturna, North and South Pender – British Columbia Historical Association, pp. 63 & 66

[30] **A Gulf Islands Patchwork:** Some Early Events on the Islands of Galiano, Mayne, Saturna, North and South Pender – British Columbia Historical Association, pp. 63 & 66

[31] **More Tales from the Outer Gulf Islands:** An Anthology of Memories and Anecdotes – British Columbia Historical Association, pp. 155 & 156

[32] **More Tales from the Outer Gulf Islands:** An Anthology of Memories and Anecdotes – British Columbia Historical Association, pp. 155 & 156

[33] **More Tales from the Outer Gulf Islands:** An Anthology of Memories and Anecdotes – British Columbia Historical Association, pp. 53 & 155

[34] **Homesteads and Snug Harbours:** The Gulf Islands – Peter Murray, pp. 180 & 181

[35] **Homesteads and Snug Harbours:** The Gulf Islands – Peter Murray, pp. 180 & 181

[36] **The Gulf Islanders:** Sound Heritage, Volume V, Number 4, pp. 60 & 61

[37] **Galiano Museum and Archives:** The Georgeson Collection – Salt Spring Archives

[38] **Galiano Museum and Archives:** The Georgeson Collection – Salt Spring Archives

[39] **Homesteads and Snug Harbours:** The Gulf Islands – Peter Murray, pp. 181

[40] **More Tales from the Outer Gulf Islands:** An Anthology of Memories and Anecdotes – British Columbia Historical Association, pp. 150

[41] **A Gulf Islands Patchwork:** Some Early Events on the Islands of Galiano, Mayne, Saturna, North and South Pender – British Columbia Historical Association, pp. 6, 15, 66 & 125

[42] **Homesteads and Snug Harbours:** The Gulf Islands – Peter Murray, pp. 182

[43] **Salt Spring:** The Story of an Island – Charles Kahn, pp. 42

[44] **A Gulf Islands Patchwork:** Some Early Events on the Islands of Galiano, Mayne, Saturna, North and South Pender – British Columbia Historical Association, pp. 6 & 7

[45] **The Akerman Family:** Growing Up With Salt Spring Island – Bob Akerman & Linda Sherwood, pp. 164 and **The Historical Pender Islands:** Limited Edition Calendar, 2006 – Pender Islands Museum Society

[46] **The Akerman Family:** Growing Up With Salt Spring Island – Bob Akerman & Linda Sherwood, pp. 164 and **The Historical Pender Islands:** Limited Edition Calendar, 2006 – Pender Islands Museum Society

[47] **Salt Spring:** The Story of an Island – Charles Kahn, pp. 226

[48] **Salt Spring Island:** Bea Hamilton, pp. 157 & 158

[49] **Salt Spring:** The Story of an Island – Charles Kahn, pp. 267 & 268

[50] **Mayne Island & The Outer Gulf Islands:** A History – Marie Elliott, pp. 96

[51] **Mayne Island & The Outer Gulf Islands:** A History – Marie Elliott, pp. 115

[52] **More Tales from the Outer Gulf Islands:** An Anthology of Memories and Anecdotes British Columbia Historical Association, pp. 11

[53] **Four Years in British Columbia and Vancouver:** An Account of their Forests, Rivers, Coasts, Gold Fields and Resources for Colonisation – Commander R.C. Mayne, R.N., F.R.G.S., pp. 1 & 445

[54] **A Gulf Islands Patchwork:** Some Early Events on the Islands of Galiano, Mayne, Saturna, North and South Pender – British Columbia Historical Association, pp. 28

[55] **Mayne Island & The Outer Gulf Islands:** A History – Marie Elliott, pp. 24

Introduction

[56] **Salt Spring Island:** An Illustrated Pamphlet With Map – Rev. E.F. Wilson, 1894, pp. 24
[57] **Mayne Island & The Outer Gulf Islands:** A History – Marie Elliott, pp. 20
[58] **Plumper Pass Lockup and Mayne Island Museum** – Mayne Island Agricultural Society, pp. 1 & 7
[59] **Plumper Pass Lockup and Mayne Island Museum** – Mayne Island Agricultural Society, pp. 1, 6 & 7
[60] **The Gulf Islands Explorer:** The Complete Guide – Bruce Obee, pp. 166
[61] **Royal Canadian Mounted Police website** – Historical Highlights
[62] **The Pender Post**: Celebrating the activities of the people of Pender Island at the Millennium, The Pender Post Society, pp. 83
[63] **A Voice from the Past** - The Gulf Islands Guardian, Spring, 1993, pp. 29 and **Salt Spring:** The Story of an Island – Charles Kahn, pp. 47
[64] **Mayne Island Post Office:** 100th Anniversary – Canada Post, pp. 2
[65] **Salt Spring:** The Story of an Island – Charles Kahn, pp. 42
[66] **The Post Offices of British Columbia:** 1858-1970 - George H. Melvin, pp. 106
[67] **A Gulf Islands Patchwork:** Some Early Events on the Islands of Galiano, Mayne, Saturna, North and South Pender – British Columbia Historical Association, pp. 131 & 170
[68] **Homesteads and Snug Harbours:** The Gulf Islands – Peter Murray, pp. 187
[69] **The Post Offices of British Columbia:** 1858-1970 - George H. Melvin, pp. 43, 71, 92, 107, 143
[70] **A Gulf Islands Patchwork:** Some Early Events on the Islands of Galiano, Mayne, Saturna, North and South Pender – British Columbia Historical Association, pp. 159
[71] **Homesteads and Snug Harbours:** The Gulf Islands – Peter Murray, pp. 182
[72] **Mayne Island & The Outer Gulf Islands:** A History – Marie Elliott, pp. 32

Mayne Island

Notes

[1] **Mayne Island Fall Fair:** Centennial Year – Mayne Island Agriculture Society, pp. 27 and **Barkerville Gold Rush website**
[2] **BC place name cards**, or correspondence between British Columbia's Chief Geographer or the Geographical Names Office – Government of British Columbia
[3] **Mayne Island & The Outer Gulf Islands:** A History – Marie Elliott, pp. 127
[4] **Mayne Island & The Outer Gulf Islands:** A History – Marie Elliott, pp. 8 & 127
[5] **Homesteads and Snug Harbours:** The Gulf Islands – Peter Murray, pp. 17
[6] **Mayne Island Fall Fair:** Centennial Year – Mayne Island Agriculture Society, pp. 27
[7] **Mayne Island Post Office:** 100th Anniversary – Canada Post, pp. 1
[8] **Mayne Island Fall Fair:** Centennial Year – Mayne Island Agriculture Society, pp. 27 and inside cover
[9] **Winifred Grey:** A Gentlewoman's Remembrances of Life in England and the Gulf Islands of British Columbia 1871-1910 – Winifred Grey, pp. 125
[10] **Four Years in British Columbia and Vancouver:** An Account of their Forests, Rivers, Coasts, Gold Fields and Resources for Colonisation – Commander R.C. Mayne, R.N., F.R.G.S., pp. 46 & 355
[11] **Four Years in British Columbia and Vancouver:** An Account of their Forests, Rivers, Coasts, Gold Fields and Resources for Colonisation – Commander R.C. Mayne, R.N., F.R.G.S., pp. 46 & 355
[12] **Mayne Island & The Outer Gulf Islands**: A History – Marie Elliott, pp. 4
[13] **Mayne Island & The Outer Gulf Islands**: A History – Marie Elliott, pp. 34
[14] **A Gulf Islands Patchwork**: Some Early Events on the Islands of Galiano, Mayne, Saturna, North and South Pender – British Columbia Historical Association, pp. 11
[15] **A Gulf Islands Patchwork**: Some Early Events on the Islands of Galiano, Mayne, Saturna, North and South Pender – British Columbia Historical Association, pp. 10
[16] **A Gulf Islands Patchwork**: Some Early Events on the Islands of Galiano, Mayne, Saturna, North and South Pender – British Columbia Historical Association, pp. 10
[17] **A Gulf Islands Patchwork**: Some Early Events on the Islands of Galiano, Mayne, Saturna, North and South Pender – British Columbia Historical Association, pp. 10
[18] **A Gulf Islands Patchwork**: Some Early Events on the Islands of Galiano, Mayne, Saturna, North and South Pender – British Columbia Historical Association, pp. 10
[19] **Mayne Island School Centennial**: 1883-1983 – Mayne Island School Centenary Committee, pp. 2
[20] **A Gulf Islands Patchwork**: Some Early Events on the Islands of Galiano, Mayne, Saturna, North and South Pender – British Columbia Historical Association, pp. 12
[21] **Homesteads and Snug Harbours:** The Gulf Islands – Peter Murray, pp. 18
[22] **Mayne Island Fall Fair:** Centennial Year - Mayne Island Agriculture Society, pp. 7
[23] **Mayne Island Fall Fair:** Centennial Year - Mayne Island Agriculture Society, pp. 7
[24] **Mayne Island & The Outer Gulf Islands**: A History – Marie Elliott, pp. 43
[25] **More Tales from the Outer Gulf Islands:** An Anthology of Memories and Anecdotes – British Columbia Historical Association, pp. 159
[26] **Indian and Northern Affairs Canada:** The View From The Ferry – Gabriele Helmig
[27] **The Terror Of The Coast:** Land Alienation And Colonial War On Vancouver Island And The Gulf Islands – Chris Arnett, pp. 128
[28] **British Columbia First Nation website**: Band Profiles, Tsartlip Band

Mayne Island

[29] **Mayne Island & The Outer Gulf Islands**: A History – Marie Elliott, pp. 13
[30] **Mayne Island & The Outer Gulf Islands**: A History – Marie Elliott, pp. 4
[31] **Mayne Island & The Outer Gulf Islands**: A History – Marie Elliott, pp. 15
[32] **Mayne Island & The Outer Gulf Islands**: A History – Marie Elliott, pp. 63
[33] **Mayne Island & The Outer Gulf Islands**: A History – Marie Elliott, pp. 80
[34] **MayneLiner Magazine:** Volume 15, Number 8, pp. 49
[35] **Mayne Island Post Office**: 100th Anniversary – Canada Post, pp. 1
[36] **Mayne Island Fall Fair**: Centennial Year - Mayne Island Agriculture Society, pp. 27
[37] **Mayne Island Post Office**: 100th Anniversary – Canada Post, pp. 3
[38] **Mayne Island Fall Fair**: Centennial Year - Mayne Island Agriculture Society, pp. 23
[39] **A Gulf Islands Patchwork**: Some Early Events on the Islands of Galiano, Mayne, Saturna, North and South Pender – British Columbia Historical Association, pp. 131
[40] **Mayne Island Post Office:** 100th Anniversary – Canada Post, pp. 4
[41] **Mayne Island Post Office**: 100th Anniversary – Canada Post, pp. 3
[42] **Mayne Island Fall Fair**: Centennial Year - Mayne Island Agriculture Society, pp. 23
[43] **Mayne Island Fall Fair**: Centennial Year - Mayne Island Agriculture Society, pp. 27
[44] **Island Heritage Buildings** – Thomas K. Ovanin, Islands Trust, pp. 108
[45] **Mayne Island Post Office**: 100th Anniversary – Canada Post, pp. 3
[46] **Mayne Island Fall Fair:** Centennial Year – Mayne Island Agriculture Society, pp. 25
[47] **Mayne Island Fall Fair**: Centennial Year - Mayne Island Agriculture Society, pp. 24
[48] **Island Heritage Buildings** – Thomas K. Ovanin, Islands Trust, pp. 108
[49] **Mayne Island & The Outer Gulf Islands**: A History – Marie Elliott, pp. 127
[50] **Mayne Island Fall Fair:** Centennial Year – Mayne Island Agriculture Society, pp. 12
[51] **Mayne Island School Centennial:** 1883-1983 – Mayne Island School Centenary Committee, pp. 1 and **Mayne Island & The Outer Gulf Islands:** A History – Marie Elliott, pp. 32
[52] **Mayne Island School Centennial**: 1883-1983 – Mayne Island School Centenary Committee, pp. 1
[53] **Mayne Island & The Outer Gulf Islands**: A History – Marie Elliott, pp. 15
[54] **Mayne Island School Centennial**: 1883-1983 – Mayne Island School Centenary Committee, pp. 2
[55] **Mayne Island School Centennial**: 1883-1983 – Mayne Island School Centenary Committee, pp. 11
[56] **Mayne Island School Centennial**: 1883-1983 – Mayne Island School Centenary Committee, pp. 3 & 4
[57] **Mayne Island School Centennial**: 1883-1983 – Mayne Island School Centenary Committee, pp. 4
[58] **Mayne Island School Centennial**: 1883-1983 – Mayne Island School Centenary Committee, pp. 4
[59] **Coast Salish Villages of Puget Sound website:** Lummi-Bellingham section
[60] **A Gulf Islands Patchwork**: Some Early Events on the Islands of Galiano, Mayne, Saturna, North and South Pender – British Columbia Historical Association, pp. 13
[61] **Mayne Island Fall Fair**: Centennial Year - Mayne Island Agriculture Society, pp. 25
[62] **A Gulf Islands Patchwork**: Some Early Events on the Islands of Galiano, Mayne, Saturna, North and South Pender – British Columbia Historical Association, pp. 13
[63] **Mayne Island & The Outer Gulf Islands**: A History – Marie Elliott, pp. 49

Mayne Island

[64] **Mayne Island & The Outer Gulf Islands**: A History – Marie Elliott, pp. 89
[65] **Mayne Island Fall Fair**: Centennial Year - Mayne Island Agriculture Society, pp. 23
[66] **BC place name cards**, or correspondence between British Columbia's Chief Geographer or the Geographical Names Office – Government of British Columbia
[67] **A Gulf Islands Patchwork**: Some Early Events on the Islands of Galiano, Mayne, Saturna, North and South Pender – British Columbia Historical Association, pp. 45
[68] **BC place name cards**, or correspondence between British Columbia's Chief Geographer or the Geographical Names Office – Government of British Columbia
[69] **Mayne Island Fall Fair**: Centennial Year - Mayne Island Agriculture Society, pp. 21
[70] **BC place name cards**, or correspondence between British Columbia's Chief Geographer or the Geographical Names Office – Government of British Columbia
[71] **The Gulf Islanders**: Sound Heritage, Volume V, Number 4, pp. 64
[72] **Homesteads and Snug Harbours**: The Gulf Islands – Peter Murray, pp. 19
[73] **Mayne Island Fall Fair**: Centennial Year – Mayne Island Agriculture Society, pp. 21
[74] **BC place name cards**, or correspondence between British Columbia's Chief Geographer or the Geographical Names Office – Government of British Columbia
[75] **Mayne Island Fall Fair**: Centennial Year – Mayne Island Agriculture Society, pp. 21
[76] **Mayne Island Fall Fair**: Centennial Year – Mayne Island Agriculture Society, pp. 21
[77] **Mayne Island Fall Fair**: Centennial Year – Mayne Island Agriculture Society, pp. 21
[78] **The Gulf Islanders**: Sound Heritage, Volume V, Number 4, pp. 64-68
[79] **Mayne Island Fall Fair**: Centennial Year – Mayne Island Agriculture Society, pp. 21
[80] **The Gulf Islanders**: Sound Heritage, Volume V, Number 4, pp. 68-69
[81] **The Gulf Islanders**: Sound Heritage, Volume V, Number 4, pp. 68-69
[82] **Mayne Island Fall Fair**: Centennial Year – Mayne Island Agriculture Society, pp. 21
[83] **Homesteads and Snug Harbours**: The Gulf Islands – Peter Murray, pp. 19
[84] **Mayne Island & The Outer Gulf Islands**: A History – Marie Elliott, pp. 17
[85] **Homesteads and Snug Harbours**: The Gulf Islands – Peter Murray, pp. 23
[86] **The Gulf Islanders**: Sound Heritage, Volume V, Number 4, pp. 50
[87] **Mayne Island Fall Fair**: Centennial Year – Mayne Island Agriculture Society, back cover
[88] **The Gulf Islanders**: Sound Heritage, Volume V, Number 4, pp. 50
[89] **The Gulf Islanders**: Sound Heritage, Volume V, Number 4, pp. 51 & 52
[90] **Homesteads and Snug Harbours**: The Gulf Islands – Peter Murray, pp. 30
[91] **The Gulf Islanders**: Sound Heritage, Volume V, Number 4, pp. 49
[92] **Mayne Island & The Outer Gulf Islands**: A History – Marie Elliott, pp. 54
[93] **Mayne Island Fall Fair**: Centennial Year – Mayne Island Agriculture Society, inside cover
[94] **Mayne Island Fall Fair**: Centennial Year – Mayne Island Agriculture Society, inside cover
[95] **A Gulf Islands Patchwork**: Some Early Events on the Islands of Galiano, Mayne, Saturna, North and South Pender – British Columbia Historical Association, pp. 29
[96] **A Gulf Islands Patchwork**: Some Early Events on the Islands of Galiano, Mayne, Saturna, North and South Pender – British Columbia Historical Association, pp. 29
[97] **A Gulf Islands Patchwork**: Some Early Events on the Islands of Galiano, Mayne, Saturna, North and South Pender – British Columbia Historical Association, pp. 29
[98] **Mayne Island & The Outer Gulf Islands**: A History – Marie Elliott, pp. 26

Mayne Island

[99] **Homesteads and Snug Harbours:** The Gulf Islands – Peter Murray, pp. 22
[100] **Island Heritage Buildings** – Thomas K. Ovanin, Islands Trust, pp. 110
[101] **A Gulf Islands Patchwork**: Some Early Events on the Islands of Galiano, Mayne, Saturna, North and South Pender – British Columbia Historical Association, pp. 47
[102] **A Gulf Islands Patchwork**: Some Early Events on the Islands of Galiano, Mayne, Saturna, North and South Pender – British Columbia Historical Association, pp. 94
[103] **A Gulf Islands Patchwork**: Some Early Events on the Islands of Galiano, Mayne, Saturna, North and South Pender – British Columbia Historical Association, pp. 94
[104] **Mayne Island Fall Fair**: Centennial Year - Mayne Island Agriculture Society, pp. 34
[105] **Plumper Pass Lockup and Mayne Island Museum** – Mayne Island Agricultural Society, pp. 7
[106] **Plumper Pass Lockup and Mayne Island Museum** – Mayne Island Agricultural Society, pp. 7
[107] **Plumper Pass Lockup and Mayne Island Museum** – Mayne Island Agricultural Society, pp. 7
[108] **Mayne Island & The Outer Gulf Islands**: A History – Marie Elliott, pp. 20 & 24
[109] **Mayne Island Fall Fair:** Centennial Year – Mayne Island Agriculture Society, pp. 27 and inside cover
[110] **Plumper Pass Lockup and Mayne Island Museum** – Mayne Island Agricultural Society, pp. 1, 6 & 7
[111] **Plumper Pass Lockup and Mayne Island Museum** – Mayne Island Agricultural Society, pp. 8
[112] **Plumper Pass Lockup and Mayne Island Museum** – Mayne Island Agricultural Society, pp. 8
[113] **Island Heritage Buildings** – Thomas K. Ovanin, Islands Trust, pp. 107
[114] **Island Heritage Buildings** – Thomas K. Ovanin, Islands Trust, pp. 107
[115] **Mayne Island Fall Fair**: Centennial Year – Mayne Island Agriculture Society, pp. 27
[116] **Mayne Island Fall Fair**: Centennial Year – Mayne Island Agriculture Society, pp. 27
[117] **Mayne Island & The Outer Gulf Islands**: A History – Marie Elliott, pp. 49
[118] **Vanishing British Columbia** – Michael Kluckner, pp. 149
[119] **Island Heritage Buildings** – Thomas K. Ovanin, Islands Trust, pp. 107
[120] **The Gulf Islanders:** Sound Heritage, Volume V, Number 4, pp. 50
[121] **Mayne Island Fall Fair**: Centennial Year - Mayne Island Agriculture Society, pp. 10 & 32
[122] **Mayne Island Fall Fair**: Centennial Year - Mayne Island Agriculture Society, pp. 10 & 32
[123] **Mayne Island Fall Fair**: Centennial Year - Mayne Island Agriculture Society, pp. 10
[124] **Mayne Island Fall Fair**: Centennial Year - Mayne Island Agriculture Society, pp. 10
[125] **A Gulf Islands Patchwork**: Some Early Events on the Islands of Galiano, Mayne, Saturna, North and South Pender – British Columbia Historical Association, pp. 173
[126] **A Gulf Islands Patchwork**: Some Early Events on the Islands of Galiano, Mayne, Saturna, North and South Pender – British Columbia Historical Association, pp. 173
[127] **A Gulf Islands Patchwork**: Some Early Events on the Islands of Galiano, Mayne, Saturna, North and South Pender – British Columbia Historical Association, pp. 173
[128] **A Gulf Islands Patchwork**: Some Early Events on the Islands of Galiano, Mayne, Saturna, North and South Pender – British Columbia Historical Association, pp. 173

Mayne Island

[129] **Homesteads and Snug Harbours:** The Gulf Islands – Peter Murray, pp. 29
[130] **Mayne Island & The Outer Gulf Islands**: A History – Marie Elliott, pp. 44
[131] **Mayne Island Fall Fair**: Centennial Year - Mayne Island Agriculture Society, pp. 11
[132] **Mayne Island Fall Fair**: Centennial Year - Mayne Island Agriculture Society, pp. 11
[133] **A Gulf Islands Patchwork**: Some Early Events on the Islands of Galiano, Mayne, Saturna, North and South Pender – British Columbia Historical Association, pp. 27
[134] **Mayne Island Fall Fair**: Centennial Year - Mayne Island Agriculture Society, pp. 11
[135] **Mayne Island Fall Fair**: Centennial Year - Mayne Island Agriculture Society, pp. 11
[136] **Mayne Island Fall Fair**: Centennial Year – Mayne Island Agriculture Society, pp. 11
[137] **Mayne Island & The Outer Gulf Islands**: A History – Marie Elliott, pp. 47
[138] **Mayne Island Fall Fair**: Centennial Year - Mayne Island Agriculture Society, pp. 6
[139] **Mayne Island & The Outer Gulf Islands**: A History – Marie Elliott, pp. 105
[140] **Mayne Island & The Outer Gulf Islands**: A History – Marie Elliott, pp. 105
[141] **Mayne Island & The Outer Gulf Islands**: A History – Marie Elliott, pp. 29
[142] **Mayne Island & The Outer Gulf Islands:** A History – Marie Elliott, pp. 57
[143] **Mayne Island Fall Fair**: Centennial Year – Mayne Island Agriculture Society, inside cover
[144] **Mayne Island & The Outer Gulf Islands:** A History – Marie Elliott, pp. 60
[145] **Mayne Island Fall Fair**: Centennial Year – Mayne Island Agriculture Society, inside cover
[146] **Mayne Island & The Outer Gulf Islands:** A History – Marie Elliott, pp. 114
[147] **Mayne Island & The Outer Gulf Islands:** A History – Marie Elliott, pp. 114
[148] **Mayne Island & The Outer Gulf Islands:** A History – Marie Elliott, pp. 62
[149] **More Tales from the Outer Gulf Islands:** An Anthology of Memories and Anecdotes – British Columbia Historical Association, pp. 273
[150] **More Tales from the Outer Gulf Islands:** An Anthology of Memories and Anecdotes – British Columbia Historical Association, pp. 171 & 218
[151] **Mayne Island Fall Fair**: Centennial Year – Mayne Island Agriculture Society, pp. 25
[152] **Mayne Island Fall Fair**: Centennial Year – Mayne Island Agriculture Society, pp. 24
[153] **More Tales from the Outer Gulf Islands:** An Anthology of Memories and Anecdotes – British Columbia Historical Association, pp. 169
[154] **More Tales from the Outer Gulf Islands:** An Anthology of Memories and Anecdotes – British Columbia Historical Association, pp. 150
[155] **Mayne Island & The outer Gulf Islands**: A History – Marie Elliott, pp. 59
[156] **Mayne Island Fall Fair**: Centennial Year - Mayne Island Agriculture Society, pp. 8
[157] **Mayne Island & The Outer Gulf Islands**: A History – Marie Elliott, pp. 37
[158] **Mayne Island & The Outer Gulf Islands**: A History – Marie Elliott, pp. 37
[159] **A Gulf Islands Patchwork**: Some Early Events on the Islands of Galiano, Mayne, Saturna, North and South Pender – British Columbia Historical Association, pp. 176 and **Mayne Island Chamber of Commerce** – Alan Cheek
[160] **Mayne Island Chamber of Commerce** – Alan Cheek
[161] **Mayne Island & The Outer Gulf Islands**: A History – Marie Elliott, pp. 37
[162] **Mayne Island Fall Fair**: Centennial Year - Mayne Island Agriculture Society, pp. 23
[163] **Vanishing British Columbia** – Michael Kluckner, pp. 150
[164] **A Gulf Islands Patchwork**: Some Early Events on the Islands of Galiano, Mayne, Saturna, North and South Pender – British Columbia Historical Association, pp. 176

Mayne Island

[165] **Vanishing British Columbia** – Michael Kluckner, pp. 150
[166] **Vanishing British Columbia** – Michael Kluckner, pp. 150
[167] **Mayne Island & The outer Gulf Islands**: A History – Marie Elliott, pp. 68
[168] **The Georgia Strait Chronicles** – Terry Glavin
[169] **Vanishing British Columbia** – Michael Kluckner, pp. 151
[170] **Vanishing British Columbia** – Michael Kluckner, pp. 151
[171] **Vanishing British Columbia** – Michael Kluckner, pp. 150
[172] **Mayne Island Fall Fair**: Centennial Year - Mayne Island Agriculture Society, pp. 22 & 23
[173] **Mayne Island Fall Fair**: Centennial Year - Mayne Island Agriculture Society, pp. 22 & 23
[174] **Vanishing British Columbia** – Michael Kluckner, pp. 150
[175] **Vanishing British Columbia** – Michael Kluckner, pp. 150
[176] **Island Heritage Buildings** – Thomas K. Ovanin, Islands Trust, pp. 106
[177] **A Gulf Islands Patchwork**: Some Early Events on the Islands of Galiano, Mayne, Saturna, North and South Pender – British Columbia Historical Association, pp. 176 and **Mayne Island Chamber of Commerce** – Alan Cheek
[178] **The Georgia Strait Chronicles** – Terry Glavin
[179] **A Gulf Islands Patchwork**: Some Early Events on the Islands of Galiano, Mayne, Saturna, North and South Pender – British Columbia Historical Association, pp. 176
[180] **Vanishing British Columbia** – Michael Kluckner, pp. 151
[181] **A Gulf Islands Patchwork**: Some Early Events on the Islands of Galiano, Mayne, Saturna, North and South Pender – British Columbia Historical Association, pp. 176
[182] **Vanishing British Columbia** – Michael Kluckner, pp. 151
[183] **A Gulf Islands Patchwork**: Some Early Events on the Islands of Galiano, Mayne, Saturna, North and South Pender – British Columbia Historical Association, pp. 176
[184] **Mayne Island Fall Fair**: Centennial Year - Mayne Island Agriculture Society, pp. 8
[185] **Mayne Island Fall Fair**: Centennial Year - Mayne Island Agriculture Society, pp. 8
[186] **Mayne Island Fall Fair:** Centennial Year – Mayne Island Agriculture Society, pp. 8
[187] **Mayne Island Fall Fair:** Centennial Year – Mayne Island Agriculture Society, pp. 8
[188] **Mayne Island Fall Fair**: Centennial Year - Mayne Island Agriculture Society, pp. 8

Saturna Island

Notes

[1] **A Gulf Islands Patchwork:** Some Early Events on the Islands of Galiano, Mayne, Saturna, North and South Pender – British Columbia Historical Association, pp. 57
[2] **The Gulf Islanders:** Sound Heritage, Volume V, Number 4, pp. 23 and **A Gulf Islands Patchwork:** Some Early Events on the Islands of Galiano, Mayne, Saturna, North and South Pender – British Columbia Historical Association, pp. 57
[3] **A Gulf Islands Patchwork:** Some Early Events on the Islands of Galiano, Mayne, Saturna, North and South Pender – British Columbia Historical Association, pp. 57
[4] **The Gulf Islanders:** Sound Heritage, Volume V, Number 4, pp. 29
[5] **A Gulf Islands Patchwork:** Some Early Events on the Islands of Galiano, Mayne, Saturna, North and South Pender – British Columbia Historical Association, pp. 50
[6] **Homesteads and Snug Harbours:** The Gulf Islands – Peter Murray, pp. 55
[7] **A Gulf Islands Patchwork:** Some Early Events on the Islands of Galiano, Mayne, Saturna, North and South Pender – British Columbia Historical Association, pp. 17 & 50 and **The Campbells of Saturna: An Oral History** – Saturna Community Club, pp. 142
[8] **A Gulf Islands Patchwork:** Some Early Events on the Islands of Galiano, Mayne, Saturna, North and South Pender – British Columbia Historical Association, pp. 17 & 50
[9] **A Gulf Islands Patchwork:** Some Early Events on the Islands of Galiano, Mayne, Saturna, North and South Pender – British Columbia Historical Association, pp. 17 & 50
[10] **A Gulf Islands Patchwork:** Some Early Events on the Islands of Galiano, Mayne, Saturna, North and South Pender – British Columbia Historical Association, pp. 50
[11] **A Gulf Islands Patchwork:** Some Early Events on the Islands of Galiano, Mayne, Saturna, North and South Pender – British Columbia Historical Association, pp. 65
[12] **The Gulf Islanders:** Sound Heritage, Volume V, Number 4, pp. 23
[13] **A Gulf Islands Patchwork:** Some Early Events on the Islands of Galiano, Mayne, Saturna, North and South Pender – British Columbia Historical Association, pp. 65
[14] **ABC Book World website**
[15] **The Gulf Islanders:** Sound Heritage, Volume V, Number 4, pp. 23
[16] **The Gulf Islanders:** Sound Heritage, Volume V, Number 4, pp. 23
[17] **The Gulf Islanders:** Sound Heritage, Volume V, Number 4, pp. 22
[18] **ABC Book World website**
[19] **A Gulf Islands Patchwork:** Some Early Events on the Islands of Galiano, Mayne, Saturna, North and South Pender – British Columbia Historical Association, pp. 65
[20] **A Gulf Islands Patchwork:** Some Early Events on the Islands of Galiano, Mayne, Saturna, North and South Pender – British Columbia Historical Association, pp. 60
[21] **Conversations with Lorraine Campbell of Saturna Island**
[22] **The Gulf Islanders:** Sound Heritage, Volume V, Number 4, pp. 38
[23] **A Gulf Islands Patchwork:** Some Early Events on the Islands of Galiano, Mayne, Saturna, North and South Pender – British Columbia Historical Association, pp. 60
[24] **The Gulf Islanders:** Sound Heritage, Volume V, Number 4, pp. 47
[25] **The Gulf Islanders:** Sound Heritage, Volume V, Number 4, pp. 47
[26] **A Gulf Islands Patchwork:** Some Early Events on the Islands of Galiano, Mayne, Saturna, North and South Pender – British Columbia Historical Association, pp. 77
[27] **The Gulf Islanders:** Sound Heritage, Volume V, Number 4, pp. 47
[28] **More Tales from the Outer Gulf Islands:** An Anthology of Memories and Anecdotes – British Columbia Historical Association, pp. 187

Saturna Island

[29] **Homesteads and Snug Harbours:** The Gulf Islands – Peter Murray, pp. 47
[30] **The Gulf Islanders:** Sound Heritage, Volume V, Number 4, pp. 21 and **A Gulf Islands Patchwork:** Some Early Events on the Islands of Galiano, Mayne, Saturna, North and South Pender – British Columbia Historical Association, pp. 52
[31] **The Gulf Islanders:** Sound Heritage, Volume V, Number 4, pp. 21 & 37
[32] **A Gulf Islands Patchwork:** Some Early Events on the Islands of Galiano, Mayne, Saturna, North and South Pender – British Columbia Historical Association, pp. 52
[33] **A Gulf Islands Patchwork:** Some Early Events on the Islands of Galiano, Mayne, Saturna, North and South Pender – British Columbia Historical Association, pp. 54
[34] **Winifred Grey:** A Gentlewoman's Remembrances of Life in England and the Gulf Islands of British Columbia, 1871-1910 – Edited by Marie Elliott, pp. 108
[35] **A Gulf Islands Patchwork:** Some Early Events on the Islands of Galiano, Mayne, Saturna, North and South Pender – British Columbia Historical Association, pp. 53
[36] **The Gulf Islanders:** Sound Heritage, Volume V, Number 4, pp. 31 & 34
[37] **The Campbells of Saturna: An Oral History** – Saturna Community Club, pp. 177
[38] **A Gulf Islands Patchwork:** Some Early Events on the Islands of Galiano, Mayne, Saturna, North and South Pender – British Columbia Historical Association, pp. 53
[39] **The Campbells of Saturna: An Oral History** – Saturna Community Club, pp. 205
[40] **Homesteads and Snug Harbours:** The Gulf Islands – Peter Murray, pp. 52
[41] **A Gulf Islands Patchwork:** Some Early Events on the Islands of Galiano, Mayne, Saturna, North and South Pender – British Columbia Historical Association, pp. 53
[42] **A Gulf Islands Patchwork:** Some Early Events on the Islands of Galiano, Mayne, Saturna, North and South Pender – British Columbia Historical Association, pp. 63
[43] **The Gulf Islanders:** Sound Heritage, Volume V, Number 4, pp. 26
[44] **A Gulf Islands Patchwork:** Some Early Events on the Islands of Galiano, Mayne, Saturna, North and South Pender – British Columbia Historical Association, pp. 56
[45] **A Gulf Islands Patchwork:** Some Early Events on the Islands of Galiano, Mayne, Saturna, North and South Pender – British Columbia Historical Association, pp. 55
[46] **Homesteads and Snug Harbours:** The Gulf Islands – Peter Murray, pp. 53
[47] **The Campbells of Saturna: An Oral History** – Saturna Community Club, pp. 175 & 177
[48] **Homesteads and Snug Harbours:** The Gulf Islands – Peter Murray, pp. 53
[49] **A Gulf Islands Patchwork:** Some Early Events on the Islands of Galiano, Mayne, Saturna, North and South Pender – British Columbia Historical Association, pp. 55
[50] **A Gulf Islands Patchwork:** Some Early Events on the Islands of Galiano, Mayne, Saturna, North and South Pender – British Columbia Historical Association, pp. 18 & 55
[51] **Island Tides newspaper:** Volume 18 Number 10, pp. 5
[52] **A Gulf Islands Patchwork:** Some Early Events on the Islands of Galiano, Mayne, Saturna, North and South Pender – British Columbia Historical Association, pp. 50
[53] **A Gulf Islands Patchwork:** Some Early Events on the Islands of Galiano, Mayne, Saturna, North and South Pender – British Columbia Historical Association, pp. 50-51
[54] **A Gulf Islands Patchwork:** Some Early Events on the Islands of Galiano, Mayne, Saturna, North and South Pender – British Columbia Historical Association, pp. 50-51
[55] **A Gulf Islands Patchwork:** Some Early Events on the Islands of Galiano, Mayne, Saturna, North and South Pender – British Columbia Historical Association, pp. 50-51

Saturna Island

[56] **A Gulf Islands Patchwork:** Some Early Events on the Islands of Galiano, Mayne, Saturna, North and South Pender – British Columbia Historical Association, pp. 50-51
[57] **A Gulf Islands Patchwork:** Some Early Events on the Islands of Galiano, Mayne, Saturna, North and South Pender – British Columbia Historical Association, pp. 50
[58] **Homesteads and Snug Harbours:** The Gulf Islands – Peter Murray, pp. 55
[59] **More Tales from the Outer Gulf Islands:** An Anthology of Memories and Anecdotes – British Columbia Historical Association, pp. 188
[60] **The Campbells of Saturna: An Oral History** – Saturna Community Club, pp. 63 & 64
[61] **The Gulf Islanders:** Sound Heritage, Volume V, Number 4, pp. 26
[62] **More Tales from the Outer Gulf Islands:** An Anthology of Memories and Anecdotes – British Columbia Historical Association, pp. 188
[63] **The Gulf Islanders:** Sound Heritage, Volume V, Number 4, pp. 23 and **A Gulf Islands Patchwork:** Some Early Events on the Islands of Galiano, Mayne, Saturna, North and South Pender – British Columbia Historical Association, pp. 57
[64] **A Gulf Islands Patchwork:** Some Early Events on the Islands of Galiano, Mayne, Saturna, North and South Pender – British Columbia Historical Association, pp. 60
[65] **A Gulf Islands Patchwork:** Some Early Events on the Islands of Galiano, Mayne, Saturna, North and South Pender – British Columbia Historical Association, pp. 60
[66] **A Gulf Islands Patchwork:** Some Early Events on the Islands of Galiano, Mayne, Saturna, North and South Pender – British Columbia Historical Association, pp. 58
[67] **A Gulf Islands Patchwork:** Some Early Events on the Islands of Galiano, Mayne, Saturna, North and South Pender – British Columbia Historical Association, pp. 58
[68] **Winifred Grey:** A Gentlewoman's Remembrances of Life in England and the Gulf Islands of British Columbia, 1871-1910 – Edited by Marie Elliott, pp. 121
[69] **The Campbells of Saturna: An Oral History** – Saturna Community Club, pp. 45 & 61
[70] **The Campbells of Saturna: An Oral History** – Saturna Community Club, pp. 117 & 118
[71] **Conversations with Lorraine Campbell of Saturna Island**
[72] **The Campbells of Saturna: An Oral History** – Saturna Community Club, pp. 190
[73] **A Gulf Islands Patchwork:** Some Early Events on the Islands of Galiano, Mayne, Saturna, North and South Pender – British Columbia Historical Association, pp. 57 and **Homesteads and Snug Harbours:** The Gulf Islands – Peter Murray, pp. 49 & 50
[74] **BC Archives website**
[75] **A Gulf Islands Patchwork:** Some Early Events on the Islands of Galiano, Mayne, Saturna, North and South Pender – British Columbia Historical Association, pp. 57
[76] **A Gulf Islands Patchwork:** Some Early Events on the Islands of Galiano, Mayne, Saturna, North and South Pender – British Columbia Historical Association, pp. 59
[77] **The Campbells of Saturna: An Oral History** – Saturna Community Club, pp. 57 & 129
[78] **The Campbells of Saturna: An Oral History** – Saturna Community Club, pp. 189
[79] **A Gulf Islands Patchwork:** Some Early Events on the Islands of Galiano, Mayne, Saturna, North and South Pender – British Columbia Historical Association, pp. 58
[80] **A Gulf Islands Patchwork:** Some Early Events on the Islands of Galiano, Mayne, Saturna, North and South Pender – British Columbia Historical Association, pp. 58

Saturna Island

[81] **A Gulf Islands Patchwork:** Some Early Events on the Islands of Galiano, Mayne, Saturna, North and South Pender – British Columbia Historical Association, pp. 58
[82] **SaturnaCAN website:** Community Access Network
[83] **The Gulf Islanders:** Sound Heritage, Volume V, Number 4, pp. 59
[84] **SaturnaCAN website:** Community Access Network
[85] **A Gulf Islands Patchwork:** Some Early Events on the Islands of Galiano, Mayne, Saturna, North and South Pender – British Columbia Historical Association, pp. 58
[86] **SaturnaCAN website:** Community Access Network
[87] **SaturnaCAN website:** Community Access Network
[88] **SaturnaCAN website:** Community Access Network
[89] **SaturnaCAN website:** Community Access Network
[90] **SaturnaCAN website:** Community Access Network
[91] **SaturnaCAN website:** Community Access Network
[92] **SaturnaCAN website:** Community Access Network
[93] **A Gulf Islands Patchwork:** Some Early Events on the Islands of Galiano, Mayne, Saturna, North and South Pender – British Columbia Historical Association, pp. 57
[94] **The Gulf Islanders:** Sound Heritage, Volume V, Number 4, pp. 28
[95] **The Gulf Islanders:** Sound Heritage, Volume V, Number 4, pp. 28
[96] **The Gulf Islanders:** Sound Heritage, Volume V, Number 4, pp. 28
[97] **The Gulf Islanders:** Sound Heritage, Volume V, Number 4, pp. 28
[98] **The Gulf Islanders:** Sound Heritage, Volume V, Number 4, pp. 37
[99] **Homesteads and Snug Harbours:** The Gulf Islands – Peter Murray, pp. 54
[100] **Homesteads and Snug Harbours:** The Gulf Islands – Peter Murray, pp. 54
[101] **Homesteads and Snug Harbours:** The Gulf Islands – Peter Murray, pp. 54
[102] **Homesteads and Snug Harbours:** The Gulf Islands – Peter Murray, pp. 54
[103] **A Gulf Islands Patchwork:** Some Early Events on the Islands of Galiano, Mayne, Saturna, North and South Pender – British Columbia Historical Association, pp. 60
[104] **The Campbells of Saturna: An Oral History** – Saturna Community Club, pp. 12
[105] **The Campbells of Saturna: An Oral History** – Saturna Community Club, pp. 12
[106] **The Campbells of Saturna: An Oral History** – Saturna Community Club, pp. 11, 12, 44 & 45
[107] **The Campbells of Saturna: An Oral History** – Saturna Community Club, pp. 107
[108] **The Campbells of Saturna: An Oral History** – Saturna Community Club, pp. 44
[109] **The Campbells of Saturna: An Oral History** – Saturna Community Club, pp. 16, 45 & 61
[110] **The Campbells of Saturna: An Oral History** – Saturna Community Club, pp. 136
[111] **The Campbells of Saturna: An Oral History** – Saturna Community Club, pp. 136
[112] **The Campbells of Saturna: An Oral History** – Saturna Community Club, pp. 121
[113] **The Campbells of Saturna: An Oral History** – Saturna Community Club, pp. 121
[114] **The Campbells of Saturna: An Oral History** – Saturna Community Club, pp. 126, 176 & 177
[115] **The Campbells of Saturna: An Oral History** – Saturna Community Club, pp. 121
[116] **A Gulf Islands Patchwork:** Some Early Events on the Islands of Galiano, Mayne, Saturna, North and South Pender – British Columbia Historical Association, pp. 17 & 59 and **The Campbells of Saturna: An Oral History** – Saturna Community Club, pp. 33

Saturna Island

[117] **The Campbells of Saturna: An Oral History** – Saturna Community Club, pp. 35, 36 & 214
[118] **The Campbells of Saturna: An Oral History** – Saturna Community Club, pp. 18 & 19
[119] **The Campbells of Saturna: An Oral History** – Saturna Community Club, pp. 18 & 19
[120] **The Campbells of Saturna: An Oral History** – Saturna Community Club, pp. 16 & 24
[121] **The Campbells of Saturna: An Oral History** – Saturna Community Club, pp. 13 & 16
[122] **The Campbells of Saturna: An Oral History** – Saturna Community Club, pp. 46 & 47
[123] **The Campbells of Saturna: An Oral History** – Saturna Community Club, pp. 47 & 50
[124] **The Campbells of Saturna: An Oral History** – Saturna Community Club, pp. 47 & 50
[125] **The Campbells of Saturna: An Oral History** – Saturna Community Club, pp. 49 & 50
[126] **The Campbells of Saturna: An Oral History** – Saturna Community Club, pp. 36
[127] **The Terror Of The Coast**: Land Alienation And Colonial War On Vancouver Island And The Gulf Islands – Chris Arnett, pp. 112

Pender Islands

Notes

[1] **More Tales from the Outer Gulf Islands:** An Anthology of Memories and Anecdotes – British Columbia Historical Association, pp. 24

[2] **A Gulf Islands Patchwork:** Some Early Events on the Islands of Galiano, Mayne, Saturna, North and South Pender – British Columbia Historical Association, pp. 19 and **More Tales from the Outer Gulf Islands:** An Anthology of Memories and Anecdotes – British Columbia Historical Association, pp. 22, 24 & 26

[3] **Island Heritage Buildings** – Thomas K. Ovanin, Islands Trust, pp. 134

[4] **More Tales from the Outer Gulf Islands:** An Anthology of Memories and Anecdotes – British Columbia Historical Association, pp. 26

[5] **Island Heritage Buildings** – Thomas K. Ovanin, Islands Trust, pp. 134

[6] **More Tales from the Outer Gulf Islands:** An Anthology of Memories and Anecdotes – British Columbia Historical Association, pp. 36

[7] **A Gulf Islands Patchwork:** Some Early Events on the Islands of Galiano, Mayne, Saturna, North and South Pender – British Columbia Historical Association, pp. 21

[8] **The Gulf Islanders:** Sound Heritage, Volume V, Number 4, pp. 12

[9] **A Gulf Islands Patchwork:** Some Early Events on the Islands of Galiano, Mayne, Saturna, North and South Pender – British Columbia Historical Association, pp. 39, 68 & 125

[10] **A Gulf Islands Patchwork:** Some Early Events on the Islands of Galiano, Mayne, Saturna, North and South Pender – British Columbia Historical Association, pp. 39, 40, 123, 128 & 129

[11] **The Gulf Islanders:** Sound Heritage, Volume V, Number 4, pp. 39 and **A Gulf Islands Patchwork:** Some Early Events on the Islands of Galiano, Mayne, Saturna, North and South Pender – British Columbia Historical Association, pp. 128 & 129

[12] **The Gulf Islanders:** Sound Heritage, Volume V, Number 4, pp. 39 and **A Gulf Islands Patchwork:** Some Early Events on the Islands of Galiano, Mayne, Saturna, North and South Pender – British Columbia Historical Association, pp. 128 & 129

[13] **The Gulf Islanders:** Sound Heritage, Volume V, Number 4, pp. 39 and **A Gulf Islands Patchwork:** Some Early Events on the Islands of Galiano, Mayne, Saturna, North and South Pender – British Columbia Historical Association, pp. 128 & 129

[14] **The Gulf Islanders:** Sound Heritage, Volume V, Number 4, pp. 39 and **A Gulf Islands Patchwork:** Some Early Events on the Islands of Galiano, Mayne, Saturna, North and South Pender – British Columbia Historical Association, pp. 128 & 129

[15] **A Gulf Islands Patchwork:** Some Early Events on the Islands of Galiano, Mayne, Saturna, North and South Pender – British Columbia Historical Association, pp. 68

[16] **A Gulf Islands Patchwork:** Some Early Events on the Islands of Galiano, Mayne, Saturna, North and South Pender – British Columbia Historical Association, pp. 129

[17] **A Gulf Islands Patchwork:** Some Early Events on the Islands of Galiano, Mayne, Saturna, North and South Pender – British Columbia Historical Association, pp. 19

[18] **More Tales from the Outer Gulf Islands:** An Anthology of Memories and Anecdotes – British Columbia Historical Association, pp. 23 & 24

[19] **More Tales from the Outer Gulf Islands:** An Anthology of Memories and Anecdotes – British Columbia Historical Association, pp. 23 & 24

[20] **A Gulf Islands Patchwork:** Some Early Events on the Islands of Galiano, Pender, Saturna, North and South Pender – British Columbia Historical Association, pp. 19

Pender Islands

[21] **More Tales from the Outer Gulf Islands:** An Anthology of Memories and Anecdotes – British Columbia Historical Association, pp. 23 & 24
[22] **More Tales from the Outer Gulf Islands:** An Anthology of Memories and Anecdotes – British Columbia Historical Association, pp. 23 & 24
[23] **More Tales from the Outer Gulf Islands:** An Anthology of Memories and Anecdotes – British Columbia Historical Association, pp. 23 & 24
[24] **More Tales from the Outer Gulf Islands:** An Anthology of Memories and Anecdotes – British Columbia Historical Association, pp. 24 & 25
[25] **A Gulf Islands Patchwork:** Some Early Events on the Islands of Galiano, Mayne, Saturna, North and South Pender – British Columbia Historical Association, pp. 20, 21 & 124
[26] **A Gulf Islands Patchwork:** Some Early Events on the Islands of Galiano, Mayne, Saturna, North and South Pender – British Columbia Historical Association, pp. 20, 21 & 124
[27] **A Gulf Islands Patchwork:** Some Early Events on the Islands of Galiano, Mayne, Saturna, North and South Pender – British Columbia Historical Association, pp. 20 & 21
[28] **Homesteads and Snug Harbours:** The Gulf Islands – Peter Murray, pp. 64
[29] **Homesteads and Snug Harbours:** The Gulf Islands – Peter Murray, pp. 64
[30] **Homesteads and Snug Harbours:** The Gulf Islands – Peter Murray, pp. 64
[31] **Island Heritage Buildings** – Thomas K. Ovanin, Islands Trust, pp. 139
[32] **Island Heritage Buildings** – Thomas K. Ovanin, Islands Trust, pp. 139
[33] **The Gulf Islanders:** Sound Heritage, Volume V, Number 4, pp. 57 & 58
[34] **Homesteads and Snug Harbours:** The Gulf Islands – Peter Murray, pp. 64
[35] **A Self-Guided Historic Tour of the Pender Islands:** The Pender Islands Museum Society, pp. 5
[36] **A Self-Guided Historic Tour of the Pender Islands:** The Pender Islands Museum Society, pp. 5
[37] **The Lost Heritage of the Penders:** Limited Edition Calendar, 2004 – Pender Islands Museum Society
[38] **More Tales from the Outer Gulf Islands:** An Anthology of Memories and Anecdotes – British Columbia Historical Association, pp. 39, 43 & 44
[39] **The Lost Heritage of the Penders:** Limited Edition Calendar, 2004 – Pender Islands Museum Society
[40] **A Self-Guided Historic Tour of the Pender Islands:** The Pender Islands Museum Society, pp. 5
[41] **More Tales from the Outer Gulf Islands:** An Anthology of Memories and Anecdotes – British Columbia Historical Association, pp. 43 & 44
[42] **More Tales from the Outer Gulf Islands:** An Anthology of Memories and Anecdotes – British Columbia Historical Association, pp. 39, 43 & 44
[43] **More Tales from the Outer Gulf Islands:** An Anthology of Memories and Anecdotes – British Columbia Historical Association, pp. 61-65
[44] **More Tales from the Outer Gulf Islands:** An Anthology of Memories and Anecdotes – British Columbia Historical Association, pp. 61-65
[45] **More Tales from the Outer Gulf Islands:** An Anthology of Memories and Anecdotes – British Columbia Historical Association, pp. 61-65

Pender Islands

[46] **More Tales from the Outer Gulf Islands:** An Anthology of Memories and Anecdotes – British Columbia Historical Association, pp. 64

[47] **More Tales from the Outer Gulf Islands:** An Anthology of Memories and Anecdotes – British Columbia Historical Association, pp. 61-65

[48] **More Tales from the Outer Gulf Islands:** An Anthology of Memories and Anecdotes – British Columbia Historical Association, pp. 61-65

[49] **The Lost Heritage of the Penders:** Limited Edition Calendar, 2004 – Pender Islands Museum Society

[50] **A Self-Guided Historic Tour of the Pender Islands:** The Pender Islands Museum Society, pp. 5

[51] **A Self-Guided Historic Tour of the Pender Islands:** The Pender Islands Museum Society, pp. 5 & 13

[52] **More Tales from the Outer Gulf Islands:** An Anthology of Memories and Anecdotes – British Columbia Historical Association, pp. 44 & 117

[53] **More Tales from the Outer Gulf Islands:** An Anthology of Memories and Anecdotes – British Columbia Historical Association, pp. 44 & 117

[54] **More Tales from the Outer Gulf Islands:** An Anthology of Memories and Anecdotes – British Columbia Historical Association, pp. 24 and **Homesteads and Snug Harbours:** The Gulf Islands – Peter Murray, pp. 61

[55] **More Tales from the Outer Gulf Islands:** An Anthology of Memories and Anecdotes – British Columbia Historical Association, pp. 24 and **Homesteads and Snug Harbours:** The Gulf Islands – Peter Murray, pp. 61

[56] **A Gulf Islands Patchwork:** Some Early Events on the Islands of Galiano, Pender, Saturna, North and South Pender – British Columbia Historical Association, pp. 131

[57] **The Pender Post**: Celebrating the activities of the people of Pender Island at the Millennium, The Pender Post Society, pp. 7

[58] **Mayne Island & The Outer Gulf Islands:** A History – Marie Elliott, pp. 79

[59] **More Tales from the Outer Gulf Islands:** An Anthology of Memories and Anecdotes – British Columbia Historical Association, pp. 24 & 25

[60] **More Tales from the Outer Gulf Islands:** An Anthology of Memories and Anecdotes – British Columbia Historical Association, pp. 24, 25 & 39

[61] **More Tales from the Outer Gulf Islands:** An Anthology of Memories and Anecdotes – British Columbia Historical Association, pp. 24, 25 & 39

[62] **A Gulf Islands Patchwork:** Some Early Events on the Islands of Galiano, Pender, Saturna, North and South Pender – British Columbia Historical Association, pp. 131 and **Homesteads and Snug Harbours:** The Gulf Islands – Peter Murray, pp. 66

[63] **A Gulf Islands Patchwork:** Some Early Events on the Islands of Galiano, Pender, Saturna, North and South Pender – British Columbia Historical Association, pp. 131 and **Homesteads and Snug Harbours:** The Gulf Islands – Peter Murray, pp. 66

[64] **A Self-Guided Historic Tour of the Pender Islands:** The Pender Islands Museum Society, pp. 3

[65] **A Gulf Islands Patchwork:** Some Early Events on the Islands of Galiano, Pender, Saturna, North and South Pender – British Columbia Historical Association, pp. 132

[66] **More Tales from the Outer Gulf Islands:** An Anthology of Memories and Anecdotes – British Columbia Historical Association, pp. 39 & 40 and **Island Heritage Buildings** – Thomas K. Ovanin, Islands Trust, pp. 136

Pender Islands

[67] **A Gulf Islands Patchwork:** Some Early Events on the Islands of Galiano, Pender, Saturna, North and South Pender – British Columbia Historical Association, pp. 132
[68] **Hope Bay Store website**
[69] **A Gulf Islands Patchwork:** Some Early Events on the Islands of Galiano, Pender, Saturna, North and South Pender – British Columbia Historical Association, pp. 132
[70] **More Tales from the Outer Gulf Islands:** An Anthology of Memories and Anecdotes – British Columbia Historical Association, pp. 41 and **Island Heritage Buildings** – Thomas K. Ovanin, Islands Trust, pp. 132
[71] **Hope Bay Store website**
[72] **More Tales from the Outer Gulf Islands:** An Anthology of Memories and Anecdotes – British Columbia Historical Association, pp. 40 & 41
[73] **Homesteads and Snug Harbours:** The Gulf Islands – Peter Murray, pp. 67
[74] **A Gulf Islands Patchwork:** Some Early Events on the Islands of Galiano, Mayne, Saturna, North and South Pender – British Columbia Historical Association, pp. 186
[75] **A Self-Guided Historic Tour of the Pender Islands:** The Pender Islands Museum Society, pp. 1
[76] **Homesteads and Snug Harbours:** The Gulf Islands – Peter Murray, pp. 67
[77] **A Gulf Islands Patchwork:** Some Early Events on the Islands of Galiano, Mayne, Saturna, North and South Pender – British Columbia Historical Association, pp. 118 & 186
[78] **A Gulf Islands Patchwork:** Some Early Events on the Islands of Galiano, Mayne, Saturna, North and South Pender – British Columbia Historical Association, pp. 118 & 186
[79] **A Gulf Islands Patchwork:** Some Early Events on the Islands of Galiano, Mayne, Saturna, North and South Pender – British Columbia Historical Association, pp. 118 & 186
[80] **Homesteads and Snug Harbours:** The Gulf Islands – Peter Murray, pp. 67
[81] **The Gulf Islands Explorer:** The Complete Guide – Bruce Obee, pp. 125
[82] **Homesteads and Snug Harbours:** The Gulf Islands – Peter Murray, pp. 68
[83] **A Gulf Islands Patchwork:** Some Early Events on the Islands of Galiano, Mayne, Saturna, North and South Pender – British Columbia Historical Association, pp. 66 & 67
[84] **A Gulf Islands Patchwork:** Some Early Events on the Islands of Galiano, Mayne, Saturna, North and South Pender – British Columbia Historical Association, pp. 66 & 67
[85] **Island Heritage Buildings** – Thomas K. Ovanin, Islands Trust, pp. 133
[86] **A Gulf Islands Patchwork:** Some Early Events on the Islands of Galiano, Mayne, Saturna, North and South Pender – British Columbia Historical Association, pp. 105 & 106
[87] **A Gulf Islands Patchwork:** Some Early Events on the Islands of Galiano, Mayne, Saturna, North and South Pender – British Columbia Historical Association, pp. 105 & 106
[88] **A Gulf Islands Patchwork:** Some Early Events on the Islands of Galiano, Mayne, Saturna, North and South Pender – British Columbia Historical Association, pp. 105 & 106
[89] **A Gulf Islands Patchwork:** Some Early Events on the Islands of Galiano, Mayne, Saturna, North and South Pender – British Columbia Historical Association, pp. 101, 105 & 106

Pender Islands

[90] **A Gulf Islands Patchwork:** Some Early Events on the Islands of Galiano, Mayne, Saturna, North and South Pender – British Columbia Historical Association, pp. 101, 105 & 106

[91] **A Gulf Islands Patchwork:** Some Early Events on the Islands of Galiano, Mayne, Saturna, North and South Pender – British Columbia Historical Association, pp. 105 & 106

[92] **A Gulf Islands Patchwork:** Some Early Events on the Islands of Galiano, Mayne, Saturna, North and South Pender – British Columbia Historical Association, pp. 23

[93] **Southern Gulf Islands:** An Altitude SuperGuide – Spalding, Montgomery and Pitt, pp. 90 and **Island Heritage Buildings** – Thomas K. Ovanin, Islands Trust, pp. 129

[94] **A Self-Guided Historic Tour of the Pender Islands:** The Pender Islands Museum Society, pp. 13

[95] **The Pender Post:** Celebrating the activities of the people of Pender Island at the Millennium, The Pender Post Society, pp. 85

[96] **A Gulf Islands Patchwork:** Some Early Events on the Islands of Galiano, Mayne, Saturna, North and South Pender – British Columbia Historical Association, pp. 114-116

[97] **A Gulf Islands Patchwork:** Some Early Events on the Islands of Galiano, Mayne, Saturna, North and South Pender – British Columbia Historical Association, pp. 114-116

[98] **A Gulf Islands Patchwork:** Some Early Events on the Islands of Galiano, Mayne, Saturna, North and South Pender – British Columbia Historical Association, pp. 114-116

[99] **A Gulf Islands Patchwork:** Some Early Events on the Islands of Galiano, Mayne, Saturna, North and South Pender – British Columbia Historical Association, pp. 114-116

[100] **A Self-Guided Historic Tour of the Pender Islands:** The Pender Islands Museum Society, pp. 3

[101] **The Pender Post:** Celebrating the activities of the people of Pender Island at the Millennium, The Pender Post Society, pp. 19

[102] **Island Heritage Buildings** – Thomas K. Ovanin, Islands Trust, pp. 140

[103] **Homesteads and Snug Harbours:** The Gulf Islands – Peter Murray, pp. 74

[104] **Island Heritage Buildings** – Thomas K. Ovanin, Islands Trust, pp. 140

[105] **A Gulf Islands Patchwork:** Some Early Events on the Islands of Galiano, Mayne, Saturna, North and South Pender – British Columbia Historical Association, pp. 5 & 171

[106] **A Gulf Islands Patchwork:** Some Early Events on the Islands of Galiano, Mayne, Saturna, North and South Pender – British Columbia Historical Association, pp. 5 & 171

[107] **A Gulf Islands Patchwork:** Some Early Events on the Islands of Galiano, Mayne, Saturna, North and South Pender – British Columbia Historical Association, pp. 5

[108] **More Tales from the Outer Gulf Islands:** An Anthology of Memories and Anecdotes – British Columbia Historical Association, pp. 26 & 35

[109] **More Tales from the Outer Gulf Islands:** An Anthology of Memories and Anecdotes – British Columbia Historical Association, pp. 26 & 35

[110] **More Tales from the Outer Gulf Islands:** An Anthology of Memories and Anecdotes – British Columbia Historical Association, pp. 26 & 35

Pender Islands

[111] **More Tales from the Outer Gulf Islands:** An Anthology of Memories and Anecdotes – British Columbia Historical Association, pp. 26 & 35

[112] **A Gulf Islands Patchwork:** Some Early Events on the Islands of Galiano, Mayne, Saturna, North and South Pender – British Columbia Historical Association, pp. 97 & 98

[113] **More Tales from the Outer Gulf Islands:** An Anthology of Memories and Anecdotes – British Columbia Historical Association, pp. 26 & 35

[114] **More Tales from the Outer Gulf Islands:** An Anthology of Memories and Anecdotes – British Columbia Historical Association, pp. 37 & 38

[115] **More Tales from the Outer Gulf Islands:** An Anthology of Memories and Anecdotes – British Columbia Historical Association, pp. 37 & 38

[116] **More Tales from the Outer Gulf Islands:** An Anthology of Memories and Anecdotes – British Columbia Historical Association, pp. 37 & 38

[117] **More Tales from the Outer Gulf Islands:** An Anthology of Memories and Anecdotes – British Columbia Historical Association, pp. 37 & 38 and **A Gulf Islands Patchwork:** Some Early Events on the Islands of Galiano, Mayne, Saturna, North and South Pender – British Columbia Historical Association, pp. 101

[118] **More Tales from the Outer Gulf Islands:** An Anthology of Memories and Anecdotes – British Columbia Historical Association, pp. 37 & 38

[119] **British Colunbia Historical News:** Volume 37 Number 2

[120] **British Colunbia Historical News:** Volume 37 Number 2

[121] **British Colunbia Historical News:** Volume 37 Number 2

[122] **Gulf Islands National Park Reserve of Canada website**: Visitor Information, Parks Canada

[123] **The Lost Heritage of the Penders:** Limited Edition Calendar, 2004 – Pender Islands Museum Society

[124] **A Gulf Islands Patchwork:** Some Early Events on the Islands of Galiano, Mayne, Saturna, North and South Pender – British Columbia Historical Association, pp. 140 and **The Gulf Islanders:** Sound Heritage, Volume V, Number 4, pp. 43 & 44

[125] **Winifred Grey:** A Gentlewoman's Remembrances of Life in England and the Gulf Islands of British Columbia 1871-1910, pp. 113 & 114

[126] **A Gulf Islands Patchwork:** Some Early Events on the Islands of Galiano, Mayne, Saturna, North and South Pender – British Columbia Historical Association, pp. 140 and **The Gulf Islanders:** Sound Heritage, Volume V, Number 4, pp. 44

[127] **A Gulf Islands Patchwork:** Some Early Events on the Islands of Galiano, Mayne, Saturna, North and South Pender – British Columbia Historical Association, pp. 78

[128] **A Gulf Islands Patchwork:** Some Early Events on the Islands of Galiano, Mayne, Saturna, North and South Pender – British Columbia Historical Association, pp. 140 and **The Gulf Islanders:** Sound Heritage, Volume V, Number 4, pp. 44

[129] **A Gulf Islands Patchwork:** Some Early Events on the Islands of Galiano, Mayne, Saturna, North and South Pender – British Columbia Historical Association, pp. 140 and **The Gulf Islanders:** Sound Heritage, Volume V, Number 4, pp. 44

[130] **A Gulf Islands Patchwork:** Some Early Events on the Islands of Galiano, Mayne, Saturna, North and South Pender – British Columbia Historical Association, pp. 140 and **The Gulf Islanders:** Sound Heritage, Volume V, Number 4, pp. 44

[131] **Winifred Grey:** A Gentlewoman's Remembrances of Life in England and the Gulf Islands of British Columbia 1871 1910, pp. 110

Pender Islands

[132] **A Gulf Islands Patchwork:** Some Early Events on the Islands of Galiano, Mayne, Saturna, North and South Pender – British Columbia Historical Association, pp. 140 and **The Gulf Islanders:** Sound Heritage, Volume V, Number 4, pp. 44

[133] **A Gulf Islands Patchwork:** Some Early Events on the Islands of Galiano, Mayne, Saturna, North and South Pender – British Columbia Historical Association, pp. 125

[134] **A Gulf Islands Patchwork:** Some Early Events on the Islands of Galiano, Mayne, Saturna, North and South Pender – British Columbia Historical Association, pp. 125 & 126

[135] **A Gulf Islands Patchwork:** Some Early Events on the Islands of Galiano, Mayne, Saturna, North and South Pender – British Columbia Historical Association, pp. 169-171

[136] **A Gulf Islands Patchwork:** Some Early Events on the Islands of Galiano, Pender, Saturna, North and South Pender – British Columbia Historical Association, pp. 36

[137] **Winifred Grey:** A Gentlewoman's Remembrances of Life in England and the Gulf Islands of British Columbia 1871-1910, pp. 113

[138] **Homesteads and Snug Harbours:** The Gulf Islands – Peter Murray, pp. 73

[139] **Homesteads and Snug Harbours:** The Gulf Islands – Peter Murray, pp. 72

[140] **A Gulf Islands Patchwork:** Some Early Events on the Islands of Galiano, Pender, Saturna, North and South Pender – British Columbia Historical Association, pp. 36

[141] **A Gulf Islands Patchwork:** Some Early Events on the Islands of Galiano, Mayne, Saturna, North and South Pender – British Columbia Historical Association, pp. 169-171

[142] **More Tales from the Outer Gulf Islands:** An Anthology of Memories and Anecdotes – British Columbia Historical Association, pp. 47-49 and **A Gulf Islands Patchwork:** Some Early Events on the Islands of Galiano, Pender, Saturna, North and South Pender – British Columbia Historical Association, pp. 170 & 171

[143] **A Gulf Islands Patchwork:** Some Early Events on the Islands of Galiano, Mayne, Saturna, North and South Pender – British Columbia Historical Association, pp. 170 & 171 and **More Tales from the Outer Gulf Islands:** An Anthology of Memories and Anecdotes – British Columbia Historical Association, pp. 47 and **Homesteads and Snug Harbours:** The Gulf Islands – Peter Murray, pp. 71

[144] **A Gulf Islands Patchwork:** Some Early Events on the Islands of Galiano, Mayne, Saturna, North and South Pender – British Columbia Historical Association, pp. 170 & 171 and **More Tales from the Outer Gulf Islands:** An Anthology of Memories and Anecdotes – British Columbia Historical Association, pp. 47 and **Homesteads and Snug Harbours:** The Gulf Islands – Peter Murray, pp. 71

[145] **A Gulf Islands Patchwork:** Some Early Events on the Islands of Galiano, Pender, Saturna, North and South Pender – British Columbia Historical Association, pp. 170 & 171 and **More Tales from the Outer Gulf Islands:** An Anthology of Memories and Anecdotes – British Columbia Historical Association, pp. 48 & 55

[146] **Homesteads and Snug Harbours:** The Gulf Islands – Peter Murray, pp. 55

[147] **A Self-Guided Historic Tour of the Pender Islands:** The Pender Islands Museum Society, pp. 3

[148] **A Self-Guided Historic Tour of the Pender Islands:** The Pender Islands Museum Society, pp. 3

[149] **Hope Bay Store website**

Pender Islands

[150] **A Self-Guided Historic Tour of the Pender Islands:** The Pender Islands Museum Society, pp. 3
[151] **Island Heritage Buildings** – Thomas K. Ovanin, Islands Trust, pp. 131
[152] **Homesteads and Snug Harbours:** The Gulf Islands – Peter Murray, pp. 67
[153] **Hope Bay Store website**
[154] **Homesteads and Snug Harbours:** The Gulf Islands – Peter Murray, pp. 67
[155] **A Gulf Islands Patchwork:** Some Early Events on the Islands of Galiano, Pender, Saturna, North and South Pender – British Columbia Historical Association, pp. 96
[156] **Hope Bay Store website**
[157] **Hope Bay Store website**
[158] **Hope Bay Store website**
[159] **Hope Bay Store website**
[160] **Island Heritage Buildings** – Thomas K. Ovanin, Islands Trust, pp. 132
[161] **Hope Bay Store website**
[162] **Hope Bay Store website**
[163] **A Gulf Islands Patchwork:** Some Early Events on the Islands of Galiano, Mayne, Saturna, North and South Pender – British Columbia Historical Association, pp. 96
[164] **A Gulf Islands Patchwork:** Some Early Events on the Islands of Galiano, Mayne, Saturna, North and South Pender – British Columbia Historical Association, pp. 79, 127 & 169
[165] **The Terror Of The Coast:** Land Alienation And Colonial War On Vancouver Island And The Gulf Islands – Chris Arnett, pp. 113
[166] **A Gulf Islands Patchwork:** Some Early Events on the Islands of Galiano, Mayne, Saturna, North and South Pender – British Columbia Historical Association, pp. 79, 127 & 169
[167] **A Gulf Islands Patchwork:** Some Early Events on the Islands of Galiano, Mayne, Saturna, North and South Pender – British Columbia Historical Association, pp. 169 & 170
[168] **Island Tides Newspaper:** Volume 16, Number 23, pp. 1
[169] **More Tales from the Outer Gulf Islands:** An Anthology of Memories and Anecdotes – British Columbia Historical Association, pp. 55
[170] **A Gulf Islands Patchwork:** Some Early Events on the Islands of Galiano, Mayne, Saturna, North and South Pender – British Columbia Historical Association, pp. 169 & 170
[171] **A Gulf Islands Patchwork:** Some Early Events on the Islands of Galiano, Mayne, Saturna, North and South Pender – British Columbia Historical Association, pp. 169 & 170
[172] **More Tales from the Outer Gulf Islands:** An Anthology of Memories and Anecdotes – British Columbia Historical Association, pp. 55
[173] **Mayne Island & The Outer Gulf Islands**: A History – Marie Elliott, pp. 82
[174] **A Gulf Islands Patchwork:** Some Early Events on the Islands of Galiano, Mayne, Saturna, North and South Pender – British Columbia Historical Association, pp. 43-44
[175] **Homesteads and Snug Harbours:** The Gulf Islands – Peter Murray, pp. 69
[176] **The Historical Pender Islands:** Limited Edition Calendar, 2006 – Pender Islands Museum Society

Pender Islands

[177] **A Gulf Islands Patchwork:** Some Early Events on the Islands of Galiano, Mayne, Saturna, North and South Pender – British Columbia Historical Association, pp. 43-44 and **The Historical Pender Islands:** Limited Edition Calendar, 2006 – Pender Islands Museum Society
[178] **A Gulf Islands Patchwork:** Some Early Events on the Islands of Galiano, Mayne, Saturna, North and South Pender – British Columbia Historical Association, pp. 69 & 70
[179] **A Gulf Islands Patchwork:** Some Early Events on the Islands of Galiano, Mayne, Saturna, North and South Pender – British Columbia Historical Association, pp. 69 & 70
[180] **A Gulf Islands Patchwork:** Some Early Events on the Islands of Galiano, Mayne, Saturna, North and South Pender – British Columbia Historical Association, pp. 69 & 70
[181] **A Gulf Islands Patchwork:** Some Early Events on the Islands of Galiano, Mayne, Saturna, North and South Pender – British Columbia Historical Association, pp. 69 & 70
[182] **A Gulf Islands Patchwork:** Some Early Events on the Islands of Galiano, Mayne, Saturna, North and South Pender – British Columbia Historical Association, pp. 100
[183] **More Tales from the Outer Gulf Islands:** An Anthology of Memories and Anecdotes – British Columbia Historical Association, pp. 24-31
[184] **More Tales from the Outer Gulf Islands:** An Anthology of Memories and Anecdotes – British Columbia Historical Association, pp. 24-31
[185] **More Tales from the Outer Gulf Islands:** An Anthology of Memories and Anecdotes – British Columbia Historical Association, pp. 30 & 31
[186] **More Tales from the Outer Gulf Islands:** An Anthology of Memories and Anecdotes – British Columbia Historical Association, pp. 30 & 31
[187] **More Tales from the Outer Gulf Islands:** An Anthology of Memories and Anecdotes – British Columbia Historical Association, pp. 31
[188] **More Tales from the Outer Gulf Islands:** An Anthology of Memories and Anecdotes – British Columbia Historical Association, pp. 29, 31 & 40
[189] **A Gulf Islands Patchwork:** Some Early Events on the Islands of Galiano, Mayne, Saturna, North and South Pender – British Columbia Historical Association, pp. 161
[190] **More Tales from the Outer Gulf Islands:** An Anthology of Memories and Anecdotes – British Columbia Historical Association, pp. 29
[191] **More Tales from the Outer Gulf Islands:** An Anthology of Memories and Anecdotes – British Columbia Historical Association, pp. 32
[192] **More Tales from the Outer Gulf Islands:** An Anthology of Memories and Anecdotes – British Columbia Historical Association, pp. 33
[193] **More Tales from the Outer Gulf Islands:** An Anthology of Memories and Anecdotes – British Columbia Historical Association, pp. 21 & 25
[194] **A Gulf Islands Patchwork:** Some Early Events on the Islands of Galiano, Mayne, Saturna, North and South Pender – British Columbia Historical Association, pp. 117
[195] **A Gulf Islands Patchwork:** Some Early Events on the Islands of Galiano, Mayne, Saturna, North and South Pender – British Columbia Historical Association, pp. 117
[196] **A Gulf Islands Patchwork:** Some Early Events on the Islands of Galiano, Mayne, Saturna, North and South Pender – British Columbia Historical Association, pp. 38
[197] **A Gulf Islands Patchwork:** Some Early Events on the Islands of Galiano, Mayne, Saturna, North and South Pender – British Columbia Historical Association, pp. 38
[198] **A Gulf Islands Patchwork:** Some Early Events on the Islands of Galiano, Mayne, Saturna, North and South Pender – British Columbia Historical Association, pp. 38

Pender Islands

[199] **Southern Gulf Islands**: An Altitude SuperGuide – Spalding, Montgomery and Pitt, pp. 21

[200] **A Gulf Islands Patchwork**: Some Early Events on the Islands of Galiano, Mayne, Saturna, North and South Pender – British Columbia Historical Association, pp. 172 & 173

[201] **A Gulf Islands Patchwork**: Some Early Events on the Islands of Galiano, Mayne, Saturna, North and South Pender – British Columbia Historical Association, pp. 172 & 173

[202] **A Gulf Islands Patchwork**: Some Early Events on the Islands of Galiano, Mayne, Saturna, North and South Pender – British Columbia Historical Association, pp. 172 & 173

[203] **Southern Gulf Islands**: An Altitude SuperGuide – Spalding, Montgomery and Pitt, pp. 232

[204] **A Gulf Islands Patchwork**: Some Early Events on the Islands of Galiano, Mayne, Saturna, North and South Pender – British Columbia Historical Association, pp. 172 & 173

[205] **A Self-Guided Historic Tour of the Pender Islands**: The Pender Islands Museum Society, pp. 15

[206] **More Tales from the Outer Gulf Islands**: An Anthology of Memories and Anecdotes – British Columbia Historical Association, pp. 39-41 and **Island Heritage Buildings** – Thomas K. Ovanin, Islands Trust, pp. 136

[207] **More Tales from the Outer Gulf Islands**: An Anthology of Memories and Anecdotes – British Columbia Historical Association, pp. 39-41 and **Island Heritage Buildings** – Thomas K. Ovanin, Islands Trust, pp. 136

[208] **More Tales from the Outer Gulf Islands**: An Anthology of Memories and Anecdotes – British Columbia Historical Association, pp. 39-41

[209] **More Tales from the Outer Gulf Islands**: An Anthology of Memories and Anecdotes – British Columbia Historical Association, pp. 40

[210] **More Tales from the Outer Gulf Islands**: An Anthology of Memories and Anecdotes – British Columbia Historical Association, pp. 39-41 & 103-105

[211] **More Tales from the Outer Gulf Islands**: An Anthology of Memories and Anecdotes – British Columbia Historical Association, pp. 41

[212] **A Self-Guided Historic Tour of the Pender Islands**: The Pender Islands Museum Society, pp. 7

[213] **Island Heritage Buildings** – Thomas K. Ovanin, Islands Trust, pp. 140

[214] **Island Heritage Buildings** – Thomas K. Ovanin, Islands Trust, pp. 140

[215] **Island Heritage Buildings** – Thomas K. Ovanin, Islands Trust, pp. 140

[216] **Island Heritage Buildings** – Thomas K. Ovanin, Islands Trust, pp. 140

[217] **A Gulf Islands Patchwork**: Some Early Events on the Islands of Galiano, Mayne, Saturna, North and South Pender – British Columbia Historical Association, pp. 21 & 107

[218] **More Tales from the Outer Gulf Islands**: An Anthology of Memories and Anecdotes – British Columbia Historical Association, pp. 39

[219] **A Gulf Islands Patchwork**: Some Early Events on the Islands of Galiano, Mayne, Saturna, North and South Pender – British Columbia Historical Association, pp. 21 & 107

Pender Islands

[220] **A Gulf Islands Patchwork:** Some Early Events on the Islands of Galiano, Mayne, Saturna, North and South Pender – British Columbia Historical Association, pp. 107
[221] **A Gulf Islands Patchwork:** Some Early Events on the Islands of Galiano, Mayne, Saturna, North and South Pender – British Columbia Historical Association, pp. 109 & 162
[222] **A Gulf Islands Patchwork:** Some Early Events on the Islands of Galiano, Mayne, Saturna, North and South Pender – British Columbia Historical Association, pp. 108 & 109
[223] **A Gulf Islands Patchwork:** Some Early Events on the Islands of Galiano, Mayne, Saturna, North and South Pender – British Columbia Historical Association, pp. 108 & 109
[224] **A Gulf Islands Patchwork:** Some Early Events on the Islands of Galiano, Mayne, Saturna, North and South Pender – British Columbia Historical Association, pp. 107 & 111
[225] **A Self-Guided Historic Tour of the Pender Islands:** The Pender Islands Museum Society, pp. 13
[226] **The Lost Heritage of the Penders:** Limited Edition Calendar, 2004 – Pender Islands Museum Society
[227] **The Lost Heritage of the Penders:** Limited Edition Calendar, 2004 – Pender Islands Museum Society
[228] **The Gulf Islands Explorer:** The Complete Guide – Bruce Obee, pp. 114
[229] **More Tales from the Outer Gulf Islands:** An Anthology of Memories and Anecdotes – British Columbia Historical Association, pp. 45 & 46
[230] **A Self-Guided Historic Tour of the Pender Islands:** The Pender Islands Museum Society, pp. 11
[231] **A Self-Guided Historic Tour of the Pender Islands:** The Pender Islands Museum Society, pp. 11
[232] **More Tales from the Outer Gulf Islands:** An Anthology of Memories and Anecdotes – British Columbia Historical Association, pp. 45 & 46
[233] **More Tales from the Outer Gulf Islands:** An Anthology of Memories and Anecdotes – British Columbia Historical Association, pp. 45 & 46
[234] **More Tales from the Outer Gulf Islands:** An Anthology of Memories and Anecdotes – British Columbia Historical Association, pp. 45 & 46
[235] **Island Heritage Buildings** – Thomas K. Ovanin, Islands Trust, pp. 132
[236] **Island Heritage Buildings** – Thomas K. Ovanin, Islands Trust, pp. 132
[237] **Island Heritage Buildings** – Thomas K. Ovanin, Islands Trust, pp. 132
[238] **More Tales from the Outer Gulf Islands:** An Anthology of Memories and Anecdotes – British Columbia Historical Association, pp. 74
[239] **Southern Gulf Islands**: An Altitude SuperGuide – Spalding, Montgomery and Pitt, pp. 90
[240] **A Gulf Islands Patchwork:** Some Early Events on the Islands of Galiano, Mayne, Saturna, North and South Pender – British Columbia Historical Association, pp. 112-113
[241] **A Gulf Islands Patchwork:** Some Early Events on the Islands of Galiano, Mayne, Saturna, North and South Pender – British Columbia Historical Association, pp. 112-113

Pender Islands

[242] **A Gulf Islands Patchwork:** Some Early Events on the Islands of Galiano, Mayne, Saturna, North and South Pender – British Columbia Historical Association, pp. 112-113
[243] **A Gulf Islands Patchwork:** Some Early Events on the Islands of Galiano, Mayne, Saturna, North and South Pender – British Columbia Historical Association, pp. 112-113
[244] **A Gulf Islands Patchwork:** Some Early Events on the Islands of Galiano, Mayne, Saturna, North and South Pender – British Columbia Historical Association, pp. 112-113
[245] **A Gulf Islands Patchwork:** Some Early Events on the Islands of Galiano, Mayne, Saturna, North and South Pender – British Columbia Historical Association, pp. 20 & 21
[246] **More Tales from the Outer Gulf Islands:** An Anthology of Memories and Anecdotes – British Columbia Historical Association, pp. 81-83
[247] **More Tales from the Outer Gulf Islands:** An Anthology of Memories and Anecdotes – British Columbia Historical Association, pp. 81-83
[248] **More Tales from the Outer Gulf Islands:** An Anthology of Memories and Anecdotes – British Columbia Historical Association, pp. 81-83
[249] **More Tales from the Outer Gulf Islands:** An Anthology of Memories and Anecdotes – British Columbia Historical Association, pp. 81-83
[250] **The Pender Post**: Celebrating the activities of the people of Pender Island at the Millennium, The Pender Post Society, pp. 51
[251] **Homesteads and Snug Harbours:** The Gulf Islands – Peter Murray, pp. 74
[252] **A Gulf Islands Patchwork:** Some Early Events on the Islands of Galiano, Mayne, Saturna, North and South Pender – British Columbia Historical Association, pp. 35
[253] **Between The Isles:** Life in the Canadian Gulf Islands - Cy Porter, pp. 171
[254] **Island Tides Newspaper:** Volume 16, Number 23, pp. 1
[255] **A Gulf Islands Patchwork:** Some Early Events on the Islands of Galiano, Mayne, Saturna, North and South Pender – British Columbia Historical Association, pp. 35 and **Southern Gulf Islands**: An Altitude SuperGuide – Spalding, Montgomery and Pitt, pp. 95
[256] **More Tales from the Outer Gulf Islands:** An Anthology of Memories and Anecdotes – British Columbia Historical Association, pp. 66-68 and **A Self-Guided Historic Tour of the Pender Islands:** The Pender Islands Museum Society, pp. 11
[257] **More Tales from the Outer Gulf Islands:** An Anthology of Memories and Anecdotes – British Columbia Historical Association, pp. 66-68 and **A Self-Guided Historic Tour of the Pender Islands:** The Pender Islands Museum Society, pp. 11
[258] **More Tales from the Outer Gulf Islands:** An Anthology of Memories and Anecdotes – British Columbia Historical Association, pp. 66-68 and **A Self-Guided Historic Tour of the Pender Islands:** The Pender Islands Museum Society, pp. 11
[259] **More Tales from the Outer Gulf Islands:** An Anthology of Memories and Anecdotes – British Columbia Historical Association, pp. 66-68
[260] **A Self-Guided Historic Tour of the Pender Islands:** The Pender Islands Museum Society, pp. 11
[261] **More Tales from the Outer Gulf Islands:** An Anthology of Memories and Anecdotes – British Columbia Historical Association, pp. 68

Pender Islands

[262] **More Tales from the Outer Gulf Islands:** An Anthology of Memories and Anecdotes – British Columbia Historical Association, pp. 66-68
[263] **The Gulf Islands Explorer:** The Complete Guide – Bruce Obee, pp. 122
[264] **More Tales from the Outer Gulf Islands:** An Anthology of Memories and Anecdotes – British Columbia Historical Association, pp. 40 & 104
[265] **More Tales from the Outer Gulf Islands:** An Anthology of Memories and Anecdotes – British Columbia Historical Association, pp. 103-105
[266] **More Tales from the Outer Gulf Islands:** An Anthology of Memories and Anecdotes – British Columbia Historical Association, pp. 103-105
[267] **More Tales from the Outer Gulf Islands:** An Anthology of Memories and Anecdotes – British Columbia Historical Association, pp. 103-105
[268] **More Tales from the Outer Gulf Islands:** An Anthology of Memories and Anecdotes – British Columbia Historical Association, pp. 102-105
[269] **More Tales from the Outer Gulf Islands:** An Anthology of Memories and Anecdotes – British Columbia Historical Association, pp. 103-105
[270] **More Tales from the Outer Gulf Islands:** An Anthology of Memories and Anecdotes – British Columbia Historical Association, pp. 103-105
[271] **More Tales from the Outer Gulf Islands:** An Anthology of Memories and Anecdotes – British Columbia Historical Association, pp. 112-115
[272] **More Tales from the Outer Gulf Islands:** An Anthology of Memories and Anecdotes – British Columbia Historical Association, pp. 112-115
[273] **More Tales from the Outer Gulf Islands:** An Anthology of Memories and Anecdotes – British Columbia Historical Association, pp. 112-115
[274] **More Tales from the Outer Gulf Islands:** An Anthology of Memories and Anecdotes – British Columbia Historical Association, pp. 112-115
[275] **More Tales from the Outer Gulf Islands:** An Anthology of Memories and Anecdotes – British Columbia Historical Association, pp. 112-115
[276] **More Tales from the Outer Gulf Islands:** An Anthology of Memories and Anecdotes – British Columbia Historical Association, pp. 112-115

Galiano Island

Notes

[1] **More Tales from the Outer Gulf Islands:** An Anthology of Memories and Anecdotes – British Columbia Historical Association, pp. 209-213
[2] **More Tales from the Outer Gulf Islands:** An Anthology of Memories and Anecdotes – British Columbia Historical Association, pp. 215
[3] **Island Heritage Buildings** – Thomas K. Ovanin, Islands Trust, pp. 98
[4] **More Tales from the Outer Gulf Islands:** An Anthology of Memories and Anecdotes – British Columbia Historical Association, pp. 209-213
[5] **Homesteads and Snug Harbours:** The Gulf Islands – Peter Murray, pp. 41 and **Galiano: Houses And People, Looking back to 1930** – Elizabeth Steward, pp. 58
[6] **Island Heritage Buildings** – Thomas K. Ovanin, Islands Trust, pp. 98
[7] **More Tales from the Outer Gulf Islands:** An Anthology of Memories and Anecdotes – British Columbia Historical Association, pp. 212
[8] **A Gulf Islands Patchwork:** Some Early Events on the Islands of Galiano, Mayne, Saturna, North and South Pender – British Columbia Historical Association, pp. 19, 131 & 144
[9] **More Tales from the Outer Gulf Islands:** An Anthology of Memories and Anecdotes – British Columbia Historical Association, pp. 265
[10] **More Tales from the Outer Gulf Islands:** An Anthology of Memories and Anecdotes – British Columbia Historical Association, pp. 265
[11] **More Tales from the Outer Gulf Islands:** An Anthology of Memories and Anecdotes – British Columbia Historical Association, pp. 265
[12] **More Tales from the Outer Gulf Islands:** An Anthology of Memories and Anecdotes – British Columbia Historical Association, pp. 265
[13] **More Tales from the Outer Gulf Islands:** An Anthology of Memories and Anecdotes – British Columbia Historical Association, pp. 265
[14] **Homesteads and Snug Harbours:** The Gulf Islands – Peter Murray, pp. 33
[15] **Homesteads and Snug Harbours:** The Gulf Islands – Peter Murray, pp. 33
[16] **Homesteads and Snug Harbours:** The Gulf Islands – Peter Murray, pp. 17
[17] **A Gulf Islands Patchwork:** Some Early Events on the Islands of Galiano, Mayne, Saturna, North and South Pender – British Columbia Historical Association, pp.139
[18] **A Gulf Islands Patchwork:** Some Early Events on the Islands of Galiano, Mayne, Saturna, North and South Pender – British Columbia Historical Association, pp 139
[19] **Mayne Island Fall Fair:** Centennial Year – Mayne Island Agriculture Society, pp. 21
[20] **Galiano: Houses And People, Looking back to 1930** – Elizabeth Steward, pp. 93 and **More Tales from the Outer Gulf Islands:** An Anthology of Memories and Anecdotes – British Columbia Historical Association, pp. 206 & 207
[21] **A Gulf Islands Patchwork:** Some Early Events on the Islands of Galiano, Mayne, Saturna, North and South Pender – British Columbia Historical Association, pp. 141 and map
[22] **A Gulf Islands Patchwork:** Some Early Events on the Islands of Galiano, Mayne, Saturna, North and South Pender – British Columbia Historical Association, pp. 141 and map
[23] **Homesteads and Snug Harbours:** The Gulf Islands – Peter Murray, pp. 41
[24] **A Gulf Islands Patchwork:** Some Early Events on the Islands of Galiano, Mayne, Saturna, North and South Pender – British Columbia Historical Association, pp. 141

Galiano Island

[25] **More Tales from the Outer Gulf Islands:** An Anthology of Memories and Anecdotes – British Columbia Historical Association, pp. 211, 212 & 244

[26] **More Tales from the Outer Gulf Islands:** An Anthology of Memories and Anecdotes – British Columbia Historical Association, pp. 211, 212 & 244 and **Galiano Island Archives website**

[27] **Galiano:** Houses And People, Looking back to 1930 – Elizabeth Steward, pp. 72 and **More Tales from the Outer Gulf Islands:** An Anthology of Memories and Anecdotes – British Columbia Historical Association, pp. 244

[28] **Galiano:** Houses And People, Looking back to 1930 – Elizabeth Steward, pp. 73

[29] **Galiano:** Houses And People, Looking back to 1930 – Elizabeth Steward, pp. 72 and **More Tales from the Outer Gulf Islands:** An Anthology of Memories and Anecdotes – British Columbia Historical Association, pp. 244

[30] **Galiano:** Houses And People, Looking back to 1930 – Elizabeth Steward, pp. 73

[31] **More Tales from the Outer Gulf Islands:** An Anthology of Memories and Anecdotes – British Columbia Historical Association, pp. 244

[32] **More Tales from the Outer Gulf Islands:** An Anthology of Memories and Anecdotes – British Columbia Historical Association, pp. 244

[33] **More Tales from the Outer Gulf Islands:** An Anthology of Memories and Anecdotes – British Columbia Historical Association, pp. 246

[34] **More Tales from the Outer Gulf Islands:** An Anthology of Memories and Anecdotes – British Columbia Historical Association, pp. 246

[35] **Galiano:** Houses And People, Looking back to 1930 – Elizabeth Steward, pp. 30 & 73

[36] **Galiano:** Houses And People, Looking back to 1930 – Elizabeth Steward, pp. 30

[37] **Galiano:** Houses And People, Looking back to 1930 – Elizabeth Steward, pp. 132

[38] **Homesteads and Snug Harbours:** The Gulf Islands – Peter Murray, pp. 34

[39] **Homesteads and Snug Harbours:** The Gulf Islands – Peter Murray, pp. 34 and **Galiano:** Houses And People, Looking back to 1930 – Elizabeth Steward, pp. 30 & 133

[40] **Homesteads and Snug Harbours:** The Gulf Islands – Peter Murray, pp. 34 and **Galiano:** Houses And People, Looking back to 1930 – Elizabeth Steward, pp. 30 & 133

[41] **Galiano:** Houses And People, Looking back to 1930 – Elizabeth Steward, pp. 30 & 133

[42] **Salt Spring:** The Story of an Island – Charles Kahn, pp. 42

[43] **Homesteads and Snug Harbours:** The Gulf Islands – Peter Murray, pp. 34

[44] **Homesteads and Snug Harbours:** The Gulf Islands – Peter Murray, pp. 34 and **Galiano:** Houses And People, Looking back to 1930 – Elizabeth Steward, pp. 133

[45] **Homesteads and Snug Harbours:** The Gulf Islands – Peter Murray, pp. 34

[46] **Homesteads and Snug Harbours:** The Gulf Islands – Peter Murray, pp.41

[47] **Galiano:** Houses And People, Looking back to 1930 – Elizabeth Steward, pp. 133

[48] **More Tales from the Outer Gulf Islands:** An Anthology of Memories and Anecdotes – British Columbia Historical Association, pp. 214-216

[49] **More Tales from the Outer Gulf Islands:** An Anthology of Memories and Anecdotes – British Columbia Historical Association, pp. 214-216 and **A Gulf Islands Patchwork:** Some Early Events on the Islands of Galiano, Mayne, Saturna, North and South Pender – British Columbia Historical Association, pp. 157

Galiano Island

[50] **More Tales from the Outer Gulf Islands:** An Anthology of Memories and Anecdotes – British Columbia Historical Association, pp. 214-216
[51] **Island Heritage Buildings** – Thomas K. Ovanin, Islands Trust, pp. 99
[52] **Galiano:** Houses And People, Looking back to 1930 – Elizabeth Steward, pp. 43
[53] **Island Heritage Buildings** – Thomas K. Ovanin, Islands Trust, pp. 99
[54] **A Gulf Islands Patchwork:** Some Early Events on the Islands of Galiano, Mayne, Saturna, North and South Pender – British Columbia Historical Association, pp. 17 & 18
[55] **A Gulf Islands Patchwork:** Some Early Events on the Islands of Galiano, Mayne, Saturna, North and South Pender – British Columbia Historical Association, pp. 17 & 18
[56] **A Gulf Islands Patchwork:** Some Early Events on the Islands of Galiano, Mayne, Saturna, North and South Pender – British Columbia Historical Association, pp. 17 & 18
[57] **A Gulf Islands Patchwork:** Some Early Events on the Islands of Galiano, Mayne, Saturna, North and South Pender – British Columbia Historical Association, pp. 17 & 18
[58] **A Gulf Islands Patchwork:** Some Early Events on the Islands of Galiano, Mayne, Saturna, North and South Pender – British Columbia Historical Association, pp. 17 & 18
[59] **A Gulf Islands Patchwork:** Some Early Events on the Islands of Galiano, Mayne, Saturna, North and South Pender – British Columbia Historical Association, pp. 17 & 18
[60] **A Gulf Islands Patchwork:** Some Early Events on the Islands of Galiano, Mayne, Saturna, North and South Pender – British Columbia Historical Association, pp. 17 & 18
[61] **A Gulf Islands Patchwork:** Some Early Events on the Islands of Galiano, Mayne, Saturna, North and South Pender – British Columbia Historical Association, pp. 17 & 18
[62] **Homesteads and Snug Harbours:** The Gulf Islands – Peter Murray, pp. 36
[63] **Southern Gulf Islands**: An Altitude SuperGuide – Spalding, Montgomery and Pitt, pp. 51
[64] **Island Heritage Buildings** – Thomas K. Ovanin, Islands Trust, pp. 102
[65] **More Tales from the Outer Gulf Islands:** An Anthology of Memories and Anecdotes – British Columbia Historical Association, pp. 223-225
[66] **Galiano:** Houses And People, Looking back to 1930 – Elizabeth Steward, pp. 2
[67] **Galiano:** Houses And People, Looking back to 1930 – Elizabeth Steward, pp. 168 and **A Gulf Islands Patchwork:** Some Early Events on the Islands of Galiano, Mayne, Saturna, North and South Pender – British Columbia Historical Association, pp. 153
[68] **A Gulf Islands Patchwork:** Some Early Events on the Islands of Galiano, Mayne, Saturna, North and South Pender – British Columbia Historical Association, pp. 153
[69] **Galiano:** Houses And People, Looking back to 1930 – Elizabeth Steward, pp. 168 and **A Gulf Islands Patchwork:** Some Early Events on the Islands of Galiano, Mayne, Saturna, North and South Pender – British Columbia Historical Association, pp. 153
[70] **Galiano:** Houses And People, Looking back to 1930 – Elizabeth Steward, pp. 168
[71] **More Tales from the Outer Gulf Islands:** An Anthology of Memories and Anecdotes – British Columbia Historical Association, pp. 227
[72] **Island Heritage Buildings** – Thomas K. Ovanin, Islands Trust, pp. 102
[73] **Captain's Quarters website**
[74] **Captain's Quarters website**
[75] **Captain's Quarters website**
[76] **Captain's Quarters website**
[77] **A Gulf Islands Patchwork:** Some Early Events on the Islands of Galiano, Mayne, Saturna, North and South Pender – British Columbia Historical Association, pp. 157

Galiano Island

[78] **Homesteads and Snug Harbours:** The Gulf Islands – Peter Murray, pp. 36
[79] **A Gulf Islands Patchwork:** Some Early Events on the Islands of Galiano, Mayne, Saturna, North and South Pender – British Columbia Historical Association, pp. 157
[80] **Galiano:** Houses And People, Looking back to 1930 – Elizabeth Steward, pp. 49
[81] **More Tales from the Outer Gulf Islands:** An Anthology of Memories and Anecdotes – British Columbia Historical Association, pp. 125 & 126
[82] **A Gulf Islands Patchwork:** Some Early Events on the Islands of Galiano, Mayne, Saturna, North and South Pender – British Columbia Historical Association, pp. 102 & 157
[83] **Galiano:** Houses And People, Looking back to 1930 – Elizabeth Steward, pp. 119
[84] **More Tales from the Outer Gulf Islands:** An Anthology of Memories and Anecdotes – British Columbia Historical Association, pp. 215
[85] **Galiano:** Houses And People, Looking back to 1930 – Elizabeth Steward, pp. 50
[86] **Galiano:** Houses And People, Looking back to 1930 – Elizabeth Steward, pp. 50
[87] **A Gulf Islands Patchwork:** Some Early Events on the Islands of Galiano, Mayne, Saturna, North and South Pender – British Columbia Historical Association, pp. 102 & 157
[88] **Galiano:** Houses And People, Looking back to 1930 – Elizabeth Steward, pp. 119-120
[89] **Galiano:** Houses And People, Looking back to 1930 – Elizabeth Steward, pp. 50
[90] **Galiano:** Houses And People, Looking back to 1930 – Elizabeth Steward, pp. 50 & 51
[91] **Between The Isles:** Life in the Canadian Gulf Islands - Cy Porter, pp. 91
[92] **A Gulf Islands Patchwork:** Some Early Events on the Islands of Galiano, Mayne, Saturna, North and South Pender – British Columbia Historical Association, pp. 102-104
[93] **A Gulf Islands Patchwork:** Some Early Events on the Islands of Galiano, Mayne, Saturna, North and South Pender – British Columbia Historical Association, pp. 95 & 102-104
[94] **Galiano:** Houses And People, Looking back to 1930 – Elizabeth Steward, pp. 36
[95] **A Gulf Islands Patchwork:** Some Early Events on the Islands of Galiano, Mayne, Saturna, North and South Pender – British Columbia Historical Association, pp. 102 & 103
[96] **Galiano:** Houses And People, Looking back to 1930 – Elizabeth Steward, pp. 64-65
[97] **More Tales from the Outer Gulf Islands:** An Anthology of Memories and Anecdotes – British Columbia Historical Association, pp. 254-256
[98] **A Gulf Islands Patchwork:** Some Early Events on the Islands of Galiano, Mayne, Saturna, North and South Pender – British Columbia Historical Association, pp.102-104
[99] **More Tales from the Outer Gulf Islands:** An Anthology of Memories and Anecdotes – British Columbia Historical Association, pp. 255
[100] **More Tales from the Outer Gulf Islands:** An Anthology of Memories and Anecdotes – British Columbia Historical Association, pp. 253-256
[101] **More Tales from the Outer Gulf Islands:** An Anthology of Memories and Anecdotes – British Columbia Historical Association, pp. 219
[102] **More Tales from the Outer Gulf Islands:** An Anthology of Memories and Anecdotes – British Columbia Historical Association, pp. 234, 257 & 258

Galiano Island

[103] **Southern Gulf Islands**: An Altitude SuperGuide – Spalding, Montgomery and Pitt, pp. 51
[104] **Southern Gulf Islands**: An Altitude SuperGuide – Spalding, Montgomery and Pitt, pp. 51
[105] **More Tales from the Outer Gulf Islands:** An Anthology of Memories and Anecdotes – British Columbia Historical Association, pp. 234, 257 & 258
[106] **More Tales from the Outer Gulf Islands:** An Anthology of Memories and Anecdotes – British Columbia Historical Association, pp. 257-258
[107] **More Tales from the Outer Gulf Islands:** An Anthology of Memories and Anecdotes – British Columbia Historical Association, pp. 257-258
[108] **Between The Isles:** Life in the Canadian Gulf Islands - Cy Porter, pp. 112
[109] **Hul'qumi'num Treaty Group website**
[110] **The Gulf Islanders:** Sound Heritage, Volume V, Number 4, pp. 69
[111] **Galiano: Houses And People, Looking back to 1930** – Elizabeth Steward, pp. 158
[112] **The Gulf Islanders:** Sound Heritage, Volume V, Number 4, pp. 69 and **Between The Isles:** Life in the Canadian Gulf Islands - Cy Porter, pp. 112
[113] **The Gulf Islanders:** Sound Heritage, Volume V, Number 4, pp. 69 & 70
[114] **The Gulf Islanders:** Sound Heritage, Volume V, Number 4, pp. 69 & 70
[115] **The Gulf Islanders:** Sound Heritage, Volume V, Number 4, pp. 69 & 70
[116] **Hul'qumi'num Treaty Group website**
[117] **A Gulf Islands Patchwork:** Some Early Events on the Islands of Galiano, Mayne, Saturna, North and South Pender – British Columbia Historical Association, pp. 136 and **Island Heritage Buildings** – Thomas K. Ovanin, Islands Trust, pp. 100
[118] **Homesteads and Snug Harbours:** The Gulf Islands – Peter Murray, pp. 47
[119] **A Gulf Islands Patchwork:** Some Early Events on the Islands of Galiano, Mayne, Saturna, North and South Pender – British Columbia Historical Association, pp. 136
[120] **A Gulf Islands Patchwork:** Some Early Events on the Islands of Galiano, Mayne, Saturna, North and South Pender – British Columbia Historical Association, pp. 136
[121] **A Gulf Islands Patchwork:** Some Early Events on the Islands of Galiano, Mayne, Saturna, North and South Pender – British Columbia Historical Association, pp. 136 & 154
[122] **A Gulf Islands Patchwork:** Some Early Events on the Islands of Galiano, Mayne, Saturna, North and South Pender – British Columbia Historical Association, pp. 136 & 154
[123] **Homesteads and Snug Harbours:** The Gulf Islands – Peter Murray, pp. 37
[124] **A Gulf Islands Patchwork:** Some Early Events on the Islands of Galiano, Mayne, Saturna, North and South Pender – British Columbia Historical Association, pp. 136 & 154
[125] **Homesteads and Snug Harbours:** The Gulf Islands – Peter Murray, pp. 37
[126] **Island Heritage Buildings** – Thomas K. Ovanin, Islands Trust, pp. 100
[127] **Galiano: Houses And People, Looking back to 1930** – Elizabeth Steward, pp. 30
[128] **Mayne Island & The Outer Gulf Islands**: A History – Marie Elliott, pp. 80
[129] **Galiano Island Archives website**
[130] **Mayne Island & The Outer Gulf Islands**: A History – Marie Elliott, pp. 96
[131] **Homesteads and Snug Harbours:** The Gulf Islands – Peter Murray, pp. 34
[132] **Homesteads and Snug Harbours:** The Gulf Islands – Peter Murray, pp. 34

Galiano Island

[133] **Southern Gulf Islands**: An Altitude SuperGuide – Spalding, Montgomery and Pitt, pp. 57
[134] **Homesteads and Snug Harbours:** The Gulf Islands – Peter Murray, pp. 34
[135] **Southern Gulf Islands**: An Altitude SuperGuide – Spalding, Montgomery and Pitt, pp. 57
[136] **Island Heritage Buildings** – Thomas K. Ovanin, Islands Trust, pp. 101
[137] **A Gulf Islands Patchwork:** Some Early Events on the Islands of Galiano, Mayne, Saturna, North and South Pender – British Columbia Historical Association, pp. 91
[138] **Island Heritage Buildings** – Thomas K. Ovanin, Islands Trust, pp. 101
[139] **Bellhouse Inn Bed and Breakfast website**
[140] **Bellhouse Inn Bed and Breakfast website**
[141] **More Tales from the Outer Gulf Islands:** An Anthology of Memories and Anecdotes – British Columbia Historical Association, pp. 275-277
[142] **More Tales from the Outer Gulf Islands:** An Anthology of Memories and Anecdotes – British Columbia Historical Association, pp. 275-277
[143] **Island Heritage Buildings** – Thomas K. Ovanin, Islands Trust, pp. 101
[144] **Island Heritage Buildings** – Thomas K. Ovanin, Islands Trust, pp. 101
[145] **Galiano:** Houses And People, Looking back to 1930 – Elizabeth Steward, pp. 17
[146] **Island Heritage Buildings** – Thomas K. Ovanin, Islands Trust, pp. 101
[147] **Bellhouse Inn Bed and Breakfast website**
[148] **Bellhouse Inn Bed and Breakfast website**
[149] **Southern Gulf Islands**: An Altitude SuperGuide – Spalding, Montgomery and Pitt, pp. 49
[150] **A Gulf Islands Patchwork:** Some Early Events on the Islands of Galiano, Mayne, Saturna, North and South Pender – British Columbia Historical Association, pp. 93
[151] **Homesteads and Snug Harbours:** The Gulf Islands – Peter Murray, pp. 39
[152] **A Gulf Islands Patchwork:** Some Early Events on the Islands of Galiano, Mayne, Saturna, North and South Pender – British Columbia Historical Association, pp. 93
[153] **Homesteads and Snug Harbours:** The Gulf Islands – Peter Murray, pp. 39
[154] **A Gulf Islands Patchwork:** Some Early Events on the Islands of Galiano, Mayne, Saturna, North and South Pender – British Columbia Historical Association, pp. 92
[155] **A Gulf Islands Patchwork:** Some Early Events on the Islands of Galiano, Mayne, Saturna, North and South Pender – British Columbia Historical Association, pp. 93 & 142
[156] **Snapshots of Early Salt Spring and other Favoured Islands:** Mouat's Trading Co. Ltd., pp. 66
[157] **A Gulf Islands Patchwork:** Some Early Events on the Islands of Galiano, Mayne, Saturna, North and South Pender – British Columbia Historical Association, pp. 103
[158] **Island Heritage Buildings** – Thomas K. Ovanin, Islands Trust, pp. 95
[159] **Galiano:** Houses And People, Looking back to 1930 – Elizabeth Steward, pp. 148
[160] **Galiano:** Houses And People, Looking back to 1930 – Elizabeth Steward, pp. 148
[161] **Island Heritage Buildings** – Thomas K. Ovanin, Islands Trust, pp. 95 and **Galiano:** Houses And People, Looking back to 1930 – Elizabeth Steward, pp. 148
[162] **Galiano:** Houses And People, Looking back to 1930 – Elizabeth Steward, pp. 148
[163] **Island Heritage Buildings** – Thomas K. Ovanin, Islands Trust, pp. 95

Galiano Island

[164] **More Tales from the Outer Gulf Islands:** An Anthology of Memories and Anecdotes – British Columbia Historical Association, pp. 225 & 226
[165] **More Tales from the Outer Gulf Islands:** An Anthology of Memories and Anecdotes – British Columbia Historical Association, pp. 225 & 226
[166] **More Tales from the Outer Gulf Islands:** An Anthology of Memories and Anecdotes – British Columbia Historical Association, pp. 225 & 226
[167] **More Tales from the Outer Gulf Islands:** An Anthology of Memories and Anecdotes – British Columbia Historical Association, pp. 225 & 226
[168] **More Tales from the Outer Gulf Islands:** An Anthology of Memories and Anecdotes – British Columbia Historical Association, pp. 225 & 226
[169] **More Tales from the Outer Gulf Islands:** An Anthology of Memories and Anecdotes – British Columbia Historical Association, pp. 225, 226 & 281
[170] **More Tales from the Outer Gulf Islands:** An Anthology of Memories and Anecdotes – British Columbia Historical Association, pp. 225 & 226
[171] **More Tales from the Outer Gulf Islands:** An Anthology of Memories and Anecdotes – British Columbia Historical Association, pp. 225 & 226
[172] **More Tales from the Outer Gulf Islands:** An Anthology of Memories and Anecdotes – British Columbia Historical Association, pp. 226 & 283
[173] **More Tales from the Outer Gulf Islands:** An Anthology of Memories and Anecdotes – British Columbia Historical Association, pp. 281-286
[174] **More Tales from the Outer Gulf Islands:** An Anthology of Memories and Anecdotes – British Columbia Historical Association, pp. 281-286
[175] **More Tales from the Outer Gulf Islands:** An Anthology of Memories and Anecdotes – British Columbia Historical Association, pp. 281-286
[176] **Galiano:** Houses And People, Looking back to 1930 – Elizabeth Steward, pp. 22
[177] **More Tales from the Outer Gulf Islands:** An Anthology of Memories and Anecdotes – British Columbia Historical Association, pp. 123-129
[178] **More Tales from the Outer Gulf Islands:** An Anthology of Memories and Anecdotes – British Columbia Historical Association, pp. 123-129
[179] **More Tales from the Outer Gulf Islands:** An Anthology of Memories and Anecdotes – British Columbia Historical Association, pp. 123-129
[180] **More Tales from the Outer Gulf Islands:** An Anthology of Memories and Anecdotes – British Columbia Historical Association, pp. 123-129 and **Snapshots of Early Salt Spring and other Favoured Islands:** Mouat's Trading Co. Ltd., pp. 46
[181] **Galiano:** Houses And People, Looking back to 1930 – Elizabeth Steward, pp. 110
[182] **More Tales from the Outer Gulf Islands:** An Anthology of Memories and Anecdotes – British Columbia Historical Association, pp. 123-129 and **Snapshots of Early Salt Spring and other Favoured Islands:** Mouat's Trading Co. Ltd., pp. 46
[183] **More Tales from the Outer Gulf Islands:** An Anthology of Memories and Anecdotes – British Columbia Historical Association, pp. 123-129
[184] **Galiano:** Houses And People, Looking back to 1930 – Elizabeth Steward, pp. 110
[185] **Southern Gulf Islands**: An Altitude SuperGuide – Spalding, Montgomery and Pitt, pp. 21
[186] **More Tales from the Outer Gulf Islands:** An Anthology of Memories and Anecdotes – British Columbia Historical Association, pp. 261-263
[187] **Galiano:** Houses And People, Looking back to 1930 – Elizabeth Steward, pp. 52

Galiano Island

[188] **More Tales from the Outer Gulf Islands:** An Anthology of Memories and Anecdotes – British Columbia Historical Association, pp. 124 & 261-263 and **Galiano: Houses And People, Looking back to 1930** – Elizabeth Steward, pp. 52

[189] **More Tales from the Outer Gulf Islands:** An Anthology of Memories and Anecdotes – British Columbia Historical Association, pp. 124 & 261-263 and **Galiano: Houses And People, Looking back to 1930** – Elizabeth Steward, pp. 52

[190] **Snapshots of Early Salt Spring and other Favoured Islands:** Mouat's Trading Co. Ltd., pp. 114

[191] **Galiano: Houses And People, Looking back to 1930** – Elizabeth Steward, pp. 53

[192] **Snapshots of Early Salt Spring and other Favoured Islands:** Mouat's Trading Co. Ltd., pp. 74 and **More Tales from the Outer Gulf Islands:** An Anthology of Memories and Anecdotes – British Columbia Historical Association, pp. 232

[193] **Snapshots of Early Salt Spring and other Favoured Islands:** Mouat's Trading Co. Ltd., pp. 74 and **More Tales from the Outer Gulf Islands:** An Anthology of Memories and Anecdotes – British Columbia Historical Association, pp. 232

[194] **More Tales from the Outer Gulf Islands:** An Anthology of Memories and Anecdotes – British Columbia Historical Association, pp. 232

[195] **More Tales from the Outer Gulf Islands:** An Anthology of Memories and Anecdotes – British Columbia Historical Association, pp. 232

[196] **Southern Gulf Islands**: An Altitude SuperGuide – Spalding, Montgomery and Pitt, pp. 55

[197] **Galiano: Houses And People, Looking back to 1930** – Elizabeth Steward, pp. 141

[198] **Galiano: Houses And People, Looking back to 1930** – Elizabeth Steward, pp. 141

[199] **Snapshots of Early Salt Spring and other Favoured Islands:** Mouat's Trading Co. Ltd., pp. 66 & 76 and **More Tales from the Outer Gulf Islands:** An Anthology of Memories and Anecdotes – British Columbia Historical Association, pp. 265

[200] **Galiano: Houses And People, Looking back to 1930** – Elizabeth Steward, pp. 73, 145 & 146

[201] **Galiano: Houses And People, Looking back to 1930** – Elizabeth Steward, pp. 73

[202] **Galiano: Houses And People, Looking back to 1930** – Elizabeth Steward, pp. 73, 145 & 146

[203] **Galiano: Houses And People, Looking back to 1930** – Elizabeth Steward, pp. 73, 145 & 146

[204] **Galiano: Houses And People, Looking back to 1930** – Elizabeth Steward, pp. 145 & 146

[205] **Southern Gulf Islands**: An Altitude SuperGuide – Spalding, Montgomery and Pitt, pp. 53

[206] **A Gulf Islands Patchwork:** Some Early Events on the Islands of Galiano, Mayne, Saturna, North and South Pender – British Columbia Historical Association, pp. 144

[207] **The Terror Of The Coast**: Land Alienation And Colonial War On Vancouver Island And The Gulf Islands – Chris Arnett, pp. 247

[208] **Mayne Island & The Outer Gulf Islands:** A History – Marie Elliott, pp. 89

[209] **More Tales from the Outer Gulf Islands:** An Anthology of Memories and Anecdotes – British Columbia Historical Association, pp. 269-272

[210] **More Tales from the Outer Gulf Islands:** An Anthology of Memories and Anecdotes – British Columbia Historical Association, pp. 269-272

Galiano Island

[211] **More Tales from the Outer Gulf Islands:** An Anthology of Memories and Anecdotes – British Columbia Historical Association, pp. 269-272
[212] **More Tales from the Outer Gulf Islands:** An Anthology of Memories and Anecdotes – British Columbia Historical Association, pp. 269-272
[213] **More Tales from the Outer Gulf Islands:** An Anthology of Memories and Anecdotes – British Columbia Historical Association, pp. 269-272
[214] **More Tales from the Outer Gulf Islands:** An Anthology of Memories and Anecdotes – British Columbia Historical Association, pp. 269-272
[215] **More Tales from the Outer Gulf Islands:** An Anthology of Memories and Anecdotes – British Columbia Historical Association, pp. 271 & 272
[216] **More Tales from the Outer Gulf Islands:** An Anthology of Memories and Anecdotes – British Columbia Historical Association, pp. 271 & 272
[217] **Galiano:** Houses And People, Looking back to 1930 – Elizabeth Steward, pp. 56
[218] **The Active Page:** Volume 14, Number 12, pp. 31

Salt Spring Island

Notes

[1] **Salt Spring:** The Story of an Island – Charles Kahn, pp. 77
[2] **A Voice from the Past** - The Gulf Islands Guardian, Spring, 1993, pp. 28 & 29
[3] **A Voice from the Past** - The Gulf Islands Guardian, Spring, 1993, pp. 28 & 29
[4] **Salt Spring Island:** Bea Hamilton, pp. 35 and **Salt Spring:** The Story of an Island – Charles Kahn, pp. 42, 46
[5] **Salt Spring:** The Story of an Island – Charles Kahn, pp. 275
[6] **Salt Spring:** The Story of an Island – Charles Kahn, pp. 46
[7] **Homesteads and Snug Harbours:** The Gulf Islands – Peter Murray, pp. 91, 92, 95 & 120
[8] **Homesteads and Snug Harbours:** The Gulf Islands – Peter Murray, pp. 97
[9] **Homesteads and Snug Harbours:** The Gulf Islands – Peter Murray, pp. 97
[10] **Salt Spring:** The Story of an Island – Charles Kahn, pp. 60
[11] **Homesteads and Snug Harbours:** The Gulf Islands – Peter Murray, pp. 91 & 120
[12] **Salt Spring:** The Story of an Island – Charles Kahn, pp. 89, 99 & 101
[13] **Salt Spring:** The Story of an Island – Charles Kahn, pp. 89, 99 & 101
[14] **Homesteads and Snug Harbours:** The Gulf Islands – Peter Murray, pp. 91 & 120
[15] **Salt Spring Island:** Bea Hamilton, pp. 35
[16] **Salt Spring:** The Story of an Island – Charles Kahn, pp. 112
[17] **Salt Spring:** The Story of an Island – Charles Kahn, pp. 37
[18] **A Voice from the Past** - The Gulf Islands Guardian, Spring, 1993, pp. 29 & 30
[19] **Homesteads and Snug Harbours:** The Gulf Islands – Peter Murray, pp. 95 & 96
[20] **A Voice from the Past** - The Gulf Islands Guardian, Spring, 1993, pp. 30
[21] **Salt Spring Island:** Bea Hamilton, pp. 39
[22] **Homesteads and Snug Harbours:** The Gulf Islands – Peter Murray, pp. 96 & 97
[23] **Salt Spring:** The Story of an Island – Charles Kahn, pp. 54
[24] **The Post Offices of British Columbia:** 1858-1970 - George H. Melvin, pp. 106
[25] **Salt Spring Island:** Bea Hamilton, pp. 39
[26] **The Post Offices of British Columbia:** 1858-1970 - George H. Melvin, pp. 143 and **Salt Spring:** The Story of an Island – Charles Kahn, pp. 97, 122 & 139
[27] **Island Heritage Buildings** – Thomas K. Ovanin, Islands Trust, pp. 60
[28] **Salt Spring:** The Story of an Island – Charles Kahn, pp. 122
[29] **Salt Spring:** The Story of an Island – Charles Kahn, pp. 122
[30] **The Post Offices of British Columbia:** 1858-1970 - George H. Melvin, pp. 106
[31] **The Post Offices of British Columbia:** 1858-1970 - George H. Melvin, pp. 43
[32] **Snapshots of Early Salt Spring and other Favoured Islands:** Mouat's Trading Co. Ltd., pp. 82
[33] **Salt Spring Island:** Bea Hamilton, pp. 89
[34] **Mouat's Landing History Hall**
[35] **A Voice from the Past** - The Gulf Islands Guardian, Spring, 1993, pp. 29 & 30
[36] **A Voice from the Past** - The Gulf Islands Guardian, Spring, 1993, pp. 29 & 30
[37] **Salt Spring:** The Story of an Island – Charles Kahn, pp. 36 & 42
[38] **A Voice from the Past** - The Gulf Islands Guardian, Spring, 1993, pp. 30
[39] **Homesteads and Snug Harbours:** The Gulf Islands – Peter Murray, pp. 96
[40] **Salt Spring Island:** Bea Hamilton, pp. 35
[41] **A Voice from the Past** - The Gulf Islands Guardian, Spring, 1993, pp. 28

Salt Spring Island

[42] **Homesteads and Snug Harbours:** The Gulf Islands – Peter Murray, pp. 93 & 94
[43] **Salt Spring Island:** Bea Hamilton, pp. 51 & 52
[44] **Homesteads and Snug Harbours:** The Gulf Islands – Peter Murray, pp. 93 & 94
[45] **Homesteads and Snug Harbours:** The Gulf Islands – Peter Murray, pp. 93 & 94
[46] **Salt Spring:** The Story of an Island – Charles Kahn, pp. 11
[47] **Salt Spring Island:** Bea Hamilton, pp. 13-16
[48] **Salt Spring Island:** Bea Hamilton, pp. 13-16
[49] **Salt Spring Island:** Bea Hamilton, pp. 13-16, 51 & 52
[50] **Salt Spring Island:** Bea Hamilton, pp. 17 & 18
[51] **Salt Spring Island:** Bea Hamilton, pp. 51 & 52 and **Salt Spring:** The Story of an Island – Charles Kahn, pp. 54
[52] **Salt Spring Island:** Bea Hamilton, pp. 51 & 52 and **Salt Spring:** The Story of an Island – Charles Kahn, pp. 54
[53] **Salt Spring Island:** Bea Hamilton, pp. 51 & 52
[54] **Salt Spring Island:** Bea Hamilton, pp. 51 & 52
[55] **Homesteads and Snug Harbours:** The Gulf Islands – Peter Murray, pp. 100 & 101
[56] **Salt Spring:** The Story of an Island – Charles Kahn, pp. 242
[57] **Salt Spring Island:** An Illustrated Pamphlet With Map – Rev. E.F. Wilson, 1894, pp. 22
[58] **Salt Spring Island:** Bea Hamilton, pp. 23 & 24
[59] **Salt Spring Island:** An Illustrated Pamphlet With Map – Rev. E.F. Wilson, 1894, pp. 22
[60] **Islands Farmers Institute** – Edward Walter, 1902
[61] **Salt Spring:** The Story of an Island – Charles Kahn, pp. 161 & 162
[62] **Salt Spring:** The Story of an Island – Charles Kahn, pp. 237
[63] **Salt Spring:** The Story of an Island – Charles Kahn, pp. 237
[64] **Salt Spring:** The Story of an Island – Charles Kahn, pp. 281
[65] **Salt Spring Island:** Bea Hamilton, pp. 68
[66] **Salt Spring Island:** An Illustrated Pamphlet With Map – Rev. E.F. Wilson, 1894, pp. 26
[67] **Salt Spring:** The Story of an Island – Charles Kahn, pp. 139
[68] **Salt Spring Island:** Bea Hamilton, pp. 129
[69] **Salt Spring:** The Story of an Island – Charles Kahn, pp. 229
[70] **The Akerman Family:** Growing Up With Salt Spring Island – Bob Akerman & Linda Sherwood, pp. 166
[71] **The Akerman Family:** Growing Up With Salt Spring Island – Bob Akerman & Linda Sherwood, pp. 166
[72] **The Akerman Family:** Growing Up With Salt Spring Island – Bob Akerman & Linda Sherwood, pp. 272 and **Salt Spring Island:** Bea Hamilton, pp. 172 & 173
[73] **Salt Spring:** The Story of an Island – Charles Kahn, pp. 37 & 42
[74] **Salt Spring:** The Story of an Island – Charles Kahn, pp. 42
[75] **Salt Spring Island:** An Illustrated Pamphlet With Map – Rev. E.F. Wilson, 1894, pp. 26
[76] **Salt Spring Island:** An Illustrated Pamphlet With Map – Rev. E.F. Wilson, 1894, pp. 26

Salt Spring Island

[77] **Salt Spring Island:** An Illustrated Pamphlet With Map – Rev. E.F. Wilson, 1894, pp. 26
[78] **Salt Spring:** The Story of an Island – Charles Kahn, pp. 174
[79] **St. Mark's On The Hill:** John Rhodes Sturdy, 1965, pp. 12
[80] **Mayne Island & The Outer Gulf Islands**: A History – Marie Elliott, pp. 96
[81] **Island Heritage Buildings** – Thomas K. Ovanin, Islands Trust, pp. 78
[82] **Island Heritage Buildings** – Thomas K. Ovanin, Islands Trust, pp. 78 and **Salt Spring:** The Story of an Island – Charles Kahn, pp. 113 & 120
[83] **Island Heritage Buildings** – Thomas K. Ovanin, Islands Trust, pp. 78 and **Salt Spring:** The Story of an Island – Charles Kahn, pp. 113 & 120
[84] **Island Heritage Buildings** – Thomas K. Ovanin, Islands Trust, pp. 78
[85] **Island Heritage Buildings** – Thomas K. Ovanin, Islands Trust, pp. 78
[86] **Salt Spring Island:** A Place To Be – Ellie Thorburn and Pearl Gray, pp. 30
[87] **Homesteads and Snug Harbours:** The Gulf Islands – Peter Murray, pp. 95 & 106
[88] **Homesteads and Snug Harbours:** The Gulf Islands – Peter Murray, pp. 106 & 107
[89] **Homesteads and Snug Harbours:** The Gulf Islands – Peter Murray, pp. 106 & 107
[90] **Salt Spring Island:** Bea Hamilton, pp. 75 & 76
[91] **Homesteads and Snug Harbours:** The Gulf Islands – Peter Murray, pp. 111 and **Salt Spring:** The Story of an Island – Charles Kahn, pp. 87
[92] **Homesteads and Snug Harbours:** The Gulf Islands – Peter Murray, pp. 111 and **Salt Spring:** The Story of an Island – Charles Kahn, pp. 87
[93] **Homesteads and Snug Harbours:** The Gulf Islands – Peter Murray, pp. 111 and **Salt Spring:** The Story of an Island – Charles Kahn, pp. 87
[94] **The Heritage of Salt Spring Island:** a Map of Treasures – Island Pathways
[95] **Gulf Islanders:** Sound Heritage, Volume V, Number 4, pp. 8
[96] **Salt Spring Island:** An Illustrated Pamphlet With Map – Rev. E.F. Wilson, 1894, pp. 21
[97] **Gulf Islanders:** Sound Heritage, Volume V, Number 4, pp. 8 & 9
[98] **Salt Spring Island:** An Illustrated Pamphlet With Map – Rev. E.F. Wilson, 1894, pp. 21
[99] **Gulf Islanders:** Sound Heritage, Volume V, Number 4, pp. 8 & 9
[100] **Island Heritage Buildings** – Thomas K. Ovanin, Islands Trust, pp. 86
[101] **Island Heritage Buildings** – Thomas K. Ovanin, Islands Trust, pp. 86
[102] **Island Heritage Buildings** – Thomas K. Ovanin, Islands Trust, pp. 86
[103] **Island Heritage Buildings** – Thomas K. Ovanin, Islands Trust, pp. 86
[104] **Island Heritage Buildings** – Thomas K. Ovanin, Islands Trust, pp. 86
[105] **Times Past:** Salt Spring Island Houses and History Before the Turn of the Century – Community Arts Council Heritage House Committee, pp. 39
[106] **Island Heritage Buildings** – Thomas K. Ovanin, Islands Trust, pp. 86-89
[107] **Salt Spring:** The Story of an Island – Charles Kahn, pp. 94
[108] **Island Heritage Buildings** – Thomas K. Ovanin, Islands Trust, pp. 88
[109] **Island Heritage Buildings** – Thomas K. Ovanin, Islands Trust, pp. 89
[110] **Salt Spring:** The Story of an Island – Charles Kahn, pp. 94
[111] **Island Heritage Buildings** – Thomas K. Ovanin, Islands Trust, pp. 86-89
[112] **Island Heritage Buildings** – Thomas K. Ovanin, Islands Trust, pp. 60
[113] **Island Heritage Buildings** – Thomas K. Ovanin, Islands Trust, pp. 60

Salt Spring Island

[114] **Island Heritage Buildings** – Thomas K. Ovanin, Islands Trust, pp. 60
[115] **Salt Spring Island Archives website**
[116] **Island Heritage Buildings** – Thomas K. Ovanin, Islands Trust, pp. 60
[117] **Salt Spring: The Story of an Island** – Charles Kahn, pp. 95
[118] **Salt Spring: The Story of an Island** – Charles Kahn, pp. 95
[119] **Salt Spring: The Story of an Island** – Charles Kahn, pp. 95 & 230
[120] **Salt Spring Island:** Bea Hamilton, pp. 79 and **Salt Spring: The Story of an Island** – Charles Kahn, pp. 103
[121] **Salt Spring Island:** Bea Hamilton, pp. 82
[122] **Salt Spring Island:** Bea Hamilton, pp. 83
[123] **Salt Spring Island:** Bea Hamilton, pp. 79 & 82 and **Salt Spring: The Story of an Island** – Charles Kahn, pp. 103
[124] **Salt Spring: The Story of an Island** – Charles Kahn, pp. 118 & 119
[125] **Salt Spring: The Story of an Island** – Charles Kahn, pp. 118 & 119
[126] **Homesteads and Snug Harbours: The Gulf Islands** – Peter Murray, pp. 105
[127] **Island Heritage Buildings** – Thomas K. Ovanin, Islands Trust, pp. 73
[128] **Salt Spring: The Story of an Island** – Charles Kahn, pp. 118 & 119
[129] **Salt Spring Island:** Bea Hamilton, pp. 98
[130] **Salt Spring Island:** Bea Hamilton, pp. 161
[131] **Salt Spring Island:** Bea Hamilton, pp. 60
[132] **The Heritage of Salt Spring Island: a Map of Treasures** – Island Pathways
[133] **Salt Spring: The Story of an Island** – Charles Kahn, pp. 108 & 111
[134] **Island Heritage Buildings** – Thomas K. Ovanin, Islands Trust, pp. 82
[135] **Island Heritage Buildings** – Thomas K. Ovanin, Islands Trust, pp. 82
[136] **Island Heritage Buildings** – Thomas K. Ovanin, Islands Trust, pp. 60
[137] **Island Heritage Buildings** – Thomas K. Ovanin, Islands Trust, pp. 60
[138] **Island Heritage Buildings** – Thomas K. Ovanin, Islands Trust, pp. 60
[139] **Gulf Islands Driftwood:** July 21, 1982, pp. 24
[140] **Salt Spring Archives website**
[141] **Salt Spring: The Story of an Island** – Charles Kahn, pp. 237
[142] **Gulf Islands Driftwood:** July 21, 1982, pp. 24
[143] **Salt Spring: The Story of an Island** – Charles Kahn, pp. 125 & 126
[144] **Mouat`s Trading Company website**
[145] **Salt Spring: The Story of an Island** – Charles Kahn, pp. 125 & 126
[146] **Mouat`s Trading Company website**
[147] **Times Past: Salt Spring Island Houses and History Before the Turn of the Century** – Community Arts Council Heritage House Committee, pp. 25
[148] **Salt Spring: The Story of an Island** – Charles Kahn, pp. 101
[149] **Salt Spring: The Story of an Island** – Charles Kahn, pp. 107
[150] **Snapshots of Early Salt Spring and other Favoured Islands:** Mouat's Trading Co. Ltd., pp. 44
[151] **Salt Spring Island:** Bea Hamilton, pp. 72
[152] **Salt Spring Island:** Bea Hamilton, pp. 72
[153] **Snapshots of Early Salt Spring and other Favoured Islands:** Mouat's Trading Co. Ltd., pp. 44 and **Salt Spring: The Story of an Island** – Charles Kahn, pp. 145 & 209

Salt Spring Island

[154] **Snapshots of Early Salt Spring and other Favoured Islands:** Mouat's Trading Co. Ltd., pp. 44 and **Salt Spring:** The Story of an Island – Charles Kahn, pp. 145 & 209
[155] **Snapshots of Early Salt Spring and other Favoured Islands:** Mouat's Trading Co. Ltd., pp. 44 and **Salt Spring:** The Story of an Island – Charles Kahn, pp. 145 & 209
[156] **The Post Offices of British Columbia:** 1858-1970 - George H. Melvin, pp. 118
[157] **Snapshots of Early Salt Spring and other Favoured Islands:** Mouat's Trading Co. Ltd., pp. 44
[158] **Salt Spring:** The Story of an Island – Charles Kahn, pp. 185
[159] **Island Heritage Buildings** – Thomas K. Ovanin, Islands Trust, pp. 69
[160] **Island Heritage Buildings** – Thomas K. Ovanin, Islands Trust, pp. 69
[161] **Island Heritage Buildings** – Thomas K. Ovanin, Islands Trust, pp. 69
[162] **Southern Gulf Islands:** An Altitude SuperGuide – Spalding, Montgomery and Pitt, pp. 114
[163] **Island Heritage Buildings** – Thomas K. Ovanin, Islands Trust, pp. 69
[164] **The Post Offices of British Columbia:** 1858-1970 - George H. Melvin, pp. 9, 16, 42 & 114
[165] **The Post Offices of British Columbia:** 1858-1970 - George H. Melvin, pp. 42 & 114 and **Salt Spring:** The Story of an Island – Charles Kahn, pp. 143
[166] **The Post Offices of British Columbia:** 1858-1970 - George H. Melvin, pp. 42 & 114 and **Salt Spring:** The Story of an Island – Charles Kahn, pp. 143
[167] **Salt Spring Island:** Bea Hamilton, pp. 88
[168] **The Akerman Family:** Growing Up With Salt Spring Island – Bob Akerman & Linda Sherwood, pp. 166
[169] **Salt Spring:** The Story of an Island – Charles Kahn, pp. 145 & 209
[170] **The Post Offices of British Columbia:** 1858-1970 - George H. Melvin, pp. 76
[171] **The Post Offices of British Columbia:** 1858-1970 - George H. Melvin, pp. 9, 42, 75 & 114
[172] **The Post Offices of British Columbia:** 1858-1970 - George H. Melvin, pp. 42 & 114 and **Salt Spring:** The Story of an Island – Charles Kahn, pp. 229 & 267
[173] **The Post Offices of British Columbia:** 1858-1970 - George H. Melvin, pp. 9 & 76
[174] **Salt Spring:** The Story of an Island – Charles Kahn, pp. 131
[175] **Salt Spring:** The Story of an Island – Charles Kahn, pp. 131
[176] **Salt Spring:** The Story of an Island – Charles Kahn, pp. 181
[177] **Salt Spring:** The Story of an Island – Charles Kahn, pp. 131
[178] **Island Heritage Buildings** – Thomas K. Ovanin, Islands Trust, pp. 49
[179] **Island Heritage Buildings** – Thomas K. Ovanin, Islands Trust, pp. 49
[180] **Salt Spring:** The Story of an Island – Charles Kahn, pp. 181
[181] **Salt Spring Island:** A Place To Be – Ellie Thorburn and Pearl Gray, pp. 63
[182] **Island Heritage Buildings** – Thomas K. Ovanin, Islands Trust, pp. 49
[183] **Salt Spring Island:** Bea Hamilton, pp. 118 and **Salt Spring:** The Story of an Island – Charles Kahn, pp. 133 & 134
[184] **Salt Spring Island:** Bea Hamilton, pp. 118 and **Salt Spring:** The Story of an Island – Charles Kahn, pp. 133 & 134
[185] **Snapshots of Early Salt Spring and other Favoured Islands:** Mouat's Trading Co. Ltd., pp. 106 and **Salt Spring Island:** A Place To Be – Ellie Thorburn and Pearl Gray, pp. 146

Salt Spring Island

[186] **Salt Spring Island:** Bea Hamilton, pp. 126
[187] **Salt Spring Island:** Bea Hamilton, pp. 126
[188] **Salt Spring Island:** Bea Hamilton, pp. 129
[189] **Salt Spring Island:** Bea Hamilton, pp. 132
[190] **Salt Spring Island:** Bea Hamilton, pp. 132 & 133
[191] **Salt Spring Island:** Bea Hamilton, pp. 129
[192] **Salt Spring:** The Story of an Island – Charles Kahn, pp. 130 & 131
[193] **Salt Spring:** The Story of an Island – Charles Kahn, pp. 150
[194] **Salt Spring:** The Story of an Island – Charles Kahn, pp. 150
[195] **Salt Spring:** The Story of an Island – Charles Kahn, pp. 225
[196] **Salt Spring:** The Story of an Island – Charles Kahn, pp. 225
[197] **Salt Spring:** The Story of an Island – Charles Kahn, pp. 225
[198] **Salt Spring:** The Story of an Island – Charles Kahn, pp. 225
[199] **Salt Spring:** The Story of an Island – Charles Kahn, pp. 224
[200] **Salt Spring:** The Story of an Island – Charles Kahn, pp. 297
[201] **Fulford Creek Guest House website**
[202] **Fulford Creek Guest House website**
[203] **Salt Spring:** The Story of an Island – Charles Kahn, pp. 167 & 181
[204] **Salt Spring:** The Story of an Island – Charles Kahn, pp. 167 & 181
[205] **Island Heritage Buildings** – Thomas K. Ovanin, Islands Trust, pp. 67
[206] **Island Heritage Buildings** – Thomas K. Ovanin, Islands Trust, pp. 67
[207] **Salt Spring Island:** Bea Hamilton, pp. 110
[208] **Salt Spring:** The Story of an Island – Charles Kahn, pp. 182
[209] **Salt Spring Island:** A Place To Be – Ellie Thorburn and Pearl Gray, pp. 59
[210] **Salt Spring:** The Story of an Island – Charles Kahn, pp. 163
[211] **The Heritage of Salt Spring Island:** a Map of Treasures – Island Pathways
[212] **Salt Spring:** The Story of an Island – Charles Kahn, pp. 280
[213] **Royal Canadian Legion Branch 92 website**
[214] **Royal Canadian Legion Branch 92 website**
[215] **Salt Spring:** The Story of an Island – Charles Kahn, pp. 144 & 145
[216] **Salt Spring:** The Story of an Island – Charles Kahn, pp. 144 & 145
[217] **Salt Spring:** The Story of an Island – Charles Kahn, pp. 144-146 & 148
[218] **Salt Spring:** The Story of an Island – Charles Kahn, pp. 144-146 & 148
[219] **Salt Spring:** The Story of an Island – Charles Kahn, pp. 144-148
[220] **Salt Spring:** The Story of an Island – Charles Kahn, pp. 144-148
[221] **Snapshots of Early Salt Spring and other Favoured Islands:** Mouat's Trading Co. Ltd., pp. 79
[222] **Snapshots of Early Salt Spring and other Favoured Islands:** Mouat's Trading Co. Ltd., pp. 51
[223] **Salt Spring:** The Story of an Island – Charles Kahn, pp. 150
[224] **Mouat's Trading Company website**
[225] **Mouat's Trading Company website**
[226] **Mouat's Trading Company website**
[227] **Island Heritage Buildings** – Thomas K. Ovanin, Islands Trust, pp. 69
[228] **The Heritage of Salt Spring Island:** a Map of Treasures – Island Pathways
[229] **Salt Spring:** The Story of an Island – Charles Kahn, pp. 176

Salt Spring Island

[230] **Mouat's Trading Company website**
[231] **Mouat's Trading Company website**
[232] **Places of Historical Interest in Ganges Village:** A Walking Tour – Salt Spring Historical Society
[233] **Island Heritage Buildings** – Thomas K. Ovanin, Islands Trust, pp. 69
[234] **Island Heritage Buildings** – Thomas K. Ovanin, Islands Trust, pp. 75 and **Salt Spring:** The Story of an Island – Charles Kahn, pp. 158
[235] **Island Heritage Buildings** – Thomas K. Ovanin, Islands Trust, pp. 75 and **Salt Spring:** The Story of an Island – Charles Kahn, pp. 158
[236] **Island Heritage Buildings** – Thomas K. Ovanin, Islands Trust, pp. 75
[237] **Salt Spring:** The Story of an Island – Charles Kahn, pp. 148 & 150
[238] **Salt Spring:** The Story of an Island – Charles Kahn, pp. 160
[239] **Salt Spring Island:** Bea Hamilton, pp. 157
[240] **Salt Spring:** The Story of an Island – Charles Kahn, pp. 295
[241] **Island Heritage Buildings** – Thomas K. Ovanin, Islands Trust, pp. 63
[242] **Island Heritage Buildings** – Thomas K. Ovanin, Islands Trust, pp. 63
[243] **Island Heritage Buildings** – Thomas K. Ovanin, Islands Trust, pp. 63
[244] **Island Heritage Buildings** – Thomas K. Ovanin, Islands Trust, pp. 63
[245] **Island Heritage Buildings** – Thomas K. Ovanin, Islands Trust, pp. 63
[246] **Salt Spring:** The Story of an Island – Charles Kahn, pp. 265
[247] **The Heritage of Salt Spring Island:** a Map of Treasures – Island Pathways
[248] **Places of Historical Interest in Ganges Village:** A Walking Tour – Salt Spring Historical Society
[249] **Salt Spring:** The Story of an Island – Charles Kahn, pp. 162
[250] **Salt Spring:** The Story of an Island – Charles Kahn, pp. 162
[251] **Salt Spring Island:** Bea Hamilton, pp. 156
[252] **Salt Spring Island:** Bea Hamilton, pp. 156
[253] **Salt Spring:** The Story of an Island – Charles Kahn, pp. 235
[254] **Salt Spring Island:** Bea Hamilton, pp. 156
[255] **Island Heritage Buildings** – Thomas K. Ovanin, Islands Trust, pp. 71
[256] **Island Heritage Buildings** – Thomas K. Ovanin, Islands Trust, pp. 71
[257] **The Heritage of Salt Spring Island:** a Map of Treasures – Island Pathways
[258] **Salt Spring:** The Story of an Island – Charles Kahn, pp. 231 & 242
[259] **Salt Spring:** The Story of an Island – Charles Kahn, pp. 231 & 242
[260] **Salt Spring:** The Story of an Island – Charles Kahn, pp. 231
[261] **Salt Spring:** The Story of an Island – Charles Kahn, pp. 231
[262] **The Akerman Family:** Growing Up With Salt Spring Island – Bob Akerman & Linda Sherwood, pp. 278
[263] **The Akerman Family:** Growing Up With Salt Spring Island – Bob Akerman & Linda Sherwood, pp. 279
[264] **Salt Spring:** The Story of an Island – Charles Kahn, pp. 236
[265] **Salt Spring Island:** Bea Hamilton, pp. 35 & 173
[266] **Salt Spring Island:** Bea Hamilton, pp. 35 & 173
[267] **Salt Spring:** The Story of an Island – Charles Kahn, pp. 236 & 237
[268] **Places of Historical Interest in Ganges Village:** A Walking Tour – Salt Spring Historical Society

Salt Spring Island

[269] **Salt Spring Archives website**
[270] **Conversations with Hastings House Country Estate staff**
[271] **Southern Gulf Islands**: An Altitude SuperGuide – Spalding, Montgomery and Pitt, pp. 117
[272] **Salt Spring:** The Story of an Island – Charles Kahn, pp. 239
[273] **Salt Spring:** The Story of an Island – Charles Kahn, pp. 301
[274] **Places of Historical Interest in Ganges Village:** A Walking Tour – Salt Spring Historical Society
[275] **Salt Spring:** The Story of an Island – Charles Kahn, pp. 246
[276] **Salt Spring:** The Story of an Island – Charles Kahn, pp. 270 & 297
[277] **Salt Spring:** The Story of an Island – Charles Kahn, pp. 270 & 297
[278] **Salt Spring:** The Story of an Island – Charles Kahn, pp. 297
[279] **Places of Historical Interest in Ganges Village:** A Walking Tour – Salt Spring Historical Society
[280] **Places of Historical Interest in Ganges Village:** A Walking Tour – Salt Spring Historical Society
[281] **Salt Spring:** The Story of an Island – Charles Kahn, pp. 267, 268 & 277
[282] **Salt Spring:** The Story of an Island – Charles Kahn, pp. 277
[283] **Salt Spring Island:** Bea Hamilton, pp. 172 & 173
[284] **The Akerman Family:** Growing Up With Salt Spring Island – Bob Akerman & Linda Sherwood, pp. 272 and **Salt Spring Island:** Bea Hamilton, pp. 172 & 173
[285] **Salt Spring Island:** Bea Hamilton, pp. 172 & 173
[286] **Salt Spring:** The Story of an Island – Charles Kahn, pp. 296
[287] **Mary Hawkins Memorial Library website**
[288] **Salt Spring:** The Story of an Island – Charles Kahn, pp. 272
[289] **Mary Hawkins Memorial Library website**
[290] **Mary Hawkins Memorial Library website**
[291] **Salt Spring:** The Story of an Island – Charles Kahn, pp. 272
[292] **Salt Spring:** The Story of an Island – Charles Kahn, pp. 296
[293] **Salt Spring:** The Story of an Island – Charles Kahn, pp. 288
[294] **Salt Spring:** The Story of an Island – Charles Kahn, pp. 289

Credits

Credits

Historical Photos

British Columbia Archives and Records Services

Royal British Columbia Museum

British Columbia Ferry Services Archives

Salt Spring Archives (Salt Spring Island)

Galiano Museum & Archives (Galiano Island)

Pender Islands Museum Society (Pender Islands)

Mayne Island Volunteer Firefighters Association (Mayne Island)

David Spalding (South Pender Island)

Donald New (Galiano Island)

Hope Bay Rising Holdings Ltd. (North Pender Island)

Kelly Irving (Pender Island)

Jim and Lorraine Campbell (Saturna Island)

Management of the Saturna Lodge (Saturna Island)

Management of The Old Farmhouse B&B (Salt Spring Island)

Credits

Current Photos

Kevin Oke Photography
Pender Island Fall Fair, Magic Lake Lantern Festival, Salt Spring Island Fall Fair, Saturday Market in the Park, Saturna Island Vineyards Harvest Celebration, Canada Day Lamb Barbeque, Cabbage Island Provincial Marine Park, Portland Island

Georgia Strait Alliance
Orca Pass International Stewardship Area

Joanie McCorry (Mayne Island)
Mayne Island Quilters Guild

Darrel Perfumo (Mayne Island)
En-Vision Gallery

Brian Haller (Mayne Island)
Bonfire in Miners Bay Community Park, Easter Egg Hunt

Charles Andre (Mayne Island)
The Hobbit House B&B

Efraim Gavrilovich (Mayne Island)
Japanese Garden lights

Ken Smith (Galiano Island)
Halloween, Galiano Fiesta, Montague Harbour Marina, Island Time 5 Star B&B, Spanish Longboat, Clowns, Slow Pitch Tournament, Galiano Triathlon

Pender Island Taxi & Tours (Pender Island)
Pender Island Taxis

The Pender Islands Artisan Co-Op (Pender Island)
Rembrandt's Birthday Art Show, Christmas Craft Fair Exhibit

Stella Roberts (Pender Island)
The Garden Party

Greg Gerke (Pender Island)
Easter Egg Hunt

Saturna Island Vineyards (Saturna Island)
Saturna Island Vineyards, Saturna Vineyards Wine Shop, Feral Goat

Boot Cove Art Studio (Saturna Island)
Boot Cove Art Studio

Everlasting Summer (Salt Spring Island)
Everlasting Summer Garden Aerial View

AppleLuscious Organic Orchards (Salt Spring Island)
Apple Festival

Graffiti Theatre (Salt Spring Island)
Seven Stories Theatrical Production

Credits

Dreamstime™
Tony Campbell, David Coleman, Galina Barskaya, Paul Wolf, Scott Pehrson, Marilyn Barbone, Steffen Foerster, Steve Degenhardt, Melissa King, Randy McKown, Kutt Niinepuu, Dennis Sabo, Jason Cheever, Ryan Tacay, Costin Cojocaru, Marilyna Barbone, Nick Stubbs, Francois etienne Du plessis, Pete Setrac, Penny Riches, Dwight Hegel, Tom Hirtreiter, Elena Ray, Norman Pogson, Hannu Liivaar, Patricia Marroquin, Franc Podgorsek, Keith Naylor, Andrew Barker, Elina Gareeva, Richard Gunion, Silas Brown, Jannelle Althoff, Bobby Deal, Yula Zubritsky, Dick Sunderland, Elena Elisseeva, Dan Bannister, Jaimie Duplass, Marilyn Barbone, Natthias Nordmeyer, Svetlana Tikhonova, Jackie Egginton, Vlad Turchenko, Emin Kuliyev, Fred Goldstein, Jennifer Westmoreland, Sue McDonald, Mark Rasmussen, David Kay, David Pruter, Mehmet Alci

Credits

Acknowledgements

The Post Offices of British Columbia: 1858-1970 - George H. Melvin

The Gulf Islanders: Sound Heritage, Volume V, Number 4

Island Heritage Buildings – Thomas K. Ovanin, Islands Trust

A Gulf Islands Patchwork: Some Early Events on the Islands of Galiano, Mayne, Saturna, North and South Pender – British Columbia Historical Association

More Tales from the Outer Gulf Islands: An Anthology of Memories and Anecdotes – British Columbia Historical Association

Homesteads and Snug Harbours: The Gulf Islands – Peter Murray

The Terror Of The Coast: Land Alienation And Colonial War On Vancouver Island And The Gulf Islands – Chris Arnett

The Gulf Islands Explorer: The Outdoor Guide – Bruce Obee

Hiking the Gulf Islands: An Outdoor Guide to BC's Enchanted Isles – Charles Kahn

Plants of the Pacific Northwest Coast – Pojar and Mackinnon

Birds of the Pacific Northwest Coast – Nancy Baron & John Acorn

Mammals of the Northwest: Washington, Oregon, Idaho and British Columbia – Earl J. Larrison

The Beachcomber's Guide to Seashore Life in the Pacific Northwest – J. Duane Sept

WetCoast Words: A Dictionary of British Columbia Words and Phrases – Tom Parkin

Mayne Island & The Outer Gulf Islands: A History – Marie Elliott

Galiano: Houses And People, Looking back to 1930 – Elizabeth Steward

The Campbells of Saturna: An Oral History – Saturna Community Club

Salt Spring: The Story of an Island – Charles Kahn

Salt Spring Island: Bea Hamilton

Author

Vicky Lindholm moved with her husband to Mayne Island, British Columbia, in December of 2004. Having authored over 30 pieces of computer courseware, she brought with her more than 20 years of writing experience.

Then And Now in the Gulf Islands is the first of its kind to be written by this author, who reviewed over 50 existing pieces of literature and explored landmarks, events, parks and beaches in order to produce this historical view of the southern Gulf Islands.

The book compares life in the Islands in the 19th and 20th centuries with that of the 21st century. It include over 700 photos, past to present, most of which the author photographed herself.

Vicky currently lives and works on Mayne Island. In addition to making a living as a writer, she manages a small gift store, as a home-based business, from her residential property.

Made in the USA
San Bernardino, CA
16 October 2018